THE
INNER
WEST

THE
INNER
WEST

An Introduction to the Hidden Wisdom of the West

EDITED AND INTRODUCED BY JAY KINNEY

JEREMY P. TARCHER / PENGUIN

a member of Penguin Group (USA) Inc.

New York

A list of rights and permissions appears on page 323.

Most Tarcher/Penguin books are available at special quantity discounts for bulk
purchase for sales promotions, premiums, fund-raising, and educational needs.
Special books or book excerpts also can be created to fit specific needs. For
details, write Penguin Group (USA) Inc. Special Markets,
375 Hudson Street, New York, NY 10014.

JEREMY P. TARCHER/PENGUIN
a member of
Penguin Group (USA) Inc.
375 Hudson Street
New York, NY 10014
www.penguin.com

Library of Congress Cataloging-in-Publication Data

The inner West : an introduction to the hidden wisdom of the
West / edited and introduced by Jay Kinney.
p.   cm.—(New consciousness reader)
Includes bibliographical references.
ISBN 1-58542-339-4 (alk. paper)
1. Occultism.   I. Kinney, Jay, 1950–   II. Series.
BF1411.I54   2004   2004043974
130'.9182'1—dc22

Printed in the United States of America
3   5   7   9   10   8   6   4   2

Book design by Chris Welch

CONTENTS

THE INNER SIDE OF THE
RELIGIONS OF THE WEST

THE SECRET TEACHINGS

ESOTERIC BROTHERHOODS

MYSTICS AND TEACHERS

ACKNOWLEDGMENTS

First and foremost, I would like to acknowledge Richard Smoley's unseen role in editing much of the material in this book. Most of the articles collected here were originally published in *Gnosis* magazine and passed through his deft editorial hands before they saw publication there.

My thanks as well to the authors who consented to be included here, and who were generous enough to write the material to begin with for less remuneration than they deserved. Research and writing on the Western esoteric traditions is invariably a labor of love, and I'm pleased to have many of the best authors in the field represented in this anthology.

I'd also like to express my appreciation to my editor at Tarcher/Penguin, Mitch Horowitz, who encouraged this book from day one, and whose patience and good suggestions have made him a pleasure to work with.

And speaking of patience, my wife Dixie deserves special thanks for standing by me, with love and support, during the stressful years of publishing *Gnosis,* and the even more stressful years since. In addition, her suggestions regarding portions of the manuscript were a great help.

Finally, in no particular order, I'd like to thank the following people who played some role (whether known or unknown) in enabling this book to be published: Katie Boyle, Michael Crisp, David Jones, the Curmudgeon Club, David Fideler, Becky Wilson, David Gilmore, Chris Farmer, Kirsten Strickland, Jay Cornell, Rashid Patch, Jeff Chitouras, Jordan Gruber, Gary Moring, Nina Nikolaeva, Frank Donnola, Refik Algan, Rosamonde Miller, the late Jerry Odum, and others unnamed.

—*Jay Kinney*

INTRODUCTION

Jay Kinney

The impulse to go in search of buried treasure must reside deep within our genes. When I was nine or ten, in Lakewood, Ohio, my brother and I were seized with the notion that something marvelous must surely reside beneath the earth. As our parents vetoed our initial plan to dig up the backyard, we were left with the meter-wide passage of bare ground between the rear of our garage and that of our back neighbor.

So it was that one summer day we marched out to that narrow corridor, shovels in hand, and started digging. The soil was hard packed and rocky, and after excavating to a depth of a foot or two, we were ready to admit defeat. The only treasure we found was a bullet of unknown age, which we excitedly showed to our parents, who promptly confiscated it and vowed to turn it over to the police. Our treasure hunt was a bust.

I was reminded of this episode when reading *The Refiner's Fire* by John L. Brooke. Brooke discusses "the divining and treasure-hunting cults that sprang up throughout the New England hinterland between the 1780s and the 1830s."[1] Fueled by "legends of treasures buried by Spaniards and pirates,"[2] and encouraged by hopes of finding lost mines and veins of precious minerals, the capital-poor settlers resorted to "cunning men," conjurers, and diviners, in generally futile attempts to strike it rich. Another wave of treasure-seeking was triggered in the California Gold Rush of 1849, this time with better luck for some.

Threaded throughout these eighteenth- and nineteenth-century efforts, according to Brooke, were notions of earthly fecundity, alchemical transmutation, and the magical control of spirits supposedly guarding their earthbound treasures—folk magical beliefs harking back to the esoteric traditions of the Middle Ages and the Renaissance.

I've brought up this recurring search for buried treasure—whether literal or metaphorical—because the subjects of this anthology are themselves a kind of buried treasure deposited within the history and culture of Western civilization.

For some thirty years, I've been engaged in a personal excavation effort with the aim of recovering the spiritual resources that the teachings of esoteric traditions represent. This hasn't been a solitary undertaking, as there is an informal network of scholars, researchers, and practitioners who have been happy to share their findings, both with each other and with the public.

For nearly fifteen years, from 1985 to 1999, much of this sharing occurred within the pages of *Gnosis: A Journal of the Western Inner Traditions,* which it was my privilege to publish. Most of the articles in this book have been drawn from that journal, although the inevitable constraints of space have meant that the selection here is but a fraction of the worthwhile material that deserves wider dissemination.

It is fair to ask just what kind of treasure the spiritual and esoteric traditions covered here represent. Is there real gold to be found, or is this a fool's errand? I believe I can best answer this by offering my own experience as an example.

LIKE MANY OTHERS who came of age as the 1960s became the 1970s, I was dissatisfied with the ordinary religious answers of my upbringing. I felt a spiritual thirst that was not quenched by merely going to church each Sunday. Inspired by figures like the Beatles, Allen Ginsberg, Ram Dass, and Alan Watts, many of us looked to Eastern religions and teachings for inspiration and guidance.

The first half of the seventies in particular saw a wave of yogis, swamis, and gurus wash up on the shores of America, each of them offering venerable methods of meditation and consciousness alteration. I took yoga classes, hung posters of Hindu gods on the walls of my dorm room, attended public talks by Swami Satchitananda, Chogyam Trungpa Rimpoche, and Maharaji, and tried to follow the advice found in Ram Dass's *Be Here Now*. But despite my efforts, I failed to find a teacher with whom I felt a profound connection. This might have been due to a strong do-it-yourself ethic on my part, but there was also something about the guru-devotee relationship that bothered me—at least as I saw it practiced by smitten Westerners.

Nearly all spiritual and mystical paths encourage seekers to minimize their egos, the better to open their consciousness to the Divine. I had no problem with that—in theory, at least—but I did have a problem with elevating another human to a God-like level and subsuming my ego to his. This seemed like an open invitation to exploitation and abuse, and as the seventies rolled on, my misgivings were confirmed as numerous swamis, yogis, and rimpoches were embroiled in scandals over just such temptations.

I also found that the cultural references—to elephant gods, blue-skinned Krishna, or Tibetan deities—were too exotic for my Western sensibility. There was too big a gap between my own symbolic vocabulary and the myths and figures of Eastern religions. I soon discovered that I was not alone in this.

The challenge—for me and others like me—was to find an approach to spiritual unfoldment that worked on every level: practical, cultural, mystical, and psychological. Over time, with the assistance of friends who ran a neighborhood metaphysical bookstore in San Francisco, I found that the esoteric and mystical traditions of my own Western culture could provide that approach.

I also found that getting a handle on this Western path was not simple. There existed few organizations providing clearcut guidance, and those that did seemed to have their best days behind them. What's more, due to the overarching power of the Church in European history, many Western esoteric traditions had led a semiunderground existence, enveloping themselves in a protective secrecy, and communicating their teachings through symbols and diagrams that were baffling to a neophyte. Modern proponents of many of these traditions claimed to trace their origins to ancient Egypt, pagan Greece, or other distant sources, but such claims were usually unproven and unprovable, and served as little more than window dressing. In short, the student who found himself or herself attracted to some element of the Inner West was forced to take a pilgrimage upon a winding path, cut away the underbrush, and simultaneously journey backward and forward in time.

This journey of discovery seemed to require a certain mindset—equal parts faith, skepticism, and common sense—and a penchant for solving puzzles. It involved familiarizing oneself with seemingly "obsolete" concepts such as the four elements (earth air, fire, and water) or the planetary spheres (the pre-Copernicus model of the Sun, Moon, and planets circling the Earth).

I found that such concepts, while obsolete as scientific descriptions of the Universe, were still useful as symbol systems to work with in exploring the subjective realms of psyche and soul.

For several years I educated myself in the basics of the Inner West, largely through reading books. This was fine, up to a point, but it ran the risk of turning my spiritual inquiry into a solely intellectual enterprise. At this point I happened upon a small, one-of-a-kind, gnostic church in the Bay Area. (Gnosticism, which is discussed in greater detail in Stephan Hoeller's essay [see chapter 3] is a Christian spiritual approach that emphasizes the importance of directly experiencing the Divine.) This church's bishop was a deeply inspired woman who had developed a present-day mystery school in which students progressed through graded clerical orders leading toward priesthood. I knew little of this prior to attending their Sunday morning mass for the first time. That mass turned out to be a pivotal event.

I had been raised in mainstream Protestant denominations whose services were shorn of almost all ritual. The gnostic mass, which was similar to the traditional Catholic mass, involved a lengthy liturgy, the consecration of wine and host, and an attitude of ritual concentration that affected me on many levels. The mass is traditionally seen as a sacrament providing a conduit for divine grace; considering how profoundly that mass affected me, I could suddenly see that this might really be the case.

Within a year's time I had entered orders at the church, and I underwent eight years of intensive training that touched on everything from the elements of ritual and the concept of sacred space to the power of music and healing prayer. This was all provided, amazingly enough, without financial obligation or dogmatic regimentation. By the time that I was ordained, I had engaged with and experienced the esoteric teachings in a way that mere book learning would never have made possible.

My point isn't that the reader should drop this book and rush to find that, or any, particular church. There are, after all, many ports in a storm. Rather, I offer my own experience as an indication that the Inner West can be initially approached through research and reading but that its real gold is likely to be found in the company of others.

YOU MAY BE wondering, at this point, what "the Inner West" refers to. It is relatively clear that when we talk about Eastern paths, for instance, these primarily refer to the Hindu, Buddhist, and Taoist religions and their associated yogic and meditative practices. But the Inner West is a bit more tangled and elusive.

Western culture has been predominantly, but not exclusively, shaped throughout much of its history by Christianity. For centuries Christianity meant the Catholic Church, which usually acted forcibly against any rivals. Because of its insistence on its sole authority, the Church insisted that any spiritual inquiry occur through the mediation of its priests, or within its other institutional structures such as monastic orders.

The mystics, gnostics, and others who sought a direct experience of God or the Unseen were commonly frowned upon when not outright persecuted. Their teachings provided a counterbalance to the biases of mainstream religion, which didn't help their popularity with the authorities. This divergence can be seen in the Inner West's use of feminine symbolic figures, such as Sophia (Divine Wisdom) and Anima Mundi (the Soul of the World); its locus of inquiry and empowerment in the individual; and its liberal, multilateral approach—all counterpoised to the masculine, collective, and unilateral posture of the Church.

In light of this, I use "the Inner West" to refer to manifestations of at least three kinds of "innerness."

First, the individual's own interior experience, both psychological and spiritual. Generally, the traditions surveyed here encourage self-observation, attentiveness to subtle changes in one's inner landscape, and spiritual unfoldment.

Second, the inner "essence" of religious truth—an essence that may not always coincide with the formal systematization of dogma and theology. Jesus' defense of "the spirit of the Law," as opposed to "the letter of the Law," suggests this.

And third, "inner" in the sense of hidden or concealed teachings. These were hidden in two ways. First, their survival in the face of Church opposition led them to take a covert or marginal existence. And second, their very nature as teachings requiring inner work meant that they only revealed themselves to determined seekers, because true knowledge must be hard won.

The Inner West, then, is the underground stream of experiential wisdom traditions (often called esoteric) that have flowed down through the centuries to the present day. That stream has had many tributaries, and the articles in this anthology are intended to provide an overview of those sources, along with looks at some of the individual currents within the stream.

One uses a metaphor at the risk of oversimplification, and in calling them a stream I don't mean to imply that the esoteric traditions of Western culture compose a unified whole. Certain elements, for instance, derive from the Hellenic Neoplatonic philosophy of the early Christian era, others from medieval Jewish Kabbalah, others from Renaissance Hermeticism, and others from pre-Christian pagan religions. Even Islam, via its esoteric traditions preserved in Sufism, can be included as a component, through its interaction with Christian and Jewish schools in Moorish Spain between the eighth and the fifteenth centuries, and its presence in southern and eastern Europe during the Ottoman Empire, from the fourteenth through the nineteenth centuries.

While some of these sources might seem mutually exclusive, they have frequently overlapped and cross-fertilized each other through the centuries. Thus the reader will find some sources, such as Hermeticism (an amalgam of ancient Greek and Egyptian philosophies) or Gnosticism, mentioned repeatedly in different articles here. Even if one is primarily attracted to only one or two approaches, it is useful to understand how all the threads weave together within the Inner West.

The question remains: What would students of these esoteric traditions hope to achieve? Why even bother deciphering complex symbol-systems or willingly take on the work of self-discipline that many of these traditions require? There are probably as many answers as there are students, but several come to the fore. One is to achieve (or be blessed with) a state of illumination or gnosis. An illumined being knows his or her true place in the greater Universe and understands the unity underlying all consciousness, whether individual or Divine. We might call this the *mystical* motivation for embracing the Inner West.

Another less encompassing goal would be the desire for contact with and guidance from higher intelligence. This might take the form of ritual interaction with angelic forces or "gods," or the exploration of astral realms that are unseen to the physical eye. This could be called the *magical* motivation for embracing the Inner West.

A third goal, which might be seen as a mixture of the preceding two, would be the wish to bring the natural world, including humankind, into a more harmonious relationship with the Divine order and with each other. Efforts toward this end might be found in nature-based religions, in the transmutations of alchemy, and in the Kabbalistic doctrine of Tikkun, the redemption of the created world. This could be called the motivation to *mend*.

I would be remiss not to mention certain risks in choosing to engage with the Inner West. Anyone who has read Hermann Hesse's novel *Steppenwolf* will recall the elusive sign at the door of the Magic Theatre: "Entrance Not For Everybody . . . For Madmen Only." This warning may overstate the case as esoteric traditions go, but it is not too wide of the mark. Contrary to the sales pitch of hundreds of New Age and pop magic books, a conscious spiritual journey is not a light-filled progression into ever more positive and clear-cut realms.

Here is a personal example. At one point, in the early 1990s, I read a book on "contacting your spiritual guides." The book advocated a fairly straightforward method, which I decided to try. I already had earthly friends who I considered genuine spiritual guides, but the notion that a disembodied guide might be waiting to help out was intriguing.

I tried the book's method of contact—which involved a form of relaxation and inner listening—and, lo and behold, words began to form in my mind's eye, which I dutifully wrote down. Over the course of a month, I made almost daily contact with the group of advisors who came through. Their perspective seemed suitably cosmic, and their advice was reasonable enough. This was hardly a case of receiving commands from a Ouija board to jump out the window.

Yet, after a month's time, following the advice of one of my material plane guides, I ceased contact with the inner guides. Here I was, seemingly in contact with high spiritual beings on an inner plane, yet I turned off the tap. Why?

The dilemma was akin to an epistemological Rubik's cube. Thoughts would form in the silence of my mind. I clothed them in words in writing them down. Were these actually just thoughts from my own Unconscious that I chose to see as coming from a source other than myself? Even if I granted that these guides might have an independent existence, what proof did I have that they weren't just disembodied busybodies who kept feeding me what I wanted to hear, in order to hold my attention and energy? There was no way of resolving such questions.

Little was lost in moving on from the cognitive cul-de-sac. I could still seek guidance in prayer and listen to the "still small voice" within. I just ceased to frequent the particular "frequency" where thoughts expressed themselves as coming from those disembodied guides. It had been an interesting experiment, but I left it at that. It seemed better to cultivate my own direct connection with God—without intermediaries—than to continue on with a dependence on guides who were unaccountable and unidentifiable.

Needless to say, anyone who is attracted to esoterica and intrigued by teachings about the Unseen risks entering a psychological twilight zone of ambiguity and projection. Such ambiguity is part of the territory, and learning to deal with it part of the challenge. However, the risks are real and shouldn't be dismissed. The occult historian Francis King memorably described the results of one early-twentieth-century magical group's residence in this territory:

> The Chiefs of the Amoun Temple in London became as addicted to mediumship and astral travel as a drug-addict is to heroin! They buried themselves in the seething images of their own unconscious minds to such good effect that two of them became schizophrenic—one of them, a clergyman, was later to die in a mental hospital—and, in 1919, Felkin [the group's leader] was forced to close the Temple down.[3]

Other challenges can arise as well. Some ten or so years ago, I undertook some apparently simple spiritual practices under the guidance of a Sufi teacher. The inner impact of these "simple practices" was considerable: I experienced the dramatic opening of an energy center within my body that was accompanied by a volcanic eruption of Unconscious material. Suddenly I was faced with a lifetime's worth of emotional "stuff" that had been carefully filed away for some rainy day. Abruptly, the rainy day had arrived, and a flood was on. Ten years later I am still processing the results of a moment's subtle energy shift.

Despite such risks, is the Inner West still worth exploring? Unquestionably. Some of us are simply not satisfied with taking our beliefs on someone else's say-so. We yearn for a greater sense of connection to both higher realms and the Universe at large. Perhaps we've had a taste of the Unseen or have had momentary flashes of a wider consciousness than the ordinary, and would like to have more. Above all, we desire to know—really know—the truth about spiritual matters. It is my own belief, based on my own experiences, that the esoteric traditions covered here can lead us toward that end. Courage, common sense, and the will to dig deep and persevere are the price of admission. But remember: "Entrance Not For Everybody . . . For Madmen Only."

THIS ANTHOLOGY BEGINS with a look at three main sources of inspiration for the Inner West: Neoplatonism, Hermeticism, and Gnosticism. At least a passing familiarity with these approaches to the inner and outer universes will be helpful in understanding later manifestations of the Inner West.

Next, we examine the mystical and esoteric currents within the three major religions of Western culture: Judaism, Christianity, and Islam. Although all three religions begin with the same line of prophets (starting with Abraham) and worship the same monotheistic God, they have each had unique approaches to mystical interiority.

We follow this with a look at some of the specific teachings of the Inner West: alchemy, magic, Tarot, astrology, the Divine Feminine, and Wicca. Most of these traditions (with the exception of astrology, which was widely disseminated) have kept a very low profile. The reasons were twofold: in order to avoid persecution by the Church, and out of a sense of protecting higher knowledge from those who would misuse it or misunderstand it. The learned mage and abbot Trithemius cautioned Cornelius Agrippa in the early 1500s: "Guard this precept: that you communicate vulgar secrets to vulgar friends but higher arcane secrets only to nobler and secret friends, giving hay to the cow but sugar to the parrot! Understand my words, lest you should be stomped upon by the hooves of cows."[4] It is only in the last century or so that it has been possible to discuss such teachings openly.

Many controversial claims have been made about secret societies and esoteric brotherhoods as the supposed protectors of occult wisdom down through the ages. However, responsible scholarship can point to only a few groups that have existed longer than a century or two at most. The next part of this book, "Esoteric Brotherhoods," examines some significant groups who are commonly considered standard-bearers of Western esotericism. The first of the three articles in this section presents the mythos of ancient wisdom spanning the centuries, with special attention to the Knights Templar. This is followed by looks at the Rosicrucians and Freemasonry.

In the final part of this book, "Mystics and Teachers," we survey some of the towering figures of the Inner West—visionaries and teachers who have made lasting contributions to esoteric understanding. Each had a different area of focus: the eighteenth-century Christian mystic Emanuel Swedenborg had remarkably detailed visions of Heaven and the life hereafter, and left behind an extensive body of writings. The Russian-born world traveler Helena P. Blavatsky founded the Theosophical Society in 1875; it has been possibly the single most influential esoteric organization of the nineteenth and twentieth centuries, and was one of the first to bridge the esotericism of East and West. The Austrian Rudolf Steiner was a powerful clairvoyant who gave particular attention to the esoteric traditions of the West and broke with the Theosophists to found his own Anthroposophical Society. The contribution of the mathematician and Egyptologist René Schwaller de Lubicz was not so much organizational as analytical: his twentieth-century perspectives on Egyptian architecture and religion have been a strong influence on some present proponents of alternate history and have opened the door to a new understanding of the depth of ancient Egypt as a civilization. The twentieth-century Russian philosopher and spiritual teacher G. I. Gurdjieff stands slightly apart from the other sources discussed here. He taught what he called the Fourth Way, a unique system of awareness (most famously discussed by his student, P. D. Ouspensky) that has since become a tradition of its own. Finally, we have a look at René Guénon and the Traditionalists, who were exponents of an esoteric perspective that stressed the need for would-be seekers to anchor themselves in one of the major religions even while exploring an esoteric inquiry that surpasses the boundaries of religion.

Should you wish to supplement your reading here with further studies of the subjects covered, the following books are recommended as accessible and reliable guides.

Twenty Essential Books on the Teachings of the Inner West

The Anatomy of Neoplatonism, by A. C. Lloyd (Oxford: Clarendon Press, 1991). A historic tour de force that covers the rise and fall of this philosophical tradition in two hundred readable pages.

The Hidden Tradition in Europe, by Yuri Stoyanov (New York: Arkana, 1994). A history of dualistic gnosis from Zoroastrianism through the Gnostics to the European heretical religions of the Bogomils and Cathars.

The Gnostic Gospels, by Elaine Pagels (New York: Random House, 1978). Interpretive quibbles aside, this remains the most readable and insightful assessment of the early Christian Gnostics as revealed in the scriptures of the Nag Hammadi Library, discovered in Egypt in 1945.

Jewish Mysticism: An Introduction, by J. H. Laenen (Louisville, KY: Westminster John Knox Press, 2001). An evenhanded and up-to-date discussion of Merkavah and Kabbalistic mysticism, especially valuable for its treatment of differing views among scholars.

Inner Christianity: A Guide to the Esoteric Tradition, by Richard Smoley (Boston: Shambhala, 2002). Provides, in an accessible and intelligent manner, a thorough introduction—both historical and experiential—to the mystical and esoteric approachs to the Christian faith.

The Sufis, by Idries Shah (Garden City, NY: Doubleday, 1971). The totality of Sufism, deftly fashioned into a page-turner that most readers will find
hard to put down.

Mystical Languages of Unsaying, by Michael A. Sells (Chicago: University
of Chicago Press, 1994). A marvelous, albeit dense, discussion of five Western
mystics (including Plotinus, Meister Eckhart, and Ibn 'Arabi) and their inten-
tional use of ambiguous and elusive language as a way to communicate ineffable mystical states.

The Occult Philosophy in the Elizabethan Age, by Frances A. Yates (London:
Ark, 1983). Yates has yet to be surpassed in providing a sympathetic and
knowledgeable understanding of the significant role that esoteric currents
played in the time of the Renaissance magician John Dee and and his patron
Elizabeth I.

Alchemy: Science of the Cosmos, Science of the Soul, by Titus Burckhardt
(Baltimore: Penguin Books, 1997). A concise overview of the often confusing
world of alchemy from one of the great Traditionalist scholars.

The Rosicrucians, by Christopher McIntosh (York Beach, ME: Samuel
Weiser, 1997). A very accessible survey of Rosicrucianism and Rosicrucian
groups from the 1600s to the present.

The Freemasons, by Jasper Ridley (New York: Arcade, 2001). If you only
have time for one book covering Freemasonry's history, this is the one.

Magic: Its Ritual, Power and Purpose, by W. E. Butler (Wellingborough,
Northamptonshire, UK: Aquarian Press, 1975). There are hundreds of books
about ceremonial magic; this slim volume provides an excellent overview
from a nonsensationalist perspective.

The Esoteric World of Madame Blavatsky, by Daniel Caldwell (Wheaton,
IL: Quest Books, 2000). An enjoyable and thought-provoking collection of
firsthand accounts of the controversial founder of Theosophy.

The Theosophical Enlightenment, by Joscelyn Godwin (Albany: SUNY
Press, 1994). A fascinating intellectual history of the esoteric and occult currents at play in the English-speaking world during the nineteenth century.

Modern Esoteric Spirituality, edited by Antoine Faivre and Jacob Needleman (New York: Crossroad, 1992). A fine source for further reading on the
topics covered in this book. Edited by two of the top scholars in the field.

Islamic Spirituality, vols. 1 and 2, edited by Seyyed Hossein Nasr (New York: Crossroad, 1987, 1991). These two volumes (the first on the history of Sufism and the second on Sufi practices and concepts) provide a reliable grounding in Islamic esotericism. These books, like the preceding one in this list, are part of Crossroad's World Spirituality series, which is a superb twenty-five-volume encyclopedic series.

Ego and Archetype, by Edward F. Edinger (Boston: Shambhala, 1992). This must be the single best explication of Carl Jung's work with Gnostic, alchemical, and religious sources. It provides an excellent introduction to Jung's psychology itself and its insights into esoteric traditions as a means to self-knowledge.

The Triumph of the Moon: A History of Modern Pagan Witchcraft, by Ronald Hutton (New York: Oxford University Press, 1999). A serious effort by a scholar of history to chart the origins of Wicca and describe its evolution to the present.

The Sword of Gnosis: Metaphysics, Cosmology, Tradition, Symbolism, edited by Jacob Needleman (New York: Methuen, 1986). This anthology is the best introduction to the challenging writings of the Traditionalist school of metaphysics.

Hidden Wisdom: A Guide to the Western Inner Traditions, by Richard Smoley and Jay Kinney (New York: Arkana, 1999). If this book has whetted your appetite, this guide by Richard Smoley and Jay Kinney is a thorough and accessible companion volume.

THE ESOTERIC ROOTS
OF THE WEST

HERMES AND ALCHEMY
THE WINGED GOD AND THE GOLDEN WORD

The inner and outer transformation that is taught in Hermeti-

cism and alchemy dates back to ancient Egypt and Greece.

Can it still have relevance for us today?

Richard Smoley

W here and when he lived, whether he was a man or god, or whether he ever existed on this planet at all, we do not know. He is variously identified with the Greek Hermes, the Egyptian Thoth, the Muslim Idris, and the biblical Enoch. Who was, or is, Hermes Trismegistus, Hermes Thrice-Greatest? Why "Thrice-Greatest"? What is Hermeticism?

Hermes Trismegistus makes his first appearance in known records in an unprepossessing fashion: on the minutes of an ancient meeting held to deal with certain abuses in the cult of an Egyptian god. In the second century A.D. devotees of Thoth were accustomed to offering sacrifices of his emblematic bird, the ibis, which then abounded on the banks of the Nile. (The popularity of the sacrifices may explain why the ibis can no longer be found there.)

Evidently there were irregularities either in the feeding of the sa-

cred birds or in their sacrifice; at any rate transactions of some meetings on this matter, written on *ostraka,* or broken potsherds, the memo
pads of antiquity, have survived. One of them reads in part: "No man
shall be able to lapse from a matter which concerns Thoth . . . Thoth,
the three times great."[1]

This title was affixed to the name of Hermes, Thoth's Greek counterpart, who stands at the head of the Hermetic tradition. The Renaissance magus Marsilio Ficino says: "They called him Trismegistus or
thrice-greatest because he was the greatest philosopher and the greatest priest and the greatest king."[2] Some Christian Hermeticists, on the
other hand, have claimed that Hermes got his title because he taught
the doctrine of the Trinity.

Hermes Trismegistus, though, is not exactly a god, but more of a
superhuman benefactor of our race. Like the bearded demigods of
Mesoamerica or the legendary emperors who begin the Chinese chron-
icles, he is at once teacher, ruler, and sage, who brought science and art
to humankind in its infancy.

During the Renaissance Hermes Trismegistus was regarded as the
"contemporary of Moses." Though few today believe this literally,
there is some justice in seeing a parallel between them, since Hermes
Trismegistus is revered as the primordial sage of the Egyptian esoteric
tradition, as Moses is of the Hebrew one. Like Moses, Hermes left
distinguished pupils: his line is said to include Orpheus, Pythagoras,
Plato, Apollonius of Tyana, and Plotinus.[3]

Over the centuries, the god Hermes metamorphosed into the master Hermes Trismegistus, and as the French scholar Antoine Faivre
notes:

> Hermes Trismegistus obviously possesses several of the essential
> attributes of the god Hermes: mobility, mutability (eclecticism),
> discourse and inspiration (hermeneutics), the function of cross-
> roads (tolerance, irenicism). . . . Like Hermes-Mercury, he runs

between various currents, linking the separate, skimming over oppositions while stealing their substance.[4]

Hence the tradition of the Thrice-Greatest one, which we call Hermeticism,[5] has as its main concern the esoteric arts of transmutation and change. One facet of this tradition is alchemy, with its well-known objective of turning lead into gold. But Hermeticism involves much more than that. It is concerned not only with changing one substance into another but also with transforming grosser substances into subtler ones. As the *Emerald Tablet,* the primordial document ascribed to Hermes, says, "you will separate the fine from the coarse, sweetly, with great ingenuity."

Taking a slightly different perspective, Peter French, in his excellent book on John Dee, defines the most basic concept of Hermeticism thus: "Man must know himself and recover his divine essence by reuniting with the divine *mens*" or mind.[6]

These two objectives—changing lead into gold and reuniting human consciousness with the divine mind—don't, on the face of it, seem to have much to do with each other. If one embodies the highest of human aspirations, the other looks like a cheesy get-rich-quick scheme. Yet they may not be so far apart.

To begin with the transmutation of lead into gold, we know that gold is good for tooth fillings and wedding rings, for stabilizing currencies, and for diversifying one's portfolio. But is it really worth all the attention it's gotten? Is it so important that the occult secrets of its manufacture were encrypted in the sculpture of the great French cathedrals, as the mysterious alchemist Fulcanelli asserts?[7] Even our own age, so roundly decried for its materialism, hasn't resorted to the ploy of putting scientific formulae on the walls of churches.

If you are sophisticated about such things, you may reply that of course alchemy isn't *really* talking about literal gold and literal lead—it's all a symbol for something in the psyche. And alchemists, in their cryptic way, seem to agree. "Our gold is not the gold of the vulgar," they say. How can we reconcile the apparent opposition between the symbolic and the substantial, or, as the *Emerald Tablet* puts it, between the "above" and the "below"?

I must state here that I'm not an alchemist; my practical knowledge of the art does not exceed the capacity to mix a few simple cocktails. All the same, in struggling with various Hermetic materials over time, I've come to some conclusions that strike me as useful.

To begin with, the Hermetic arts speak of two fundamental principles, *sol* and *luna.* The epithets applied to them are numerous and confusing: *sol* is Sun, gold, heaven, light; *luna* is Moon, silver, water, stone, ocean, night, and many more. It is far from clear at first what these terms mean. Baron Julius Evola, the quirky Italian esotericist whose book *The Hermetic Tradition* offers perhaps the clearest discussion of the alchemical process, says such strings of words "are symbols in the hermetic cipher language that refer, often in the same passage, to one continuous object and thereby create an enormous difficulty for the inexperienced reader."[8]

Evola goes on to quote Cornelius Agrippa: "No one can excel in the alchemical art without knowing these principles *in himself;* and the greater the knowledge of self, the greater will be the magnetic power attained thereby and the greater the wonders to be realized."[9]

So what are these principles in ourselves? "We can say that in general the Sun is 'form' and the power of individuation," Evola writes, "while the Moon—which preserves the archaic Mother and Woman symbols—expresses the 'material' and universal: to the undifferentiated vitality, to the cosmic spirit or the ether-light, corresponds the feminine."[10]

Still a bit abstract. To simplify further, we could say that *sol,* the Sun, gold, represents the principle of consciousness, that which *experiences*—the "I." The Theosophist Annie Besant calls this the Self, the

Knower, "that conscious, feeling, ever-existing One that in each of us knows himself as existing."[11]

Luna, on the other hand, is a name for that which *is experienced.* The Greeks called it ὑλη, *hyle.* This word is usually translated as "matter," but it seems more to resemble Éliphas Lévi's "astral light"—a watery astral substance that has no shape of its own but can take on the shapes of specific things.

This is to say that experience has no qualities in a pure state; we never just experience, but rather we experience *something,* and we experience it *as* something—a table, book, chair, or what-have-you. This is matter in its fixed state, or "lead."

If so, then Hermeticism, in one of its many dimensions, could have to do with transmuting the "lead" of ordinary experience into the "gold" of consciousness. Alchemists say you have to have gold in order to make gold. This would mean that you have to start with the raw material of your own experience ("lead"), using what consciousness you already have ("gold") to create more consciousness.

The alchemical process, then, can be seen as an elaborate allegory of the descent of consciousness into the matter and the means by which it returns to its pristine state. Other metals such as copper and iron, as well as the stages such as *nigredo, albedo,* and *rubedo,* would refer to intermediate steps in this process.

The idea of "mercury," for example, serves as a symbol for the means by which mind "mediates" between the knower and the known. Mercury, or quicksilver, as you know, is what we have in our thermometers; changing shape, it tells us the temperature. In the same way our own perceptions "change their shape" to reflect how the world is. (The accuracy of their reporting has always been a subject of lively debate among philosophers. And of course you'll remember that Hermes is the trickster among the gods.)

Similarly the stage of *nigredo* or blackness is associated with Venus or desire. (This points to one interpretation of the symbol of the Black Madonna, sometimes identified with Isis.) At this stage the "I" or *sol* becomes conscious of its own desire and its attachment to that desire. One of Venus's names, as Fulcanelli reminds us, is Cypris, in Greek Κυπρις or "the impure one."[12] Like Venus, desire has this dual aspect: it is beneficent, life-giving, but it cements us to our own experience, bringing death and destruction.

To realize this truth at a deep level brings about the next stage: whitening or *albedo*—the triumph of purity, the freedom from attachment to desire. Evola suggests that this purification can be accomplished in two opposite ways. There is the familiar means of asceticism (associated with Mars or iron, suggesting struggle and discipline), which is the conquest of desire, but there is also the possibility of embracing desire, especially sexual passion, and transforming it. But, Evola bluntly warns, "This is an extremely dangerous path!"[13]

Assuming that the *albedo* is accomplished without mishap, consciousness becomes purified. In this stage the "I" is known as White Gold, White Sulfur, "matter that turns copper white"—possibly meaning that it makes desire pure. (Copper, you'll remember, is the metal of Venus.)[14]

And finally, the last stage, *rubedo,* or reddening. If white is associated with purity, redness is associated with warmth. We all know people who have been stuck at the stage of *albedo:* they may well seem pure, ethereal, clean, but they also exude a certain remoteness or disembodiment. *Rubedo* adds, or reveals, another characteristic of consciousness. Evola characterizes it as the "return to earth" of purified consciousness. As the *Emerald Tablet* says, "its power is intact, if it shall have been turned toward earth."

That is to say, consciousness, the "I," *sol,* having become purified and detached from the dross of experience, must now return to give it warmth and light. This stage brings to mind the myth of the Buddha's enlightenment: having achieved supreme illumination, he yields to the entreaties of the gods and returns to earth to teach the Dharma.

This is, as you can see, an extremely brief and schematic view of the Hermetic transformation; there are many stages and substages that I've left out. (Earlier alchemists, for example, described another phase, *xanthosis* or yellowing, after the *rubedo*. This stage lays additional stress on illumination or gnosis, symbolized by the color yellow, as a characteristic of the perfected *sol*.) Clearly it's not possible to go into all these variations here, but I think the general outline holds true.

Alchemical texts are well known for their obscurities and omissions, so it comes as no surprise that we are left wondering just what technique enables this transmutation to take place.

The answers are as varied as spiritual experience itself. C. G. Jung, for whom alchemy furnished an elaborate blueprint for his view of individuation, favored work with dream figures, images, and symbols through "active imagination."

While admitting that these images are endowed with unimaginable profundity, I feel tempted to sound a note of caution here. The psychic world of dreams and images is notorious as a realm of delusion and fascination; we can wander in and forget how to find our way out. Hence dream and imagery work can prove dangerous and disorienting unless one makes a serious effort to ground oneself in ordinary work and life. (This does not seem to be a mistake that Jung himself fell into, but it does seem to be one that some Jungians fall into.)

There is, however, another means of approach, which involves a practice that probably goes back to the ancient Egyptian mysteries. It has acquired a new name in the modern world: *proprioception,* or the ability to sense one's own body. In choosing the matter on which to perform the Great Work, one alchemist advises: "Take some *real earth, well impregnated with the rays of the sun, the moon, and the stars.*"[15] This could refer to bodily sensation and experience, "real earth" impregnated with celestial and cosmic influences as manifested in our own psyches.

Sol, then, would here be conscious attention, the ability to sense and experience the body from the vantage point of "I." This is simultaneously a separation from and an immersion in the experience of the body here and now. If carried out properly, the "lead" of ordinary sensation, dull, inert, nearly dead, becomes "gold," bright, lustrous, and untarnishable. The life force itself, which begins as a thing of the earth, doomed to die like a plant or beast, becomes adamantine and immortal. Evola writes:

> The goal of Hindu alchemy was to introduce consciousness into this vital force, causing it to become part of it; then to reawaken and retrace all the phases of the organization, reaching thereby an actual and creative rapport with the completed form of one's own body, which could then literally be called regenerated. "The living man," as opposed to the tradition of the "sleeping" and the "dead," esoterically would be precisely the one who has realized such direct contact with the innermost source of his corporeal life.[16]

Isha Schwaller de Lubicz teaches that much the same is true of Egyptian esotericism:

> The way is the conscious reanimation of the entire body, the confirmation of the interplay between its functions and all its vital reactions. . . .
>
> No earthly man can perceive Spirit except in his own flesh. And this is no mere literary simile, but a most positive reality. You can only find your God by generating Him in yourself, in the darkness of your own body.
>
> For when He takes cognizance of a substance, then He becomes its God.[17]

This process of transformation through conscious attention to the body could even offer a key to the central myth of ancient Egypt, the legend of Isis and Osiris. Osiris, or the force of consciousness, is slain by Set, the force of oblivion. Osiris's limbs are scattered all over Egypt. Esoterically this could mean that consciousness in the ordinary state forgets its own embodiment; our own limbs and body parts are "scattered" in the sense that we are normally oblivious to them. Only attention and integration, represented by the gods Horus and Isis, manage to defeat Set and restore Osiris to life.

Specific techniques of proprioception, or conscious sensing of the body, are still taught today in various esoteric schools, some of which trace their practices back to Egypt itself.[18]

We can perhaps accept that alchemy, so far from being an archaic collection of nonsense, has deep symbolic import. C. G. Jung certainly thought so. In works like *Mysterium Coniunctionis,* he traces an elaborate correlation between alchemical images and the images that arise in the psyche. Jung, however, had little interest in practical alchemy, and he insisted more than once that "the alchemists did not know what they were writing about."[19]

I think one would need to be very cautious in making such a statement. Every so often one encounters a practicing alchemist who contends that the transmutation of lead into gold is meant very literally indeed. And a great deal of alchemical writing, it seems to me, makes no sense unless it is so understood.

If so, then practical alchemy is an analogous process to what I've sketched here: the alchemist goes through parallel procedures in the laboratory and in himself. The matter in his beaker is transformed alongside the matter of his body.

Exactly how this is done in concrete terms I can't say, and you are very much at liberty to disagree. But for the moment grant me my point. Let's suppose an alchemist can change ordinary, physical lead into gold. The literature is full of warnings about doing it for reasons of greed. And the operation is secret, so there can be no question of proving a point to somebody. So why go through this procedure?

As I've stated it here, alchemical transformation involves taking something with only a minimal amount of life and intelligence in its ordinary state and refining and perfecting it until it reaches a state of higher being. Hermes Trismegistus says: "As above, so below." What does this enable us to conclude about laboratory alchemy?

Here you might recollect an idea that appears often in esoteric thought: the notion that everything in the universe is endowed with consciousness. Even a sodium atom, which we normally regard as having no intelligence at all, "knows" how to recognize, and bind with, a chlorine atom. An atom's consciousness is very narrow and rigidly determined, but it does have consciousness nonetheless.

Hence it would stand to reason that some substances have more "consciousness" or "knowledge" than others. Gold is in this sense more "intelligent" than lead: it "knows" how to shine, and unlike baser metals, such as copper, iron, or silver, it also "knows" how to stay free from tarnish or rust. To transmute lead, a comparatively dull and dense substance, into an intelligent one is thus a means of raising the consciousness of matter.

Again, though, what's the point? Even if an alchemist were able to transmute several pounds of lead into gold, this is still an infinitesimal quantity of all the matter known to exist. Can the consciousness of the universe really be raised by this procedure?

Here it's important to avoid a common trap. As good Americans, we automatically assume that more is better. But it may not always be so. The point of alchemical transmutation may not lie in the size of the final product but in the transmutation itself. There may be something in the procedure that acts like a homeopathic remedy, stimulating the growth of consciousness in the universe in ways we can't imagine. After all, consciousness, like life, wants and needs to perpetuate itself.

At this point we stand on the borders of other schools and other disciplines. To liberate the infinitesimal shards of intelligence that groan under the oppression of dullness, to produce "gold," not only in the literal sense but by increasing the consciousness of an inert substance, calls to mind, for example, the idea in Lurianic Kabbalah that "sparks" of the primordial Light are imprisoned in all things and that it is the duty of the righteous to liberate them. I don't imagine the Hermetic Great Work (or for that matter Lurianic Kabbalah) is the *only* way of enacting such a liberation. But it may be one way.

This all may sound rather superstitious. It's not so superstitious, though, to think that the world, inanimate as well as animate, possesses an interiority that can be either neglected and despised or awakened and cultivated. It's even possible that this great secret offers a clue to our purpose on earth, which we've forgotten as we've become identified with the shifting shapes of our own mercurial perceptions. Does the *Emerald Tablet* allude to this purpose when it says, "This is the father of all consecration of the whole world"?

Enough, perhaps, about Hermeticism for now. What of Hermes himself? I hesitate to use words like "god" or "archetype," but possibly we can think of him as a superhuman intelligence who not only reminds us of our function in linking the "above" and the "below," but who regulates the great spiritual streams of humankind.

Hermes Trismegistus has stood at center stage in world history three times so far. Of his first manifestation, in predynastic Egypt or earlier, we can say nothing; it is all but completely obscured by its remoteness. The second time he comes to the fore, this time in a historical epoch, is in late antiquity, when the gods of the Pagan pantheons had grown weak and old. Here the Hermetic works served as a bridge between the ancient faiths and the new Christian milieu that would supplant them.

Then Hermes reappears in the Renaissance, when the Christian stream itself had grown tired and corrupt. At this point the *Corpus Hermeticum,* rediscovered among the ruins of Byzantium in 1460, helped inspire the Renaissance and served as a midwife for the birth of modernity, which over the past century has grown into the first truly global civilization.

Today modernity seems to have reached its own state of exhaustion. Is Hermes reappearing in our own age to reformulate his tradition once again? Certain impulses suggest it. There is on the one hand the looking backward of certain streams of contemporary Neopaganism, which are trying to revive the worship of the gods of Greece and Egypt. There is also the looking forward of various new religions, with their admixtures of old forms with contemporary science and psychology.

Though both of these directions are valuable and necessary, I'm not sure that any of the current attempts at reformulation have arrived at their goal. It seems unlikely that bird-headed figures will inspire worship in the humanity of the third millennium. On the other hand, any new religion will have to join the pack of squabbling faiths that are already crying for the allegiance of humankind.

Perhaps the Hermetic impulse today, rather than reformulating the traditions of the past, will have as its chief objective the tolerance and irenicism of which Antoine Faivre speaks. That is to say, rather than inventing a new faith, it may instead try to teach the ones that already exist to live in peace. At the same time it may also remind them of the goal that lies at the heart of each: the transformation of the "lead" of ordinary being into the "gold" of true consciousness.

THE STAR-GODS OF NEOPLATONISM

The teachings of Plato and his later followers are among the most

influential of the Inner West. Their belief that the stars were

gods, mediating between eternity and mortal life on earth,

provides a fascinating glimpse of their perspectives.

Kenneth Stein

I n modern times we think of the stars as enormous gaseous bodies in
outer space. It can come as a shock to learn that the Neoplatonists
thought of them as visible gods circling the earth. Were these ancient philosophers merely naïve? Or did they have some knowledge
that we lack?

Neoplatonism was the last phase of the philosophical school originally founded by Plato (c. 428–347 B.C.E.). Modern scholars believe that
Plato tried to explore the nature of truth through dialectical discussions in his dialogues rather than setting out a definite doctrine. But
the Neoplatonists present Plato's ideas as a systematic occult philosophy that is implicit in his writings; they considered themselves to be
simply continuing Plato's teaching. Indeed the doctrines of the Neoplatonists are all to be found in Plato, but with different emphases than
they seem to have in his works.

Ammonius Saccas (175–242 c.e.) apparently initiated this phase of
Platonic thought during the early third century in Alexandria, which
was a hub of Platonic ideas. Little is known about Ammonius, except
that his pupils included Plotinus (205–270), the greatest of the Neoplatonists. Other significant figures include Porphyry (c. 234–c. 305),
Plotinus's pupil and biographer; Iamblichus (c. 250–c. 330); and Proclus (c. 410–485), who has the distinction of being considered the last
major Pagan Greek philosopher.

Neoplatonism was concentrated in several centers. Athens was the
primary one (the Academy, an institution of higher learning founded
by Plato himself, was located there), but Plotinus taught in Rome,
while others worked in Alexandria and Syria. Regional differences
sometimes paralleled differences in emphasis. Plotinus's approach
stressed the metaphysical and speculative, whereas the Syrian school,
represented by Iamblichus, focused more on theurgy, by which the aspirant could contact higher realms.

The Neoplatonists worked out a fully developed esoteric philosophy. When they refer to the stars, we may think their intent is to explain them as modern science does, and we see immediately that their
knowledge of physics and astronomy is mistaken. But the Neoplatonists were concerned with a holistic conception of things, a system of
interconnected and interacting wholes and its meaning for human
beings. It is from this perspective that we must understand their view
of the earth and stars. To grasp it is to understand much, not least of all
ourselves, in terms of a different order of reality.

To the Neoplatonists, all things in the changing, visible Cosmos (the
heavens and the earth) are linked to an invisible realm, eternal and unchanging, composed of divine beings: "The All persists: the ground of
all the change must itself be changeless," as Plotinus states in *The Enneads*.[1] For them the "spiritual" implied not so much piety or holiness
but the invisible reality from which everything comes. Through the

senses human beings perceive an imperfect realm, but through the mind they can reach the true nature of things.

Neoplatonism, like astrology, sees the realm of the fixed stars and the seven planets as being above the earth, linking man with the invisible spiritual realm beyond. (The ancient schema counted the sun and the moon with the five visible planets, Mercury, Venus, Mars, Jupiter, and Saturn, because, unlike the fixed stars, they seem to change their positions in the sky.)

The stars—and I shall use the term here to include the seven planets—are in some sense material, since they are visible. But they are quite different from earthly things because they have the marks of divinity: "The sun is a God because it is ensouled; so too the stars."[2] They are spherical in shape and move in circular, self-renewing orbits around the earth. They also give off light (to the Neoplatonists an immaterial substance), another sign of divinity. The stars are not composed of the ordinary four elements, but of a refined mixture of them. Moreover these starry bodies do not lose their light; they live forever. As such, they are intermediate gods, linking our fragmentary, partial experiences on earth with the divine whole.

The worldview of Neoplatonism is like a vertical chain. The One, the source of all things, eternally emanates three basic planes through modifications in its own nature: Divine Mind (Intellect), which contains the gods and the Forms or Platonic Ideas; Soul, which is life; and the Cosmos, the visible physical realm. Beneath these at the lowest level is Matter, an invisible principle that is formless, indeterminate, and always in flux, producing instability and evil on earth. Even so the earth is not all evil; it also contains the gods, Forms, and principles within it.

Plotinus emphasizes that the stars do not completely cause events on earth. Though they exercise general providential functions, they are not responsible for the accidents and evils of human life; they are only one influence on man. Plotinus emphasizes that the stars are a sign system: "In such a total, analogy will make every part a Sign."[3] They recall a divine reality to people on earth. Since they can indicate future events in a general way, they are a help to mankind. But being divinities, they are not worried, rushing around, or meddling in human affairs; they are above human concerns. Eternal, perfect, and beautiful, the stars express on a lower, visible level the eternal order of the immaterial divine world. Any unexpected irregularity in the heavens, such as the appearance of shooting stars or comets, is a general sign from the star-gods of some unusual good or evil to come, not an indication of any true imperfection.

For Neoplatonism the visible world, existing in ever-fluctuating matter, time, and space, is an imperfect reflection of the divine realm. "As above, so below," as the key Hermetic text, *The Emerald Tablet,* puts it. Plotinus says we know what is "there," in the divine world, by considering what is "here," "the Intellectual against the sensible."[4] "Here" there is sexual differentiation; thus gods and goddesses must exist in the higher realm. We see different types of animals and vegetation on our earth; thus their essences, the Forms that generate each type, live "there." Even abstract principles, such as geometric figures, numbers, qualities, and relations, exist in the unchanging world. Soul links the two realms. But we must put away our notions of time, space, and matter. There are no time, space, and matter in the divine, but a higher interrelation of unities, a holistic reality: "It is in virtue of unity that beings are beings."[5]

Thus things in the earthly realm are copies of the perfect unities of the divine. These unities exist on three levels: on the highest they are gods; on an intermediate level they are Forms; on the lowest they are principles.[6] All three operate in the manifestation of the visible Cosmos.

Reality, then, is like a chain of links from the One through the realm of the invisible gods to the visible stars and finally to the corporeal, visible earth. Each link in the chain produces the one beneath it without losing its own full nature, and each lower level receives from and participates in the higher, of course in its fashion: "Anything that produces another is superior to the nature of that produced."[7] For Proclus, there are three levels of manifestation of the planets—higher, intermediate, and lower—each of which exhibits the same basic characteristic on progressively weaker levels.

The sphere of the fixed stars, which revolves changelessly around the earth, represents the "Same," that is, the eternal invisible god-realm beyond. The planetary stars, however, represent the "Different," since they move in varied orbits and thus reflect the changes in life.

In his *Commentary on Plato's Timaeus,* Proclus explains the nature of the fixed stars and the seven planets. They are made of all four elements, fire, air, water, and earth, but in a refined state, with fire, or visibility, dominant and earth, or tangibility, recessive. There is a descending chain of stars and planets with one of the four elements ruling in each, until we reach the earth, where the four elements are cruder and in constant flux and the element earth, or tangibility, is dominant and fire, or light, recessive. Thus there is a whole from the stars to the earth in descending scheme from perfection to imperfection.[8] But the invisible divine realm, beyond time, space, and matter, is always fully accessible to the visible universe and to every point in it, including human beings.[9]

In the same commentary Proclus describes the rulerships of the gods of the planets. The moon is generation, or nature; Mercury is symmetry and also imagination; Venus is appetite and beauty; the sun gives light, truth, sight, and visibility; Mars engenders division, heat, irascibility; Jupiter indicates excellent temperament and vitality; and Saturn causes connectedness, coldness, and intellectual powers.[10]

HUMAN BEINGS AND THE STARS

In the Neoplatonic view, human beings are originally part of the realm of the stars, which is the seedbed for human souls. Choosing a life on earth, souls descend. In this process they forget their divinity even though they carry some memories of it, which are the source of our implicit striving for perfection. Human beings thus are microcosms that recapitulate the macrocosm. Within each person there are planes: the highest mind, which retains the intuitive imprints of the divine god-forms; the rational soul; the imagination; and finally the lowest aspect, which governs sense perception and memory and also maintains the bodily functions. Each individual human replicates the entire chain: Divine Mind, Soul, and Body.

Each soul that descends to earth comes from a particular planetary star-group and contains some aspect of the god that rules it. Thus there are Saturnian, Jovial, and Mercurial types, for example. Human beings who correctly identify with their planetary soul can even attain godlike characteristics. An example is Asclepius, the god of healing, originally a human being who attained divine status because of his identification with his god.[11]

Above all, implicit in our higher soul is a sense of the divine Forms. Though we draw geometric figures, we can never make a perfect square or circle. Even in our imagination we cannot picture them perfectly. Nonetheless we have ideas of them in our higher soul. The same is true of such abstract concepts as justice and love; everything here is a copy of the perfect paradigms above. In order for us to know anything there must be unchanging Forms; sense perception will give us only uncertain opinions. To know is to recollect the Forms.

When the individual soul descends from its original place in the stars, it comes within the range of effluences that constitute the "starry-formed vehicle," which contains the soul itself. As it descends, the highly attenuated nature of this astral body, which is at this stage more like air, takes on moisture, which makes it congeal to some extent; finally, it takes on an external corporeal nature.[12] If at death the starry body is not sufficiently pure because of its activities during life, it sinks down and reincarnates; but if it has been purified through philosophic knowledge and theurgy, it will ascend.

The starry body, the primary vehicle for spiritual activity, contains the imagination, which is the human faculty for visualization. There is a lower aspect to this astral body that is closer to the material (the emotions), as well as a higher aspect (reason). At death the person goes to the divine realm, but only when the lower vehicle is purified.[13]

During corporeal life, the astral body can to one degree or another leave the body. In dreams, for example, we have the sense of moving in time and space, even though we are really projecting these dimensions within the space of the imagination.

Another example is the practice of geometry. Proclus explains that when the mind makes geometric figures, it is projecting them within the space of the imagination. Geometry is a lower-level method of going beyond the corporeal and activating the visualizing faculty within the astral body. Mathematics is an even stronger example of the ability of the astral body to dispense with the material, since mathematical calculations don't require the use of geometric diagrams like circles and triangles.[14]

But on earth, sense perception distracts us with its variety, intensity, and complexity. We fall into partial modes of thinking—materialistic, opaque, and drawn to the passions, which can distort, depress, and unbalance us. We can try to accept the imperfect world, but it gives no satisfaction. Enlightenment consists of seeing the whole reality; it aligns us with the genuine order of things.

Through various meditative practices, we can recall the god-forms and our forgotten origin; we can elevate ourselves above the corporeal passions and commune with higher levels of reality, producing discernible effects in ourselves and the world. Above all, we can escape the cycles of reincarnation and return to the divine.

This return does not require asceticism but temperance, awakening the higher emotions and intellect, and overcoming the passions. By these means we can become gods and rule in eternal bliss. This ultimate bliss is not merely intellectual; it is an elevation of both intellect and emotion, a fullness of Being.[15] It focuses on our identification with the True, the Beautiful, and the Good. To return to the divine realm is to rule in one's spiritual body with spiritual perception, to act as a god spontaneously and without labor, in essential harmony with the Whole.

THE LAW OF SYMPATHY

Human beings are linked in a real way with the stars and beyond. The Neoplatonists call this connecting link "sympathy," which is far more than an emotion; it is the principle of like-to-like attractions and similarities within and among the planes of reality.[16] Everything in the Neoplatonic universe is interrelated. All things are full of gods, Forms, and principles. All things seek their own kind amid the antipathies caused by Matter.

The entire visible Cosmos is a sympathetic reflection of the divine in matter, time, and space. Plotinus sought to explain the physical capacity of sight on the basis of sympathy. Sympathy also accounts for psychological influences among human beings. It can cause visions or communications from the gods or spirits as well as phenomena like positive coincidences and sudden healings. It can even have effects in the verbal realm: the Neoplatonists interpreted the Greco-Roman myths and Homeric poems to show how the truths of the Neoplatonic teaching are concealed within them.

Sympathy is not a dead, external similarity, but a living, magnetic principle. Iron particles are drawn to the lodestone. The moonstone is connected with the moon because of its opalescence; so is the cat, since its eyes enlarge and narrow like the waxing and waning of the moon. The sunflower relates to the sun, since its blossom follows the sun's movement. Proclus also cites the burning caused by a flame as an example of sympathy. When someone puts a piece of paper in the vicinity of a flame without touching it, the paper can burst into fire. Thus the flame emanates its power in sympathetic gradations into the area around it.

Others have observed sympathy in modern times. Goethe calls it "electric and magnetic powers" by which we exercise an attractive and repelling force in our world. Paul Kammerer refers to it as "seriality," the ordering of natural things and events in apparent "coincidences." C. G. Jung calls it "synchronicity," a principle connecting events beyond ordinary physical causation. Quantum theory speaks of it as "nonlocal causation," by which effects can occur in any part of the universe.

Sympathy is seen in meditation or contemplation.[17] All things contemplate; it is their link with Being. The Demiurge, one of the invisible gods, contemplates the gods, Forms, and principles of the divine realm, and the visible, material Cosmos springs into existence. Plotinus himself considered purely external action to be inferior to contemplative thought. And although human beings are necessarily involved in external activity, those who understand the law of sympathy can employ it beyond merely physical action.

In man, this fundamental link with the Whole gives rise to magic, theurgy, and mysticism, enabling us to overcome the evils caused by Matter and realize the transcendent. Magic operates within the visible Cosmos; it is the use of quasi-material means, like spells and incantations, to produce effects in the material world. Through theurgy one can attain experience of the gods themselves.

Plotinus explains magic as the responses of the star-gods to spells.[18] Some of his students objected: magicians sometimes ask for immoral things and receive them. Could the star-gods be responsible for that?

In answer, Plotinus stressed that the star-gods are not conscious of their role. The effects of magic are a sympathetic, superconscious effect of their power, like a string producing a sound when it is plucked. It is the magician who has to be moral. For Plotinus, magical effects pass through the Cosmos by way of the star-gods, since all is interconnected in the Whole. We live among invisible realities.

Although Plotinus exercised magical and clairvoyant powers, he is critical of magic because it entangles man in lower, worldly desires when he should detach himself from them. Magic may be a real force, but the sage remains untouched by it because it is beneath him. Instead he is concerned with higher sorts of sympathy, theurgy, and ultimately union with the Supreme One. Man must return to his original unfallen state. How? By the practice of theurgy.

THE STARRY VEHICLE

In its later stages Neoplatonism largely came under the influence of the "divine Iamblichus," most of whose works have perished except for a defense of theurgy entitled *On the Mysteries*. In this work, Iamblichus maintained that, to reach the higher planes, theurgy is superior to philosophy. All knowledge of the Forms is incomplete, he held, but theurgy gives experience. Proclus, the authoritative later interpreter of Neoplatonism, was strongly influenced by theurgy, which he considered "more excellent than all human wisdom."[19] Theurgy included a range of activities to induce trance states similar to those in modern séances. But it also included meditative activities.[20]

Proclus wrote a commentary on the *Chaldean Oracles,* a second-century transmission by a theurgist named Julian that survives only in fragments.[21] Proclus's commentary (itself fragmentary) is of the greatest interest because it contains instructions for private meditation, which he explicitly relates to theurgy. This meditative activity involved turning away from sense perception and the fluctuating opinions derived from it, as well as from ordinary reasoning, to rise to the "celestial regions" through sympathy. "A forgetfulness of eternal reasons is the cause of the departure of the soul from the Gods," Proclus writes, "and . . . a recollection of the knowledge of the eternal Forms is the cause of the return to them." Furthermore he observes that symbols enable one to recollect these higher realms. The symbol, by its suggestiveness, focuses and energizes the starry body, inducing imaginative experience in the spiritual realm.

In theurgy we are not merely knowing by means of sense perception or ordinary reasoning. We are establishing a rapport, a sympathetic link, between our higher reason, which contains the god-forms, and the higher realms. In this realm of intuition, the identity of the individual soul is not lost but realizes its fullness.

The Neoplatonists give us a holistic science; one must grasp their intent and procedures to understand them. They saw the imperfect, visible Cosmos and human beings as living reflections of the perfect, invisible realm beyond. The stars enable man to recollect the Same, the eternal realm of mind, as well as the Different, the changing realm of sense perception. Through the Neoplatonic teaching, especially theurgy, man can use the stars as a medium for recalling his identity with the eternal structure of Being.

3

THE QUEST FOR SPIRITUAL FREEDOM

THE GNOSTIC WORLDVIEW

The alternative worldview of the ancient Gnostics provides a
startling solution to the problem of suffering and injustice
in the Universe.

Stephan A. Hoeller

Gnosticism is the teaching based on Gnosis: the knowledge of
transcendence arrived at by way of interior, intuitive means.
Although Gnosticism thus rests on personal religious experience, it is a mistake to assume that all such experiences result in Gnostic recognitions. It is nearer the truth to say that Gnosticism expresses
a specific religious experience, an experience that does not lend itself to
the language of theology or philosophy, but is best expressed through
the medium of myth. Indeed, one finds that most Gnostic scriptures
take the forms of myths. The term "myth" should not here be taken to
mean "stories that are not true," but rather, truths that are expressed as
stories.

ORIGINS AND BACKGROUND OF GNOSTICISM

The Gnosticism with which we are most familiar flourished among Christian sects in the first few centuries of the Christian era, until it was overpowered by the organized Church.

What was the origin of Gnosticism and how is it best understood? For a very long time the normative and prevalent answer to this question came from the heresiologist Church Fathers of the second through fourth centuries, c.e. These sources, which included authors entirely hostile to the Gnostics (Irenaeus, Hippolytus, Tertullian, Epiphanius) and some mildly antagonistic ones (Clement and Origen), put forth the view that Gnosticism is a Christian heresy, that is, a body of teachings that represents a deviant and corrupted form of the "real" or mainstream Christianity. However, this position was effectively attacked, if not outright demolished, by prominent nineteenth-century scholars, mainly of German nationality. Beginning with the works of F. C. H. Baur of the Tübingen school, and augmented by the researches of Adolf von Harnack, Richard Reitzenstain, and many others, this scholarly tendency contended that Gnosticism could not have been a heresy because in its time there did not exist anything like a normative orthodoxy. Instead, there existed a number of approaches to the Christian religion that functioned simultaneously and at times competed with each other. What came to be known later as Gnostic schools were simply some of these early variants.

Another explanation that arose from the "paganizing" inclinations of some scholars declared that Gnosticism was a form of Paganism with a Christian coating. Some slight internal evidence was advanced to prove this contention: Gnosticism was far less rigidly monotheistic than either Judaism or later, mainstream Christianity; and the feminine emphasis in many Gnostic teachings may have had a relation to Egyptian or Greek goddess worship. Similarly, the prominent empha-

sis of Gnosticism on a secondary, world-creating quasi-deity called the
Demiurge had a precedent in the teachings of Plato and his followers.
Still, it is well known that prominent Pagan teachers, including the
Neoplatonist Plotinus, attacked the Gnostics. Moreover, a Pagan vari-
ant of Gnosticism, called Hermeticism, existed side by side with Chris-
tian Gnosticism. These circumstances contradict the notion that
Gnostics were simply Pagans masquerading in quasi-Christian dress.
Certainly the religious thought of Mediterranean Pagan cultures was
not excluded from the thinking of the Gnostics, but it was far from being its core.

Yet another tendency, powerfully present in nineteenth- and early
twentieth-century scholarship tried to locate the origins of Gnosticism
in cultures outside the Mediterranean matrix. Persia, India, and southeast and northwestern Asia were considered as possible sources of the
Gnostic tradition. Much was made of the "dualist" attitude that is
shared by Gnostics and Zoroastrians. What these scholars neglected
was the fact that significant differences separate Zoroastrian dualism
from the Gnostic variety. The former may be considered radical dualism while the latter appears to be of a more qualified kind. That similarities exist between Gnosticism and both Hinduism and Buddhism
cannot be denied. Both of these great Eastern traditions recognize
a form of Gnosis, called *Jnana* in Sanskrit, which is regarded as a
salvific form of enlightening knowledge. Still, no historical trajectories
have been discovered that would point to Asia as the cradle of the
Gnostic tradition.

In the latter portion of the twentieth century, scholarship increas-
ingly came to view the Gnostic religious phenomenon as largely of
Jewish historical provenance. The researches of the late Gershom
Scholem and particularly the content of the Nag Hammadi library of
Gnostic writings contributed powerfully to this view. Scholem linked
Gnosticism with Jewish Chariot-mysticism and with the origins of the
Kabbalah. The scriptures contained in the Nag Hammadi collection

suggest a link with secret, underground currents in Judaism that appear to have existed for a considerable time in opposition to the official orthodoxy of the priestly cultus of Jerusalem. The Essene groups who were responsible for writing the Dead Sea Scrolls, as well as other heretical groups of Jews, may indeed have been responsible for much of the membership not only of Gnostic Christian schools but of the entire Christian movement. Forerunners of this Jewish Gnosticism can certainly be discerned in the Wisdom literature of the Old Testament, where the deific feminine figure of the Gnostic Sophia appears in an early form as the majestic Chokmah of Proverbs, Ecclesiastes, Ecclesiasticus, and of the Book of the Wisdom of Solomon.

In sum, the historical context indicates that Gnosticism (as it came to be called some hundreds of years later) was originally a Jewish esoteric spirituality that assumed a Christian form after the coming of the Christian dispensation. It was subsequently repressed by a self-declared orthodoxy that itself was originally but one of several variants within a diverse fold of the followers of the great Teacher of Nazareth. The majority of the original sources of the Gnostic tradition tell us that this tradition was always in the world and that its principal teachers and hierophants were certain prophets and patriarchs of the Old Testament, beginning with Adam and his son, Seth. While obviously mythological in nature, these statements reveal to us truths often more profound than the so-called objective data of history. Gnosis and Gnosticism have always been in the world and have taken different forms in different cultures. The Gnostic tradition associated with Christianity and with Western culture in general originated in the Mediterranean area and more specifically within the Semitic matrix, although, like Christianity itself, it was no stranger to the kindred spirituality of Greece, Rome, and Egypt.

In the following summary, I will attempt to encapsulate in prose what the Gnostic myths express in their distinctively poetic and imaginative language.

THE COSMOS

All religious traditions acknowledge that the world is imperfect. Where they differ is in the explanations that they offer to account for this imperfection and in what they suggest might be done about it. Gnostics have had their own—perhaps quite startling—view of these matters: they hold that the world is flawed because it was created in a flawed manner.

Like Buddhism, Gnosticism begins with the fundamental recognition that earthly life is filled with suffering. In order to nourish themselves, all forms of life consume each other, thereby visiting pain, fear, and death upon one another (even herbivorous animals live by destroying the life of plants). In addition, so-called natural catastrophes—earthquakes, floods, fires, drought, volcanic eruptions—bring further suffering and death in their wake. Human beings, with their complex physiology and psychology, are aware of these painful features of earthly existence. They also suffer from the frequent recognition that they are strangers living in a world that is flawed and absurd.

Many religions advocate that humans are to be blamed for the imperfections of the world. Supporting this view, they interpret the Genesis myth as declaring that transgressions committed by the first human pair brought about a "fall" of Creation resulting in the present corrupt state of the world. Gnostics respond that this interpretation of the myth is false. The blame for the world's failings lies not with humans, but with the Creator. Since—especially in the monotheistic religions—the Creator is God, this Gnostic position appears blasphemous, and is often viewed with dismay even by nonbelievers.

Ways of evading the recognition of the flawed Creation and its flawed Creator have been devised over and over, but none of these arguments have impressed Gnostics. The ancient Greeks, especially the Platonists, advised people to look to the harmony of the universe, so that by venerating its grandeur they might forget their immediate afflictions. But since this harmony still contains the cruel flaws, forlornness, and alienation of existence, this advice is considered of little value by Gnostics. Nor is the Eastern idea of Karma regarded by Gnostics as an adequate explanation of Creation's imperfection and suffering. Karma at best can only explain how the chain of suffering and imperfection works. It does not inform us in the first place why such a sorrowful and malign system should exist.

Once the initial shock of the "unusual" or "blasphemous" nature of the Gnostic explanation for suffering and imperfection of the world wears off, one may begin to recognize that it is in fact the most sensible of all explanations. To appreciate it fully, however, a familiarity with the Gnostic conception of the Godhead is required, both in its original essence as the True God and in its debased manifestation as the false or creator God.

DEITY

The Gnostic God concept is subtler than that of most religions. In its way, it unites and reconciles the perspectives of monotheism and polytheism, as well as of theism, deism, and pantheism.

In the Gnostic view, there is a true, ultimate, and transcendent God, who is beyond all created universes and who never created anything in the sense in which the word "create" is ordinarily understood. While this True God did not fashion or create anything, He (or It) "emanated" or brought forth from within Himself the substance of all there is in all the worlds, visible and invisible. In a certain sense, it may therefore be true to say that all is God, for all consists of the substance of God. By the same token, it must also be recognized that many portions of the original divine essence have been projected so far from their source that they underwent unwholesome changes in the process. To worship the cosmos, or nature, or embodied creatures is thus tantamount to worshipping alienated and corrupt portions of the emanated divine essence.

The basic Gnostic myth has many variations, but all of these refer to Aeons, intermediate deific beings who exist between the ultimate, True God and ourselves. They, together with the True God, comprise the realm of Fullness (Pleroma) wherein the potency of divinity operates fully. The Fullness stands in contrast to our existential state, which in comparison may be called emptiness.

One of the aeonial beings, who bears the name Sophia ("Wisdom"), is of great importance to the Gnostic worldview. In the course of her journeyings, Sophia came to emanate from her own being a flawed consciousness, a being who became the Creator of the material and psychic cosmos, all of which he created in the image of his own flawed nature. This being, unaware of his origins, imagined himself to be the ultimate and absolute God. Since he took the already existing divine essence and fashioned it into various forms, he is also called the Demiurgos or "half-maker." There is an authentic half, a true deific component within Creation, but it is not recognized by the half-maker and by his cosmic minions, the Archons or "rulers."

THE HUMAN BEING

Human nature mirrors the duality found in the world: in part it was made by the false creator God and in part it consists of the light of the True God. Humankind contains a perishable physical and psychic component, as well as a spiritual component that is a fragment of the divine essence. This latter part is often symbolically referred to as the "divine spark." The recognition of this dual nature of the world and of the human being has earned the Gnostic tradition the epithet of "dualist."

Humans are generally ignorant of the divine spark resident within them. This ignorance is fostered in human nature by the influence of the false creator and his Archons, who together are intent upon keeping men and women ignorant of their true nature and destiny. Anything that causes us to remain attached to earthly things serves to keep us in enslavement to these lower cosmic rulers. Death releases the divine spark from its lowly prison, but if there has not been a substantial work of Gnosis undertaken by the soul prior to death, it becomes likely that the divine spark will be hurled back into the pangs and slavery of the physical world.

According to Gnosticism, not all humans are spiritual (pneumatics) and thus ready for Gnosis and liberation. Some are earthbound and materialistic beings (hyletics), who recognize only the physical reality. Others live largely in their psyche (psychics). Such people usually mistake the Demiurge for the True God and have little or no awareness of the spiritual world beyond matter and mind.

In the course of history, humans progress from materialistic sensate slavery, by way of ethical religiosity, to spiritual freedom and liberating Gnosis. As the scholar Gilles Quispel wrote: "The world-spirit in exile must go through the Inferno of matter and the Purgatory of morals to arrive at the spiritual Paradise." This kind of evolution of consciousness was envisioned by the Gnostics, long before the concept of evolution was known.

SALVATION

Evolutionary forces alone are insufficient, however, to bring about spiritual freedom. Humans are caught in a predicament consisting of physical existence combined with ignorance of their true origins, their essential nature, and their ultimate destiny. To be liberated from this predicament, human beings require help, although they must also contribute their own efforts.

From earliest times Messengers of the Light have come forth from the True God in order to assist humans in their quest for Gnosis. Only a few of these salvific figures are mentioned in Gnostic scripture; some of the most important are Seth (the third son of Adam), Jesus, and the prophet Mani. The majority of Gnostics always looked to Jesus as the principal savior figure (the Soter).

Gnostics do not look to salvation from sin (original or other), but rather from the ignorance of which sin is a consequence. Ignorance—whereby is meant ignorance of spiritual realities—is dispelled only by Gnosis, and the decisive revelation of Gnosis is brought by the Messengers of Light, especially by Christ, the Logos of the True God. It is not by His suffering and death but by His life of teaching and His establishing of mysteries that Christ has performed His work of salvation.

The Gnostic concept of salvation, like other Gnostic concepts, is a subtle one. On the one hand, Gnostic salvation may easily be mistaken for an unmediated individual experience, a sort of spiritual do-it-yourself project. Gnostics hold that the potential for Gnosis and thus of salvation is present in every man and woman, and that salvation is not vicarious but individual. At the same time, they also acknowledge that Gnosis and salvation can be—indeed must be—stimulated and facilitated in order to effectively arise within consciousness. This stimulation is supplied by Messengers of Light, who, in addition to their teachings, establish salvific mysteries (sacraments), which can be administered by apostles of the Messengers and their successors.

One needs to also remember that knowledge of our true nature—as well as other associated realizations—is withheld from us by our very condition of earthly existence. The True God of transcendence is unknown in this world: in fact He is often called the Unknown Father. It is thus obvious that revelation from on high is needed to bring about salvation. The indwelling spark must be awakened from its terrestrial slumber by the saving knowledge that comes "from without."

CONDUCT

If the terms "ethics" or "morality" are taken to mean a system of rules, then Gnosticism is opposed to them both. Such systems usually originate with the Demiurge and are covertly designed to serve his purposes. If, on the other hand, morality is said to consist of an inner integrity arising from the illumination of the indwelling spark, then the Gnostic will embrace this spiritually informed existential ethic as ideal.

To the Gnostic, commandments and rules are not salvific; they are not substantially conducive to salvation. Rules of conduct may serve numerous ends, including the structuring of an ordered and peaceful society, and the maintenance of harmonious relations within social groups. Rules, however, are not relevant to salvation; that is brought about only by Gnosis. Morality therefore needs to be viewed primarily in temporal and secular terms; it is ever subject to changes and modifications in accordance with the spiritual development of the individual.

As noted in the foregoing discussion, "hyletic materialists" usually have little interest in morality, while "psychic disciplinarians" often grant to it a great importance. In contrast, "pneumatic spiritual" persons are generally more concerned with other, higher matters. Different historical periods also require variant attitudes regarding human conduct. Thus both the Manichaean and Cathar Gnostic movements, which functioned in medieval times when purity of conduct was regarded as an issue of high import, responded in kind. The present period of Western culture perhaps resembles in more ways that of second- and third-century Alexandria. It seems therefore appropriate that Gnostics in our age adopt the attitudes of classical Alexandrian Gnosticism, wherein matters of conduct were largely left to the insight of the individual.

Gnosticism embraces numerous general attitudes toward life: it encourages nonattachment and nonconformity to the world, a "being in the world, but not of the world"; a lack of egotism; and a respect for the freedom and dignity of other beings. Nonetheless, it falls to the intuition and wisdom of every individual "Gnostic" to distill from these principles individual guidelines for personal application.

DESTINY

When Confucius was asked about death, he replied: "Why do you ask me about death when you do not know how to live?" A Gnostic might easily have given this answer. To a similar question posed in the Gnostic Gospel of Thomas, Jesus answered that human beings must come by Gnosis to know the ineffable, divine reality from whence they have originated, and whither they will return. This transcendental knowledge must come to them while they are still embodied on earth.

Death does not automatically bring about liberation from bondage in the realms of the Demiurge. As previously mentioned, those who have not attained to a liberating Gnosis while they were in embodiment may become trapped in existence once more. It is quite likely that this might occur by way of the cycle of rebirths. Gnosticism does not emphasize the doctrine of reincarnation prominently, but it is implicitly understood in most Gnostic teachings that those who have not made effective contact with their transcendental origins while they were in embodiment would have to return into the sorrowful condition of earthly life.

In regard to salvation, or the fate of the spirit and soul after death, one needs to be aware that help is available. Valentinus, the greatest of Gnostic teachers, taught (circa the second century) that Christ and Sophia await the spiritual man—the pneumatic Gnostic—at the entrance of the Pleroma, and help him to enter the bridal-chamber of final reunion. Ptolemaeus, a disciple of Valentinus, taught that even those not of pneumatic status, the psychics, could be redeemed and live in a heaven-world at the entrance of the Pleroma. In the fullness of time, every spiritual being will receive Gnosis and will be united with its higher Self—the angelic Twin—thus becoming qualified to enter the Pleroma. None of this is possible, however, without earnest striving for Gnosis.

GNOSIS AND PSYCHE:
THE DEPTH PSYCHOLOGICAL CONNECTION

Throughout the twentieth century the new scientific discipline of depth psychology has gained much prominence. Among the depth psychologists who have shown a pronounced and informed interest in Gnosticism, a place of signal distinction belongs to C. G. Jung. Jung was instrumental in calling attention to the Nag Hammadi library of Gnostic writings in the 1950s because he perceived the outstanding psychological relevance of Gnostic insights.

The noted scholar of Gnosticism G. Filoramo wrote: "Jung's reflections had long been immersed in the thought of the ancient Gnostics to such an extent that he considered them the virtual discoverers of 'depth psychology'. . . Ancient Gnosis, albeit in its form of universal religion, in a certain sense prefigured, and at the same time helped to clarify, the nature of Jungian spiritual therapy."[1] In the light of such recognitions one may ask: Is Gnosticism a religion or a psychology? The answer is that it may very well be both. Most mythologems found in Gnostic scriptures possess psychological relevance and applicability. For instance, the blind and arrogant creator-Demiurge bears a close resemblance to the alienated human ego that has lost contact with the ontological Self. Also, the myth of Sophia resembles closely the story of the human psyche that loses its connection with the collective unconscious and needs to be rescued by the Self. Analogies of this sort exist in great profusion.

Many esoteric teachings have proclaimed: "As it is above, so it is below." Our psychological nature (the microcosm) mirrors metaphysical nature (the macrocosm); thus Gnosticism may possess both a psychological and a religious authenticity. Gnostic psychology and Gnostic religion need not be exclusive of one another but may complement each other within an implicit order of wholeness. Gnostics have always held that divinity is immanent within the human spirit, although it is not limited to it. The convergence of Gnostic religious teaching with psychological insight is thus quite understandable in terms of time-honored Gnostic principles.

CONCLUSION

Some writers make a distinction between "Gnosis" and "Gnosticism." Such distinctions are both helpful and misleading. Gnosis is undoubtedly an experience based not in concepts and precepts, but in the sensibility of the heart. Gnosticism, on the other hand, is a worldview based on the experience of Gnosis. For this reason, in languages other than English, the word *Gnosis* is often used to denote both the experience and the worldview (*die Gnosis* in German, *la Gnose* in French).

In a sense, there is no Gnosis without Gnosticism, for the experience of Gnosis inevitably calls forth a worldview wherein it finds its place. The Gnostic worldview is experiential and based on a certain kind of spiritual experience of Gnosis. Therefore, one might argue, it will not do to omit, or to dilute, various parts of the Gnostic worldview, for were one to do this, the worldview would no longer conform to experience.

Theology has been called an intellectual wrapping around the spiritual kernel of a religion. The more that theology dominates, the greater the danger of religions being strangled and stifled by their wrappings. Gnosticism does not run this danger, because its worldview is stated in myth rather than in theology. Myths, including the

Gnostic myths, may be interpreted in diverse ways. Transcendence, numinosity, as well as psychological archetypes, along with other elements, play a role in such interpretation. Still, such mythic statements tell of profound truths that will not be denied.

Gnosticism can bring us such truths, for it speaks with the voice of the highest part of the human—the spirit. Of this spirit, it has been said: "It bloweth where it listeth." This then is the reason why the Gnostic worldview could not be extirpated in spite of many centuries of persecution.

The Gnostic worldview has always been timely, for it has always expressed the "knowledge of the heart" that is true Gnosis. For those who long for that knowledge, Gnosticism remains a living tradition, not merely a historical one.

THE INNER SIDE
OF THE RELIGIONS
OF THE WEST

4

KABBALAH AND JEWISH MYSTICISM

AN OVERVIEW

The Jewish mystical tradition continues to renew itself through

its creative interpretation of scripture and religious practice.

Pinchas Giller

What is today called "Kabbalah" is the mystical tradition of classical Judaism. As a movement and a mode of thinking, it has always seen itself as the primordial, inner perception of Rabbinic Judaism. The Hebrew word "Kabbalah" literally means "that which is received." Because of this priority given to handed-on teachings, some early Kabbalistic circles even discouraged creativity and disqualified extemporaneous religious experience as a source for esoteric knowledge. In place of these, Kabbalists reviewed the vast exoteric Jewish tradition until the inner dynamics of that tradition began to emerge. Kabbalistic truths emerge with greatest numinosity when considered in the context of their source tradition, for Kabbalah is the product of the reconsideration of the universe of symbols provided by the extensive literature of the Second Temple period (526 B.C.E.–500 C.E.).

Jewish mystical spirituality results from the paradoxes inherent in the informing mythos of Judaism. This mythos consists of the notion of the One God, existing in ontic and historical relationship with the individual and with the Jewish community. This mythos emerges, with growing complexity, in the chronology of the Hebrew Bible. The familiar, somewhat anthropomorphic God of the Garden of Eden reaches out to form a covenant with Abraham and his progeny.

At Mount Sinai, this relationship becomes moral and contractual, with the repeated stipulation (Deut. 11) "Guard yourselves, lest your hearts be seduced, and you run off, worshipping other gods, bowing down to them . . ." Idol worship, the pursuit of illusion, is defined as humankind's great potential catastrophe. The love relationship described by Jeremiah (2:2), "I remember the giving of your youth, your consuming love, when you followed me through the desert, an unplanted land," becomes the betrayal invoked by Hosea (3:1), "God said to me, go love a promiscuous and adulterous woman, like God, when he loves the children of Israel, and they turn to other gods . . ." This erotic metaphor of love and betrayal is sustained and transformed in the eroticism of the Zoharic and Lurianic writing, two central expressions of Kabbalah.

In the Wisdom literature, the last works of the Hebrew Bible, God's relationship to the individual becomes even more complex. The Psalmist moves from exultation to despair. Ecclesiastes wonders how life can be lived without the promise of final justice. Job suffers God's capricious and arbitrary cruelty. The Bible can be read as a parable of the loss of innocence. After Job and Ecclesiastes, the next step could only be the gnostic rejection of this existence as wholly evil. Far from this imperfect, secular world and its disappointments, perhaps one could posit a sublime, pure divinity.

This was a step that Judaism never took. For all its loss of innocence with regard to life's possibilities, Judaism never renounced the redemptive potential of this world. It didn't condemn the physical and never "cut the seedling" of holiness in present existence. It could never embrace the Christian myth of the noble young god, sent down to redeem the evil world, only to be destroyed in the process. True, Kabbalah did conduct an ongoing flirtation with the gnostic myth of a distinction between present reality and the separate realm of the Divine. However, in the Kabbalistic worldview, this was not a complete separation, but rather God's emanation through the ten S'firot, the dimensions or realms of existence.

There is much secondary material on Kabbalah available in English, but it is largely unsuccessful in portraying its inner nature. Modern scholarship in Kabbalah has been dominated by historiography, which isolates various historical periods, or graphs the development of individual ideas. In the midst of this type of study, the constant images and symbols are often lost, though they are sometimes retained as psychological symbols.

For instance, the biblical love relationship between God and Israel may have transmuted into the erotic metaphor of the *Mysterium Coniunctionis*, the union of the transcendent and earthly manifestations of God. This idea has parallels in alchemical literature and even in Canaanite notions of fertility that predate the Bible. For the Jews, in the synagogue of the Sabbath Eve, rising to greet the "Sabbath Bride," it makes no difference that they are invoking a symbol of spiritual transformation as defined by the studies of Jung and Neumann. They only want to enhance their own Sabbath experience with the image of the Divine Eros, to celebrate the erotic energy suffusing the world on that night, as the Zohar describes so many times.

Kabbalah, particularly the hermeneutic tradition of the Zohar, grew out of Judaism's sanction of the practice of ongoingly reinterpreting itself. The Pharisaic Judaism of the Second Temple period canonized the Hebrew Bible. Yet it also encouraged the existence of an amorphous, creative "oral" tradition. This creative tradition had many applications. It might alter the interpretation of a particular law of the

Pentateuch, altering its nature entirely. Or a biblical narrative might be expanded to include more colorful, legendary elements. This process of oral tradition is a battle that Judaism wages against alienation from its own roots, an alienation that is a natural result of the experience of exile. This method of biblical interpretation is called Midrash, and it is the central literary mode of the Zohar, the central Kabbalistic text.

An example of this process would be the reinterpretation of the biblical passages dealing with the Tabernacle and the sacrificial cult. When the Temple in Jerusalem was functional, these passages, which comprise much of the books of Exodus and Leviticus, were immediately relevant. How could they retain their immediacy, with the Temple long in ruins and the Jews exiled in Europe and the Near East for many centuries? The Midrashic traditions, with the Zohar at its farthest reaches, interpreted the passages on the dimensions of the Tabernacle as relating, in fact, to the dimensions of the Universe. The Tabernacle was an earthly paradigm of the Cosmos; to ponder its constituent elements was to ponder the Divine superstructure.

With this view of the meaning of scripture, a novel inversion took place. Texts that were overtly meaningful, that gave ethical instruction or narrated the history of the Jewish commonwealth, were relegated to a secondary position. Texts that described any kind of static relationship, on the other hand, be they the dimensions of the Tabernacle, the stratified social roles of the book of Proverbs, or the seduction imagery of the Song of Songs, were given primary consideration. The static images of these passages, coupled with their timeless relevance, were perceived as the encoded secrets of the Universe.

One striking effect of this inversion of importance was in the vast realm of ritual and practice. According to the mystical perception of Jewish law, the precepts, or *Mitzvot,* possess an esoteric as well as an exoteric character. The Ten Commandments and other precepts with overt moral validity have an exoteric function, while the more obscure strictures, such as not mixing milk and meat or not blending wool and linen, have a more esoteric nature. Since they are less obviously of this world, the more obscure and esoteric Mitzvot were potentially more profound, since they related to another realm entirely.

In order to discern this esoteric understanding of the Bible, a school of Kabbalistic Midrash came into being, epitomized by the Zohar and its related literature. The Zohar itself achieved the status of canon fairly soon after its compilation. Eventually, passages of Zohar were incorporated into the synagogue liturgy, the highest accolade that the Jewish tradition affords its literature. The subliminal message of the Zohar is that the highest mystical experience lies in the inspired creation of exegesis of the Bible. Not incidentally, this perception conforms with the most conservative of Jewish values, that Torah study and dissemination is the central redemptive activity.

A second form of Kabbalistic expression came from the ecstatic, prophetic tradition inherent in biblical Judaism. Even in the biblical period, extemporaneous prophetic ecstasy aroused some consternation, though Moses himself yearned: "O that all the people of God were prophets, that God would give his spirit to them!" (Num. 11:29). Popular, mantic prophecy seemed to fade at the beginning of the Second Temple period, with apparent Rabbinic attempts to forcibly drive it from the public imagination (Mishnah Sotah 9:12). The tradition of mystical ecstasy continued in closed circles, among a group known as the "descenders of the Chariot" (Yordei Mercavah). The imagery of this tradition combined the chariot vision of Ezekiel 1 with the idea of ascent/descent into graduated celestial chambers and palaces. Interestingly, a number of hymns from the Mercavah tradition have survived in the standard liturgy and are sung in thousands of synagogues every Sabbath.

This mantic tradition reemerged, or perhaps regenerated sponta-

neously, in the works of the thirteenth-century mystic Abraham Abu-
lafia. The mystical hermeneutics of the Zohar were also being compiled at this time, and the two traditions initially found themselves in
opposition to each other. Subsequent medieval systems of Kabbalah
sought to combine these intellectual and ecstatic elements, particularly
in the traditions of Tsfat, the small Galilean town that served as a
haven for the Kabbalah after the Spanish expulsion in 1492. In Tsfat,
systematizers of the Kabbalah such as Rabbi Moshe Cordovero and
Rabbi Isaac Luria combined the hermeneutic and ecstatic forms into
unified systems. Today, the surviving Near Eastern, Lithuanian, and
Hassidic schools of Kabbalah have functional systems of meditation as
well as vast theoretical literature.

Since the Middle Ages, Kabbalists have often found themselves in
conflict with proponents of religious rationalism. In this conflict, the
rational, conscious mind of the philosopher is often pitted against
the symbolic unconscious of the mystic. In Judaism, it was generally
the Kabbalists who prevailed, usually by subsuming and subverting the
conclusions of the philosophers.

Maimonides, the twelfth-century Spanish Aristotelean who synthe-
sized all of Rabbinic Judaism in his legal and philosophical works, was
adamantly opposed to anthropomorphism, the visualization of God in
physical terms. It was, in fact, very authentically Jewish of him to defend the abstraction of the idea of God's unity. Unfortunately for Maimonides, this notion of the God who is One tended to break its own
paradoxes. The Bible further complicated the issue with images such as
humankind being created "in his image, in the form of the image of His
structure" (Gen. 1). The editor of the Idra Rabbah, the most flagrantly
anthropomorphic passage of the Zohar, added the following disclaimer.

To remove all stumbling-blocks from the path of those interested, on whom the light of Kabbalah has not yet shown, let the

hearer hear, and the seer see, that all the words which the Godly Rabbi Shimon Bar Yochai brought in this holy book, such as "brown of the skull," "hairs of the head," "cranium," "nostrils of the ancient," "ears," "hands," "feet," and so forth from the physical vessels and other images with which he described the Blessed God, specifically in the Holy Great Idra and the Holy Lesser Idra (for in these places, such descriptions are particularly profuse); these all indicate dimensions and spheres and inner, cerebral concepts. All the limbs about which the sages euphemized, are for the imagination, indications of hidden and obscure things, not for any physical or material thing, God forbid, for there is no image between the Holy One and ourselves, in any sense, and especially not in the physical realm. May God save us from error, Amen-may-it-be-Thy-Will! (Zohar 3:127b)

For Maimonides, God had no physical form and it was forbidden to imagine Him thus. For the Kabbalist, it was acceptable to portray God's attributes in physical terms, on the understanding that it was an appropriate understanding of something that was beyond all corporeal expression. This convoluted reasoning was in fact already acceptable Jewish practice. Any Jew knows that God has no physical form, even as he or she sits at the Passover meal and recites: "We were slaves in the land of Egypt and the Blessed Holy One brought us out with a mighty hand and an outstretched arm."

A second area of conflict between philosophical and mystical Judaism was in the rationale of the Laws of the Torah. For the rationalist, the Torah's laws have a perfecting effect on the human character. Failing this rationale, the Torah's laws have a commemorative function. For example, the prohibition against eating blood (Deut. 12:23) is explained by Maimonides, in the *Guide of the Perplexed,* as being the avoidance of a certain pagan rite in which blood was eaten ceremonially. Maimonides' Kabbalistic opponent, Nachmanides, gives a differ-

ent understanding, in his explanation of Leviticus 17:11 ("for the soul
of all flesh is in the blood"):

> Nobody with a soul should consume another soul (i.e. the blood),
> for the souls all belong to God, the human soul and the animal
> soul are His, the same thing happens to them in the end, this
> one's death is like the other's death, they all have one spirit. . . .
> That which is eaten returns in the body of the eater. Were a man
> to eat the soul of another creature, he would absorb all of that
> creature's coarseness and stupidity.[1]

As a mystic, Nachmanides discerns a malevolent power in the pro-
hibited substance. As previously mentioned, Kabbalah generally saw
the Mitzvot as relating to present and transcendent reality simultaneously. Philosophical rationalism, with its commitment to present reality above all, could hardly compete. By the Renaissance, the Zohar and
Lurianic writings were ascendant and the *Guide of the Perplexed* often
unavailable. It remained for philosophical Judaism to reemerge in the
mid-nineteenth century, when European society saw fit to emanci-
pate the Jews and accept them, for a time, as part of the Western community.

Today, it seems that religious rationalism is once again in a state of
decline. The West is in the grip of an outbreak of millennial fundamentalism. Eschatological circles in Christianity, Judaism, and Islam
toy with the idea of a coming apocalypse, each group assuming that it
will emerge, unscathed, from the rubble. At the same time, American
Judaism, long denuded of its mythic, symbolic content, sees its numbers steadily decreasing.

In the Israel Museum, in Jerusalem, there is a wooden synagogue
from eastern Europe, preserved in its entirety. All the others like it
were destroyed by the Nazis in the 1930s. On the walls and ceiling of
the synagogue, the whole mythic bestiary and aviary of the Midrash

and Kabbalah gambol and frolic: the Leviathan, the Primal World-Snake, the Unicorn and Dragon, the forgotten population of the Jewish Unconscious. Will a new generation reclaim the Kabbalistic view of reality? I would hope that the Kabbalistic worldview can survive as a mode through which humankind realizes the preciousness of its own existence.

5

THE MYSTICISM OF CHRISTIAN TEACHING

Christianity is about a personal relationship with God. But it's
also an inner work that aims for the deification of the seeker.

Theodore J. Nottingham

The word "esoteric" has been largely misunderstood. It has often been used to represent groups that are secretive or occult
in some form. But the essential meaning of the word can be
translated as "inner." It is part of the concentric circles defined as *exoteric, mesoteric,* and *esoteric*—from the outer form to the inner teaching. Once this understanding of the word is clear, one can link the idea
of esotericism with that of mysticism, which also represents the work
of inner transformation at the heart of spiritual teachings.

In exploring the inner teachings of a religion such as Christianity, it
is necessary to go beyond the standard dogmas that are passed on
through catechism, Sunday-school classes, and theological seminaries.
From the very beginning there was an inner understanding of the
teachings that had to be uncovered. Jesus said to his disciples: "To you

has been given the secret of the kingdom of God, but for those outside, everything is in parables" (Mark 4:11).

THE TEACHING

Christianity is not the worship of a cult figure. It is the very process of transformation that makes a human being another *Christos,* an awakened child of the Creator. Perhaps few of us will achieve Christ's level of oneness with the cosmic forces that brought all things into being, but that may be because few of us are willing to sacrifice and love as fully as he did. We can each be temples of the spirit, new creations liberated from our pettiness and blindness and empowered to bless the world. But how badly do we want this compared to all other distractions, conveniences, and enticements offered to us at every instant?

Christian teaching describes both crucifixion and resurrection. These words are not only metaphors, nor are they simply events that happened in antiquity. Rather they are concepts that apply to the human ego—the one thing that stands in the way of our development.

The ego is grounded in unevolved natural forces (the survival instinct, infantile self-centeredness), in unconscious behavior (parental imitation, environmental influence), and in imagination (fantasy of self-importance). It is an impostor that is the source of our misery and distorted relationships to others.

The Christ says: Cut it loose, jump off the cliff of your false identity; don't turn back, or, in the language of the Bible, "Sell all you have and follow me." This is a radical, unadulterated, all-consuming teaching. At the same time it is centered on active compassion, irrepressible hope, and ecstatic joy. It encompasses the yin and yang, the death and rebirth recognized by all visionaries as being at the core of reality itself.

Severe ascetics and fanatic followers have often violated the purity of this old teaching. But it is easy to find the authentic reflection of a

life in Christ among Christianity's best representatives, such as Francis
of Assisi, Teresa of Avila, and, in our day, Thomas Merton. The great
saints and mystics were lovers of God and therefore lovers of all beings. One of them, the twelfth-century monk Bernard of Clairvaux,
expressed the nature of Christian inner work with sublime simplicity:
"The measure of love is to love beyond measure."

WATCHFULNESS

One key to opening the door to our true nature is found in the most
common element in our psyche—attention. Early Christian teachers
recognized it as central to spiritual development.

An elementary definition of attention might be that it is a focusing of
our energy onto a subject of interest. We all know instinctively when this
inner power waxes and wanes. We can remember from school days how
often we found our attention wandering off into realms of fantasy or to
the scenery outside the window. With maturity, we may have found it
necessary to develop that "muscle" of concentration to keep ourselves engaged on a task. Many people have not realized that this same intangible
power of attention is critical to spiritual awakening. If we let it dissipate
into the countless distractions of life, we will find that our life force is
drained, unavailable for our ultimate task of conscious existence.

Most of us lack the self-awareness that is required to realize the dignity of being human. From the character driving down the highway
more focused on his daydreams than on the lives of those around him
to the thoughtless parent who humiliates his child, this lack of inner
attention is the cause of our continual stumbling.

Self-awareness and the subsequent discovery of the Divine are rare
in human behavior because they require energy. We squander most of
the psychic "gold" of our attention on things from fidgeting to out-
bursts of anger. Such wastage can wipe out a whole day's ration of energy, as can constant talking, daydreaming, and worrying.

Watchfulness requires us to pay attention to the thoughts, impulses, and desires that vie for expression and satisfaction. This very attention may prevent them from taking control. Through this effort we acquire self-mastery and establish a stable foundation for inner transformation.

Nothing can be accomplished if we are not dependable or mindful of our commitment. We cannot be of use to ourselves or to anyone else if we are constantly tossed about by the waves of inner chaos. We gain a "clear sight" when we lift ourselves above the thoughts and feelings that struggle within us. This is not merely a psychological trick, but makes room for the inflow of a higher power.

Christ, understood not as a man from the Judean hill country but as the incarnation of the conscious core of all creation, tells us in clear terms how essential it is that we find our center: "He who abides in me, and I in him, he it is that bears much fruit" (John 15:5).

To abide in Christ is not a matter of religious belief but of alignment with the very nature of reality. As the Belgian priest and theologian Louis Evely has said, "Jesus' greatest liberation is to have liberated us from religion! He wanted us all to have free, direct, and joyful access to God."

This access is free, but it does require specific efforts on our part, the first one being the *watch of the heart,* so central to the inner teaching of early and monastic Christianity.

DETACHMENT AS ILLUMINED PRESENCE

Spiritual teachers throughout the Christian tradition tell us that learning how not to respond to external stimuli is a necessary step for inner development. This does not imply a cold, disconnected relationship to life. Detachment, as understood in the mystical tradition, is removal, not from life, but from one's own uncontrolled emotions.

The teachings gathered in the *Philokalia* from the great masters of

Orthodox Christianity offer specific ways of developing these inner powers. Turned inward, attention stands guard over images coming in from without and thoughts arising from within. Persistent awareness ensures that both stimuli are kept from further influencing our behavior. Once an image is allowed to penetrate within, it is on the way to being materialized into action.

The early masters list the following capacities developed through inner watchfulness:

- The guarding of the intellect
- Continuous insight into the heart's depths
- Stillness of mind unbroken even by thoughts that appear to be good
- The capacity to be empty of all thought

Thus protected, the heart can give birth to thoughts of a more conscious nature. External reality now comes to us without the filters of expectations, prejudices, and judgments that otherwise mar our view. Experts in inner warfare tell us that we should wage this war with a focused and united will that disperses fantasies. The intellect then no longer pursues them "like a child deceived by some conjurer" (*Philokalia,* saying 105).

The masters further claim that such watchfulness gives us knowledge previously unattainable by our intellect while we were still "walking in the murk of passions and dark deeds, in forgetfulness and in the confusion of chaos" (*Philokalia,* saying 116).

THE INDWELLING OF THE UNCREATED

The ancient scriptures that are the foundation of Christianity invite us to seek after the mystery and power that we name God. They tell us that this unknown and yet very present creative force of the universe responds to us individually. But they add that a personal contact must be established to enable us to participate in this new consciousness: "It is no longer I who live, but Christ who lives in me" (Gal. 2:20).

These words express the indescribable intimacy possible between human beings and the Divine. The experience of this encounter yields a transformation that is the entrance into another dimension of reality, known as life eternal. "And this is eternal life, that they know the only true God, and Jesus Christ whom thou hast sent" (John 17:3).

Evelyn Underhill (1875–1941), one of the great scholars of Christian spirituality, defines mysticism as "the hunger for reality, the unwillingness to be satisfied with the purely animal or the purely social level of consciousness."[1] This is the first stage in the development of a mystical consciousness. Mysticism calls for a relentless effort in the concentration of thought, will, and love upon the eternal realities that are commonly ignored. An attitude of attention, best described as a state of prayer, is required.

Underhill writes that

> the readjustments which shall make this attention natural and habitual are a phase in man's inward conflict for the redemption of consciousness from its lower and partial attachments. The downward drag is incessant, and can be combatted only by those who are clearly aware of it, and are willing to sacrifice lower interests and joys to the demands of the spiritual life.[2]

The mystic way is therefore a process of sublimation, carrying the self to higher levels than ordinary states of awareness. But this is no selfish journey. For as the mystic grows nearer the source of true life and participates in the creative energies of the Divine, he or she is capable of greater activity on behalf of others. Among the mystics in the Christian tradition are found missionaries, prophets, social reformers, poets, founders of institutions, servants of the poor and the sick, and instructors of the soul.

In her book *Practical Mysticism,* Underhill insists that "the mystic is not merely a self going out on a solitary quest of Reality. He can, and must, and does go only as a member of the whole body, performing as it were the function of a specialized organ. What he does, he does for all."[3]

We learn from the writings of the mystics that such a consciousness has the power to lift those who possess it to a plane of reality that no struggle, no cruelty, no catastrophe can disturb.[4] This "inner sanctuary" is the point where God and the soul touch. In the fourteenth century, John Tauler, a student of Meister Eckhart, referred to this place as "the ground of the soul." Catherine of Siena spoke of the "interior home of the heart," Teresa of Avila knew it as the "inner castle," and John of the Cross described it as the "house at rest in darkness and concealment." These metaphors suggest a secret dwelling in the center of our being that remains permanently united with God's creative act. The self in its deepest nature is more than itself. To move into oneself means ultimately to move beyond oneself.

Out of her vast study and experience, Underhill offers us one of the finest definitions of the essence of esoteric work: "Mysticism is the way of union with Reality. The mystic is a person who has attained that union in greater or lesser degree; or who aims at and believes in such attainment."[5]

The history of the Christian religion cannot be separated from the history of its mystics, for its doctrines represent their experiences translated into dogma. The Church's language concerning new birth, divine sonship, regeneration, and union with Christ are all of mystical origin: they are derived from concrete experiences rather than speculation. Such experiences are not the exclusive possession of spiritually sensitive persons. In the state of humble receptivity, any human spirit can apprehend a reality greater than itself.

One teacher who greatly affected the spiritual evolution of the West through esoteric teaching in our century is George Ivanovich Gurdjieff (1866?–1949). He points to the one of the main problems in the mystical search: "Christianity says precisely this, to love all men. But this is impossible. At the same time it is true that it is necessary to love. First one must be able, only then can one love. Unfortunately, with time, modern Christians have adopted the second half, to love, and lost view of the first, the religion which should have preceded it."[6]

Throughout Western history, Christianity has emphasized the goal of human life and neglected the means by which this goal may be reached. The result has been a certain recognizable personality and behavior that is an imitation rather than the outcome of real inner transformation. Jacob Needleman, a major contributor to the modern spiritual journey, asks in his book *Lost Christianity:* What is the bridge that can lead a person from the state of submersion in egoistic emotions to that incomparable range of life known under the simple term "love of God"?

FAITH AND BELIEF

We are part of a culture in which religion is mostly a matter of words, exhortations, and philosophy rather than practical guidance for directly experiencing the truth of the teachings. Methods and exercises, such as are found in the writings of the Desert Fathers of the third and fourth centuries, once brought the possibility of growing beyond a self-centered psychology. But our age has cast them aside in its disdain for anything that is not entirely at the disposal of the rational mind.

Because of this prejudice, the sacred response of faith that emanates from a higher level within us has become confused with a kind of "belief" that Needleman calls "one of the numerous egotistic mechanisms within the mind that seem designed solely for the purpose of making people feel they are in the right and that everything is going to be all right."[7]

Maurice Nicoll, a leading teacher of esotericism as inner psychological transformation, presents a reply: "Faith is a continual inner effort, a continual altering of the mind, of the habitual ways of thought, of the habitual ways of taking everything, of habitual reactions. To act from faith is to act beyond the range of the ideas and reasons that the sense-known side of the world has built up in everyone's mind."[8]

The dichotomy between knowing and believing rests on the fact that what the intellect thinks may contradict what the heart believes. Christianity has always recognized that thinking by itself cannot change human nature. Christ's teachings do not merely offer an explanation of life but rather a means of making life different. It is an obvious fact that, while we may think great thoughts, we may not be able to live according to what we know to be true.

As long as our emotional life remains the same, full of self-justification and negativity, all the right thinking in the world will not change our essential nature. It is not that the mind cannot form a thought of God, but that such thoughts in themselves cannot change anything in us. Something else is required. The tradition tells us that there is within us a force that draws us toward Truth, and this force is neither the thinking nor the emotional function. This is what the word "faith" is meant to stand for, but it cannot be equated with simple emotional conviction.

Thomas Merton tells us that faith is neither an emotion nor an opinion. "It is not some personal myth of your own that you cannot share with anyone else, and the objective validity of which does not matter either to you or God or anybody else."[9] For Merton, faith does not bypass the mind but perfects it. "It puts the intellect in possession of Truth which reason cannot grasp by itself."[10] The act of faith is also a contact, a communion of wills. Merton observed that in the state of faith we experience the presence of God. "Faith is the opening of an inward eye, the eyes of the heart, to be filled with the presence of the Divine light."[11]

Something must be awakened in us that is both highly individual, the holistic blossoming of our true self, and at the same time free from mere subjectivity, something intensely our own yet free of the ego's tyranny. This is the heart of esoteric teaching.

TEACHINGS ON THE SOUL

One of the great errors of the exoteric Christian tradition may be that it takes for granted the presence of a soul already formed and functioning. Yet the soul is not a fixed entity but an actual energy that is activated in the experiences of daily life. The assumption of a soul in finished form within human nature has led to identifying our ordinary thoughts and emotions with the higher part of ourselves, and thus to the mistaken effort of trying to perfect our being by perfecting our thoughts and emotions. But spiritual growth does not come merely through intellectual or emotional development. There is another state of being to be reached, another quality of awareness that reveals new aspects of reality.

All religious traditions call for a change of spiritual focus and for an attuning of the whole soul to what is beyond and above ourselves. It is a turning of our being toward spiritual things. As spiritual things are simple, *recollection* is a simplification of our state of mind. It gives us the kind of peace and vision of which Jesus speaks when he says: "If your eye is sound, your whole body will be full of light" (Matt. 6:22).

Christian teaching refers to recollection as more than a mere turning inward upon ourselves. This method does not necessarily mean the denial of external things. Recollection makes us aware of what is most significant in the moment of time in which we are living. When the outward self is submissive and ordered by the inward being, then the soul is in harmony with itself, with the realities around it, and with God. When we are not present to ourselves through recollection, we are only aware of the mode of being that turns outward to created things, and thereby we lose ourselves in them. Recollection aligns the outward self with the inward self and gives us access to the Spirit.

An example of this condition is given to us by the German psychotherapist and spiritual teacher Karlfried Graf Dürckheim. He tells us that the simple act of watering a flower can be done merely because the plant needs water. But it can also be undertaken as an act of love. The moment is then transformed from an ordinary activity into a profound and memorable experience that introduces us into the presence of spiritual reality both within ourselves and in the material world.

But this manifestation of love is possible only to the degree that a person has transmitted the truth to the whole of himself or herself. This requires some kind of self-mastery and unrelenting commitment.

The wisdom teachers of early Christianity developed a method of self-study that is of timeless value. These enlightened elders tell us that "temptation" (or influences from our fragmented thoughts that arise from both the inner and the outer worlds) occur in the following manner:

- It begins innocently by a simple *suggestion* through some word or picture.
- If the soul communicates with it, then comes the *assent,* when, as John Climacus says, "the object lodges for a long time in the soul, which gets used to it."
- Finally comes the *captivity,* where the heart is dragged along involuntarily, this alien thought now having become a dominant force in the psyche.

The ultimate wisdom of these ancient mystics is that continual inner attention is made possible by a form of perpetual prayer. This is the basis of a state of higher consciousness putting one in touch with eternity at the heart of the passing moment.

THEOSIS

At the heart of the Eastern Orthodox tradition, which is rooted in the earliest developments of Christianity, is a very mysterious word: *theosis*. Around this word revolved the whole spirituality of the ancient Church.

Theosis means divinization. The Eastern Fathers spoke of God becoming human in order to deify humanity. They did not mean to suggest that human beings can share in the Divine substance, but rather that we can experience the Divine energies of relationship and communion.

Deification is a relationship of love brought about by the Incarnation. *Theosis,* in this context, means participation in the Divine nature. Such transformation, or rebirth, involves a penetration into the depths of reality and a confrontation with all forms of illusion in ourselves and in society. The road to God then becomes one of darkness and mystery, in which all human concepts are seen as relative.

The early Church strongly believed in this unknowability of God. Gregory of Nyssa stated that not only is the essence of God unknowable, but even the essence of an ant is unknowable. Only in that darkness which Moses entered on Mount Sinai can we come close to God. We know through "unknowing." Here Christian esoteric teaching and Eastern spirituality reach common ground.

Christians often forget that, although the witness of the New Testament is Christocentric, Jesus himself is theocentric. The Church has tended to deify Jesus in doctrine, art, and hymns. In doing so, Christians often succumbed to the dangers of a personality cult that has almost lost sight of the underlying fact that God is all in all. Jesus is then seen as a kind of cult figure over against other religious figures. But the encounter between the Divine and the human in Jesus Christ should not be distorted into a confrontation between Christianity and non-Christian religions.

Theosis is both a change and a recovery of that which is deepest and most personal in ourselves. The first birth is a preparation for the second birth, which is the spiritual awakening of the mind and heart. This is a consciousness that takes us beyond the level of the individual ego. Mystical rebirth is not a single event, but a continual inner renewal that occurs many times in our lives. We not only grow in love, we become love.

The cross symbolizes the supreme power of God to transform defeat into triumph through sacrificial love. Since life is the spirit, the power, the energy, and manifestation of God, death is to be seen as another state of being in which the spirit continues to live in God. The Resurrection is the link between the two, enabling one who is transformed by inner purification to experience conscious awareness of the eternal. Call it esoteric, mystical, or inner Christianity—this is the original spark that came from the historical event in the first century A.D. that still transforms people to this day.

6

SUFISM

A PATH TO HUMAN WHOLENESS

Sufism doesn't ask for renunciation of life in the world. Instead it

can be seen as a way to become more fully human.

Kabir Helminski

If you came to a crossroads and the signs read "This way to Life" and "This way to God," which would you choose? How many people have believed that the way to the Divine reality is in the opposite direction from the path of a human life? How many have developed pathologies because they took the road away from life, away from their own humanity? For me the compelling quality of Sufism is its humanity, its integration of the highest spiritual attainment with a fully lived human life. For the Sufi, the realization of the Divine is the realization of complete humanness.

Sufism has taken form over the last fourteen hundred years within the matrix of the Qur'anic revelation, the most recent of the major sacred traditions. Its spiritual power is generated by the enlightened state received by the prophet Muhammad and passed on in a verifiable

81

esoteric lineage. Its style and flavor come from the lived example (*sunnah*) and words (*hadith*) of Muhammad.

Within classical Sufism, the Qur'anic revelation and the *sunnah* of the Prophet provide a matrix within which the human being matures and comes to completion. In this tradition it is believed that the Reality we are seeking is also seeking us and has offered guidance in the form of revelation and inspired teachings. It is assumed that the sincere seeker will be guided step by step by his or her Lord (in Arabic, *Rabb,* which also means "educator"). And so Sufism consists of a balance between revealed guidance and individual spiritual experience.

When I came to Sufism, I felt that I had long since "graduated" from conventional religion and had entered the path of experiential spirituality. Nevertheless, what I encountered in Sufism, especially as I experienced it in the Middle East, challenged my indifference to the ideas of prophethood and revelation and helped me to be more receptive to Islam and the Qur'an. Over more than fifteen years of questioning and experience, I gradually came to accept that the Qur'an is an authentic manifestation of Divine Intelligence, or, in its own words, "a guidance for mankind" (2:185), a revelation that is intelligible and applicable in any historical, geographical, or cultural milieu.

> In this, behold, there is indeed a reminder for everyone whose heart
> is wide awake and surrenders their ears with a conscious mind.

> Will they not, then, try to understand this Qur'an? Had it issued
> from any but God, they would surely have found in it many inner contradictions.[1]

SUFISM AS SYNTHESIS

Sufism has been a vital spiritual and historical impulse that has guided and integrated the spiritual energies of hundreds of millions of people for over fourteen centuries. It is a mistake to think of it as an Eastern, or even Middle Eastern, tradition. Its spiritual claim to universality is based on an understanding of the Qur'an as the inspired synthesis and reconciliation of earlier revelations. Its historical claim to universality lies in its power to assimilate the spiritual attainments of the cultures of the whole region from Spain through Africa, Arabia, Turkey, Iran, India, China, and central and southeast Asia.

Sufism integrates the Eastern and the Western, the impersonal and the personal dimensions of Spirit. Like the Eastern traditions, it recognizes the importance of deep contemplation and meditative awareness and looks beyond appearances to the essential oneness of Being. Like the Western traditions, it recognizes the importance of a deeply personal relationship with the Divine as well as love and practical service to our fellow human beings and the natural world.

Sufism is a path emphasizing individual presence, human affection, esthetic beauty, practicality, and Divine love. It is in harmony with human nature and does not oppose spiritual attainment to individual, social, or family life. It does not see seclusion, asceticism, celibacy, monasticism, social parasitism, or religious professionalism as either necessary or helpful to attaining spiritual maturity. The Sufi model of enlightenment is not the reclusive sage who has cut his ties with the world or the enlightened master elevated and served by a cult of followers. Sufis do not regard spirituality as a profession or specialization separate from life. The Sufi is likely to be married and have a family and is generally self-supporting through a socially useful occupation. He or she would not accumulate personal power or wealth through spiritual activities but would exemplify the qualities of servanthood and self-effacement. "A Sufi is a handful of dust passed through a sieve, then moistened with a few drops of water. Stepped on, he neither bruises nor muddies the foot of the passer-by."[2]

Sufism developed in many dimensions: social, cultural, esthetic, scientific. The Sufi centers (*tekkes, dergahs,* and *khaneqas*) were typically places of continual learning. Not only did they offer spiritual training and service, but they were cultural and intellectual centers as well, introducing the highest values and cultural achievements into their respective societies.

The late Jelaluddin Çelebi, until his death the head of the Mevlevi Order and a descendant of Jelaluddin Rumi, the order's founder, was born and raised in a Mevlevi *tekke* in Aleppo, Syria. He has described to me his precious memories of this place, where spirituality flourished side by side with learning, art, and agriculture, and where the sounds of music, discourse, and prayer were heard from every quarter. He told how one *dede,* a great violinist, could often be heard playing the classical compositions of the Mevlevi tradition, as well as Bach and other Western composers, with tears streaming down his cheeks. This Mevlevi community was also progressive in its attitudes, often introducing technological change, such as tractors, radios, and telephones, into the wider community.

More than a thousand years ago, Sufis started the professional guilds that spiritualized the arts and crafts of the Islamic world and whose principles, in a more secularized form, later spread to Europe. The principles of chivalry, or heroic service, are also from an Islamic mystical source, the Futtuwah Orders, and were likewise carried to Europe. Sufi groups were responsible for the restoration of agriculture to central Asia after the Mongol devastation in the thirteenth century. In the Ottoman Empire, the Mevlevi Order contributed many of the finest examples of design and calligraphy, classical music, and literature. Today Sufis are at work making profound contributions in the fields of human rights and conflict resolution, in the frontiers of consciousness and transpersonal psychology, and in the arts and social services.

A HUMAN WAY OF LIFE

Sufism consists of both essence and form. Its essence is a state of loving mind. This state of loving and enlightened mind is supported by and integrated with a way of life that is its form. Sufism involves inner verification, a spiritual empiricism, but it is not only that. It is spiritual practice guided by revelation, a revelation that, moreover, suggests a normative human life. In the West this may be its least understood aspect, especially today, when liberal, secular culture offers no particular value system other than a tolerance based on the relativity of all value systems.

In the West, Sufism has sometimes been taken out of context and superficially understood in terms of methods and techniques, ideas, ceremonies, and states. Other sacred traditions have suffered a similar fate: Buddhism, for instance, has often been effectively reduced to a technique of meditation while its religious law, the Eightfold Noble Path, is left in the background. If Sufism is understood as a system of techniques for engendering ecstatic states, it is understood only partially. We cannot steal the fire. We must enter it. "Seven hundred Sufi masters have spoken of the Path, and the last said the same as the first. Their words were different, perhaps, but their intention was one. Sufism is the abandonment of affectation. And of all affectations, none is weightier than your 'you-ness.'"[3]

Sufism could be seen as a recovery program for those addicted to the separate self. It is theoretically possible to overcome this addiction without any program, but the power of the addiction is easily underestimated and often denied. Overcoming it can be like trying to scale a high wall: one's best efforts can be frustrated unless one has a ladder of the right height with its rungs in place.

Classical Sufism involves a way of life, a pattern of submission that includes regular ablution, prayer, and fasting, as well as the qualities it sees as normative for human life, including affection, gentleness, patience, generosity, hospitality, sobriety, modesty, intelligence, and restraint. Practices taken out of this context are at best incomplete and at worst may contribute to the illness rather than to the cure, furthering the addiction to self.

THE SUFIS, ESPECIALLY the Mevlevis, have created a system of human development grounded in love and using the power of love to awaken and transform human beings. Rumi taught that it is everyone's potential to master the art of loving. Using the typical Sufi context of a group or spiritual family, the Mevlevis have created a milieu in which human love was so strong that it naturally elevated itself to the level of cosmic love. "Ishq olsun," they say: "May it become love." They have cultivated a kindness and refinement in which love ferments into a fine wine. They encourage service to humanity as an expression of the love they feel. And they accept a rigorous discipline in order to keep the fire of love burning strongly.

> The porter runs to the heavy load and takes it from others,
>   knowing burdens are the foundation of ease
>   and bitter things the forerunners of pleasure.
> See the porters struggle over the load!
> It's the way of those who see the truth of things.
> Paradise is surrounded by what we dislike;
>   the fires of hell are surrounded by what we desire.[4]

Although even some of the greatest minds have asserted that love is a complete, unknowable mystery, Sufism proposes that there is a knowledge of love, that it desperately needs to be shared, and that in fact no knowledge is more valuable and essential. On the one hand,

Rumi has said: "Whatever I have said about love, when love comes, I am ashamed to speak." On the other hand, if love is the essential power within this universe and within ourselves, no subject has greater precedence. It may be that failure in any field is essentially a failure of love.

LOVE'S UNIVERSE

From the Sufi point of view, this universe is an expression of love. We live in an ocean of love, but because it is so near to us, we sometimes need a shock to remind us of its constant presence. A story goes to illustrate this: A little fish was told it could not live without water, and it became very afraid. It swam to its mother and, trembling, told her about this substance without which they would die. The mother said, "Water, my darling, is what we're swimming in."

We experience a profound forgetfulness when we come into this world. Its greed, drudgery, and arrogance can seem a cruel trap. But after we acknowledge the centrality of love, everything that happens is part of the process of awakening to the fact that love brought us here, that we are loved by a beneficent unseen Reality, and that the core of our being is love. Love is seeking to discover itself; indeed the whole purpose and meaning of creation is to discover the secret of love.

We begin to see the infinite power of love as the greatest cause in the universe, and little by little we begin to serve it. In order for us to serve, love needs to be grounded in knowledge. Love without knowledge is dangerous. With love alone we could burn ourselves and others; we could become lunatics. Love is such an extraordinary and complex power, and the human being has such a great capacity for it, that to dismiss it as an unknowable mystery is like standing in awe before a fire and saying we don't know what this is, how it started, or what to do with it.

Love is both mystery and knowledge. Furthermore, it is a mystery that has spoken to us about itself in the form of those revelations and exemplars that have profoundly altered the course of human history.

For the Sufi, Muhammad is the foremost exemplar. Without the character of Muhammad, who is called "the living Qur'an," the whole spirit of Sufism is inconceivable. Thanks to his influence, the impulse of Islam arose from what had been the decadent backwater of Arabia to foster a vast civilization based on human equality, social justice, and divine remembrance. In the West we are generally unaware of the historical significance of Islamic civilization and the degree to which it established justice and equality, furthered scientific inquiry, and guaranteed religious tolerance for more than a thousand years. In these areas it maintained precedence over other civilizations, at least until its relatively recent decline in the last few centuries. It was Muhammad who bestowed upon the Muslim community the magnetism and inspiration that gave birth to this high level of culture.

Ali, the prophet's son-in-law, into whom the secrets of Sufism were breathed, preserved these words that he heard from Muhammad:

> *Meditation in God is my capital.*
> *Reason and sound logic are the root of my action.*
> *Love is the foundation of my existence.*
> *Enthusiasm is the vehicle of my life.*
> *Contemplation of Allah is my companion.*
> *Faith is the source of my power.*
> *Sorrow is my friend.*
> *Knowledge is my weapon.*
> *Patience is my clothing and virtue.*
> *Submission to the Divine Will is my pride.*
> *Truth is my salvation.*
> *Worship is my practice.*
> *And in prayer lies the coolness of my eye*
> *and my peace of mind.*[5]

Muhammad's character, which exemplified a life of love, became a model for all Sufis; the study of his sayings and deeds has always been central to the Sufi curriculum. The Sufis in their turn expanded the prophet's impulse into an ever more explicit expression of love.

The Sufi seeks to uncover and grasp the principles by which we can cooperate with this power of love. We can reconnect our isolated wills to love's will. It is possible to open up to the experience of love through the practice of active submission. ("Islam" literally means "submission.")

Active submission is being receptive to the intelligence of Spirit and living accordingly. This submission is the natural state of the essential self, free of selfishness, anxiety, and fear. With this submission to Spirit, the human being discovers his or her finest and noblest capacities and achieves a balance of spiritual receptivity and energetic activity in relation to his or her life in the world.

The opposite of this submission is the neurotic anxiety and compulsive living that is accepted as normal today. Because we have cut ourselves off from Spirit, we have swelled with false pride and thrown the world out of balance. Our bodies and minds, our relationships, and our whole ecology are suffering the consequences.

THE SCHOOL OF LOVE

The great thirteenth-century Turkish Sufi Yunus Emre said: "Let us master this science and read this book of love. God instructs; Love is His school."[6]

Perhaps the most important thing that Sufism can offer is the deepening realization that we are all students in the school of love, although it may take us a long time to admit this fact. It is amazing how stubborn and slow we can be to realize this, and how often we still forget. We forget whenever we see our own desires and goals as being more important than the feelings and well-being of those we love. We forget whenever we blame others and lose sight of the fact that in this school of love, it is love that we all are trying to learn.

We have all been failures in love. This is our conscious starting point. We can practice meditation and seek spiritual knowledge for years and still overlook the central importance of love. In fact the subtlest of all forms of egoism comes when we try to be "more spiritual" than others. But love forgives even that.

I do not really know if this modern world is further from the truth than many civilizations that have preceded it. Yet so much of what occupies our attention seems a fiction, leading us to lives of delusion, selfishness, and loneliness. Behind our anxiety is a lack of meaning and purpose, a lack of love. Unless we look with the eyes of love, we cannot see things as they are.

One of the most painful experiences for any person is recognizing that most human beings take themselves as the exclusive goal and center of their thoughts, feelings, and activities. It can be terrifying for a sensitive soul to live in a world where everyone is so busy achieving his or her own goals that real human needs are trampled in the process. For most people, even "love" is primarily a form of self-gratification. And for many of us spirituality begins as a way of feeling good about ourselves. Yet this self-centered way of being is exactly the "sin" that all authentic spiritual traditions would save us from.

It doesn't matter what we have accomplished, what recognition we have received, what we own; there is nothing as sweet as loving—not necessarily being loved, but just loving. The more we love, the richer we are. Nothing is more beautiful or sacred than the impulse of love we feel for a friend, a child, a parent, a partner. Nothing would be sweeter than to be able to love everywhere and always.

One of the essential concepts in Sufism is that of *adab,* spiritual courtesy, respect, appropriateness. Through *adab* the seeker begins to melt some of his or her egoism. *Adab* is not formality; it helps to create the context in which we develop our humanness in this school of love. Every situation and relationship has its proper *adab:* relations between students on the path, relations with family members and elders, relations with one's shaikh. Every level of being has its *adab.* Coming into the presence of Truth has its *adab,* too.

The assimilation of *adab* has been fundamental to my own experience of Sufism. It is one of the first things that our shaikh stressed as Sufism was being introduced to Westerners. "Help them to learn *adab,*" he would say.

As one begins to become aware of the benefits and possibilities of *adab,* it becomes strikingly clear how much has been lost in contemporary culture in the name of some hypothetical freedom and individuality. By contrast, *adab* is taking complete responsibility for oneself, for one's thoughts, feelings, and actions. A few of its principles might be conveyed as follows.

To be straightforward, sincere, and truthful.

To cultivate awareness of and regret for our own faults rather than finding fault with others.

To do what one does for Allah's sake, not for the sake of reward or fear of punishment.

To be free of the preoccupations, worries, vanities, and ambitions of the world.

To be indifferent to the praise or blame of the general public.

To ignore any extraordinary states that occur during one's worship or practice.

To adopt an appropriate humility and invisibility in public and in the meetings of the dervishes.

To serve the good of one's brothers and sisters with all one's resources.

To heal any wound you may have caused to another and to correct any misunderstanding within three days if possible.

To know that no good will come out of the expression of anger or
   excessive hilarity.

To be patient with difficulties.

To be indifferent to favor or benefit for oneself, even to "receiving
   one's due."

To be free of all forms of spiritual envy and ambition, including
   the desires to lead or teach.

To make one's practices inwardly sincere rather than outwardly
   apparent.

To increase one's knowledge of Sufism (including the Qur'an,
   hadith, and the wisdom of the saints).

To struggle with one's ego as much as it prevents one from
   following proper *adab,* and to realize that the greatest ally is love.

To have a shaikh whom one loves and is loved by, and to cultivate
   this relationship.

As Shaikh Tosun Bayrak al-Jerrahi has said, "As difficult as it may
be to find a perfect shaikh, it is more difficult to be a minimal dervish"
(i.e., a humble student of Sufism).

Where does all of this lead? This poem from *The Walled Garden of
Truth,* written in the twelfth century by Hakim Sanai, offers a distilla-
tion of Sufism's essence and a foretaste of the state of completion:[7]

While reason is still tracking down the secret,
you end your quest on the open field of love.

The path consists in neither words nor deeds:
only desolation can come from these,
and never any lasting edifice.

Sweetness and life are the words
of the man who treads this road in silence;

when he speaks it is not from ignorance,
and when he is silent it is not from sloth.

My friend, everything existing
exists through him;
your own existence is a mere pretense.

No more nonsense! Lose yourself,
and the hell of your heart becomes a heaven.
Lose yourself, and anything can be accomplished.

Your selfishness is an untrained colt.
Melt yourself down in this search:
venture your life and your soul
in the path of sincerity;
strive to pass from nothingness to being,
and make yourself drunk with the wine of God.

You have broken faith,
yet still he keeps his faith with you:
he is truer to you
than you are to yourself.
He created your mental powers;
yet his knowledge is innocent
of the passage of thought.
Love's conqueror is he
whom love conquers.

When you reach the sea,
stop talking of the stream.
There's no duality in the world of love:
what is all this talk of "you" and "me"?

THE SECRET
TEACHINGS

THE QUEST OF THE MAGUS

A SUMMARY OF THE WESTERN
MAGICAL TRADITION

Magic has been the object of much suspicion through the
centuries. What is its real purpose and intent?

Thomas D. Worrel

THE PREHISTORIC ORIGINS OF MAGIC

The origins of magic are deeply buried in the remote infancy
of the human race. The people living in those early times
were more immersed in the intricacies of nature, and more
aware of the subtle nuances and changes in their environment than we
are today. Not only were they intimately familiar with the powers of
plants to nourish, spice, heal, or kill, they also saw similar and more
complex characteristics of powers and attributes in animals and the
world about them. Everyday life made them aware of basic categories
of nature: earth and solids, water and liquids, winds and the mysterious breath, fire and the warmth of living beings. Below the surface of
the land, in the sea, and in the sky were mysterious forces that seemed
to have power and influence over all the land and its inhabitants. The

sky indicated to them where they were in the year and what was to come. The plants and animals would behave as the sky directed; its power was awesome. The sun seemed most powerful, for no one could even look at it without consequences. When the sun drew near, the world came to life; when it withdrew, the world began to die. The moon had hidden mysterious powers in relation to the night, ocean tides, females, and time. Five other lights in the sky (the planets) moved in unique patterns while the rest of the stars moved in unison from some even more remote sphere.

The origins of magic must be found within that matrix. I say that because many of those same elements are found in Western magical tradition as it evolved from the earliest treatises on up to current theories. Magic has systematized an appreciation and knowledge of the characteristics and powers of natural forces and attempts to communicate with the supernatural intelligences behind them. The core structure of magical work has always been based upon the schematic of the four elements, the seven planets, and the fixed stars, along with the powers and intelligences that they either embody or represent.

As we move into the historical period we can see how obviously older practices began to be recorded. Ancient records from various cultures are available, and some of the most important come from the early Egyptian civilization. Even those aspects of magic that had no direct link with Egypt were commonly thought to have come from that mysterious land. Thus ancient Egypt and the surrounding civilizations mark the beginning of the formulation of magic in Western civilization. From this point on, magic was continually systematized, developed, and refined as it absorbed new information.

With the advent of hieroglyphics, the means of recording and conveying this information took giant leaps forward. Down through the history of ancient Egypt we find more and more evidence of magical documents, amulets, spells of all kinds, and the acts of magicians. Of particular note are the concepts of realms in the afterlife, and the use of spells to help one access these realms as well as deal with the entities one finds there. We will see many of these notions present in later magical practices.

CHARACTERISTICS AND DEFINITIONS
OF THE MAGICAL UNIVERSE

What do we mean by magic; and, to what are we referring when we use the phrase "the Western magical tradition"? Of course we do not mean the sleight-of-hand techniques and trickery familiar to us as stage magic. Magic, as defined here, refers to ceremonial and ritual practices used for specific purposes, usually within a spiritual context. Before we go further into the defining process, it is helpful to look at the context in which magic finds itself and the assumptions underlying its practice.

Three of the most important structural components of the magical universe must include: (1) a living hierarchically structured universe; (2) the presence of links or interconnections between, and correspondences with, all these living parts; and (3) the belief that the magician, through his ceremonies and ritual practices, gains access to, communicates with, influences, or is influenced by, the powers behind nature's manifestations.[1]

The first important concept is that nature and the whole universe is alive or vital in all its parts and aspects. A part of this concept is that nature is divided into gradations from the outermost, seemingly infinite phenomena of nature to the innermost unity of the divine world. Not only does nature have kingdoms or realms such as mineral, plant, animal, and human, but there are inner or spiritual kingdoms as well. The world is multidimensional and multilayered.

The second important concept is the idea of the interconnections and correspondences that exist between different areas and levels of the vital world. Our universe is a vast network of connections between the different dimensions. These connections are sometimes explained as being derived from the Platonic World of Forms whose eternal presence filters down through myriad worlds till different combinations manifest. Or to put it another way, "lower" levels of manifestation are linked to other higher, more spiritual levels. These interconnections and subtle correspondences act as doorways between the various planes. Because these correspondences exist within the human mind as well, the magician has the potential of access.

The third necessary component is the medium of access available to the ceremonial magician. Given the first two components just listed, it is still necessary for the magician to (1) have access or some connection to these realms, and (2) be able to affect or be affected by the powers and spirits once that connection is made. The particular medium in question is the magician himself. The Hermetic notion that man is a microcosm of the greater cosmos comes prominently into play in this regard. It does so through mirroring the previous two components: that man's total being is multidimensional and hierarchical in a fashion parallel with nature and that there are interconnections and correspondences throughout his being that link him with resonant aspects in the macrocosm.

A magician uses ritual, prayers, incantations, symbolic instruments, designs, and other objects as well as song, dance, and gestures to awaken and open his awareness to these usually hidden spiritual realms. The art and craft of magic then is to create and utilize all of these components to achieve the magician's purpose.

These ideas set the stage for the workings of all types of magic, the high and the low, the spiritual and the mundane. With this model, we can readily see the possibility of sympathetic magic (seeking to affect one thing by means of an associated thing) and imitative magic.

A further nuance of magical definition necessary for our purpose is that of theurgy. Theurgy comes from the Greek *theourgia,* wherein *theos* means god and *ergos* means working, thus translating as "god-working." One definition that has been given is: "By theurgy we mean the knowledge of the theory and practice necessary to connect us with gods and spirits, and not only through raising our understanding but also through concrete rites and material objects that set into motion divine influences where and when we want."[2] But this definition does not carry the full weight of what is involved in theurgy. Theurgy is not just communication or connection with mediating entities; its ultimate purpose is to ascend to the realm of the gods, if not the One itself. The aim of theurgy is extremely similar to yoga in that the climax of the more advanced rites propels the consciousness to an ecstatic state. The ultimate aim, in some forms of theurgy, is a type of mystical union with God.

With these definitions, we can begin to look at the development of magic and particularly theurgy in the Western world.

THE GREEK CONTRIBUTION TO THE MAGICAL TRADITION

While we may see very early formulations of magical development in the ancient land of Egypt, it is in the Greco-Roman period that magic, or theurgy, emerges as a coherent and consistent spirituality. The many religious and philosophical currents that emerged during this time period seemed to propel its development to even higher levels. For at this time we can clearly see the emergence of the recurring schematic of the four elements, the seven "planets," and the fixed sphere.

The philosophical doctrine of the four elements originated with the Greek philosopher Empedocles (fifth century B.C.E.), who wrote: "By accepting four distinct elements, or 'roots of all things,' [one] is able to explain natural change as a result of the combination, separation, and regrouping of indestructible entities. There remains, of course, something illusory about the kaleidoscopic appearance of change. . . . In reality there is only the mixing, unmixing, and remixing of permanent entities."[3]

Although the seven wandering luminaries were always known, their particular ordering differed among cultures. Eventually a set order was formulated that lasted till the heliocentric paradigm supplanted it, but for magical purposes it is still used today. Jim Tester, a scholar in Classics, informs us that

> the order called "Chaldaean," which was undoubtedly Greek and astronomical, derived from the planets' periods of rotation round the ecliptic, and hence their assumed distances from the earth, was moon, Mercury, Venus, sun, Mars, Jupiter, Saturn. It is this order, which becomes standard from the second century B.C.E., which is used in Greek astrology.[4]

Later we see this exact planetary order imposed on the Kabbalistic Tree of Life. But it was during an even earlier period when the ideas regarding the fixed sphere became standard. Tester informs us that "the twelve from Aries to Pisces seem to have emerged as standard form no earlier than the end of the fifth century B.C., and the first mention of twelve equal signs, as opposed to the constellations (of unequal extent in the heavens), was in 419 B.C."[5]

By the time Iamblichus, a Syrian Platonist (240–325 C.E.), was born, many of the currents of earlier thought had already taken root in the classical pagan mind. From the wisdom of Egypt to the Neo-Pythagoreans and the Neoplatonists, the several concepts of the mathematical basis of the universe, the immortality of the soul, the mythical theme of the fall and reintegration of the soul, the progression of souls after death, the mediating process through the hierarchical worlds represented by the planets and stars were all well established.

In the writings of Iamblichus we have a coherent and complete view of the theory and practice of ceremonial magic. It is actually some of the earliest material available that articulates the place of magical work in spiritual pursuits within a philosophical framework. Iamblichus augmented the Neoplatonic philosophy by inclusion of Pythagorean teachings and Egyptian and pagan religion, as well as the *Chaldean Oracles*. The *Chaldean Oracles* were important in many philosophical circles. They are a collection of hexameter verses from the late second century c.e. that had enormous influence. There now remain only fragments that have been collected from the many authors who quoted them. Regardless, we know they were considered authoritative revelations and accorded the highest respect. All of these elements help compose Iamblichus's system of magical attainment.

For Iamblichus, theurgy is the way for the soul to participate in the divine. It is the vehicle for the soul's ascent back to the celestial order and the world soul. By practicing the correct rites the magician could bring the powers within him into alignment with the powers of the cosmos and thus achieve access to the Demiurge. The Demiurge is defined as follows: "The God, *Demiurgos,* is not the creator of matter, but when he receives it, as eternal, he molds it into forms and organizes it according to numerical ratios."[6] He is, in a sense, the architect or designer of the universe.

It was believed that the Demiurge created the soul with particular harmonic ratios and divine symbols. The ratios were identical with the ratios perceived in the sky but became distorted in the process of incarnation. Theurgic rites restored their proper alignment. The harmonic ratios were active in the soul, but the symbols remained inactive until by the practice of theurgy the magician could awaken them. Particular ritual actions set into motion certain powers within the soul that would allow it to reunify with the heavenly powers. These activated powers brought the soul into deeper alignment with the cosmic Will, thus making the theurgist a vehicle of the gods. As this alignment strengthened, the soul realized its place in the universe. This was the way of uniting the microcosm with the macrocosm.[7]

How did magic achieve this awakening? We can consider planetary rites for example. It had long been thought that the Egyptian priests used the vowels in specific ways in their hymns. Gregory Shaw, in his book on Iamblichus, from which the foregoing material is largely derived, writes that "Iamblichus believed that the seven vowels were connatural with the seven planetary gods."[8] Shaw also reports that "Iamblichus used the term *rhoizos* to describe the sounds emitted by the stars whose intervals served as the bases for theurgical chants and melodies."[9] And it is through the use of chanting the names and vowels in the rites that the soul could participate in the "energy" of the gods and ascend to their sphere. Or, conversely, set up the conditions for the gods to descend into the magician.

After the outlawing and destruction of the pagan schools and sanctuaries, and with the rise of the power of the Church, the practice of magic faded into the Dark Ages, along with many other things of the Latin West. Its reemergence was slow, usually in exceptional individuals and small groups, but it did survive in various forms, often as folklore.

A major renewal in the history of the Western magical tradition occurred at the beginning of the Italian Renaissance in the city of Florence. As in the time of Iamblichus, several major philosophical and religious traditions began to converge in this period. Many rediscoveries set the stage for a renewal of the magical tradition. The work of Marsilio Ficino and his students, friends, and patrons impacted European magical thought so strongly that in some ways the waves have yet to fully reach the shore. We will consider Ficino's work and trace some of the influences that issued from his Florentine academy, influencing several subsequent magicians.

MARSILIO FICINO'S MAGICAL RENAISSANCE

In fifteenth-century Florence, ruled by the great Medici dynasty, Marsilio Ficino (1433–1499) became one of the most influential philosophers of Europe. He began several translation projects under the patronage of Cosimo de Medici: he finished the translations of the *Hymns of Orpheus* and the *Sayings of Zoroaster* by 1462, the *Corpus Hermeticum* by 1463, and Plato by 1469. And between 1484 and 1492 he translated and commented upon Plotinus (the *Enneads*), Porphyry, Iamblichus, and Proclus. His work had an extensive effect. In the introduction to a collection of Ficino's published letters, the editor says that "Ficino's Academy awoke Europe to the deep significance of the Platonic tradition" and that "it was Ficino more than anyone else who took from Plato, Plotinus, and the Hermetic writings the concept that part of the individual soul was immortal and divine, a concept that was all-important to the Renaissance."[10] Cosimo gave Ficino use of his villa at Careggi outside of Florence where he translated and held discussions and taught.

Not only was Marsilio Ficino a philosopher and priest but he was also a magus, a magician. As far as we know, he was not taught magic by anyone but learned by his own work. Some of his knowledge must have been easily accessible, but some had come through his translation projects. D. P. Walker surmises that

> Peter of Abano and other mediaeval writers on magic, such as Roger Bacon, Alkindi, Avicenna, and "Picatrix," are probably important sources for Ficino's talismans, and would suggest invocations to planets. But far more important are certain Neoplatonic texts: Proclus' *De Sacrificiis et Magia,* Iamblichus' *De Mysteriis* and *Vita Pythagorae,* Porphyry's *De Abstinentia,* the *Hermetica,* especially the *Asclepius.* Most of these Ficino translated or paraphrased.[11]

As is common in magic, Ficino was an astrologer too. One of the main qualities of Ficino's work is his concern for the health of the soul, an area where he could utilize his astrological counsel. Noel Cobb in his foreword to Thomas Moore's book on Ficino's astrological psychology gives us Ficino's view of soul:

> Psyche, as World Soul, . . . is scattered throughout everything; everything manifests soul's interiority and depth. The planets mirror their metaphors within. They are also persons with characters, physiognomies, styles of speech and action, who form complex relationships among themselves. . . . The Gods are embodied, astronomically, in the planets, but psychologically in myths and in the phenomenological texture of the sensible world. Ficino's psychology is one which would imagine the divinity within each thing, the God in each event.[12]

To better understand the magic of Ficino, it is helpful to use the more modern terminology of depth psychology. Planetary rites promote a nourishing and continual reciprocity with the divine archetypes within the psyche—the planetary counterparts deep in the mind. Speaking of Ficino, Joscelyn Godwin says he "sang his Orphic poems in order to set his spirits (spiritus) in motion and thereby open himself up to the influences of the benefic planets, descending by way of the subtle air. In Ficino's belief, such operations of musical magic only worked because man himself is in a natural state of resonance with the higher powers."[13]

The ideas of Ficino were developed further by other magicians such as Giordano Bruno. Bruno used elaborate mnemonic devices to develop the will and imagination in these same directions. "Bruno's magic memory system thus represents the memory of a Magus, one who both knows the reality beyond the multiplicity of appearances through having conformed his imagination to the archetypal images, and also has powers through this insight. It is the direct descendent of Ficino's Neoplatonic interpretation of the celestial images, but carried to a much more daring extreme."[14]

Ficino's influence was truly great and spread throughout Europe. One can trace from his lineage to great mystics and magicians for generations to come.

INFLUENCES POURING FORTH FROM THE CAREGGI CIRCLE

Many scholars came to Florence to participate in what was happening there. One of them was Giovanni Pico della Mirandola (1463–1494), who is considered the first non-Jewish Renaissance Kabbalist. He was a student and friend of Ficino. It was Pico who began the process of merging the Hermetic and Neoplatonic philosophy with the scriptures, after studying the Kabbalah, which made its way to Italy with Spanish Jews fleeing from Spain. Pico is thought of as the first Christian Kabbalist.

Johann Reuchlin (1455–1522) was influenced by Pico and was a professor of law (one of the foremost jurists and legal scholars of his day), a humanist, and a student of classical philology and philosophy. He was also proficient in Latin, Greek, and Hebrew. Reuchlin is considered the first non-Jew to write a book on the Kabbalah—*De Arte Cabalistica* (1517).

Another figure influenced by Pico was Francesco Giorgi (1466–1540), who drew together Neoplatonism, Neo-Pythagorianism, the teachings of Hermes Trismegistus, Kabbalah, angels, planets, harmony and number, and the architectural symbolism of Vitruvius into a coherent system. His work was later studied by the English Renaissance magus John Dee.

These men had a far-reaching influence. One important instance of the extent of this influence is the relationship of Reuchlin to Johannes Trithemius. Trithemius (1462–1516) was a Christian monk of the Benedictine Order. Leaving home as a young man, he traveled and came into association with Reuchlin. Later elevated to abbot, he was an avid scholar and amassed a library of some two thousand volumes. He knew both Greek and Hebrew (helped by Reuchlin) and studied Pythagoras, Hermetics, and the Kabbalah. Although his work was not published until 1606, it was long known and read in manuscript form. His was the main Renaissance manual of practical Kabbalah or angel-conjuring. Trithemius's work was another influence on John Dee.

In 1509, Trithemius was visited by Cornelius Agrippa (1486–1535). Agrippa had already been influenced by Reuchlin's *De Verbo Mirifico*.[15] It is reported that Agrippa was deeply impressed with Trithemius, and a teacher/pupil relationship probably developed. Agrippa's *Three Books of Occult Philosophy* has been considered the foundational work of all Western magic since its publication. Some magical societies today still issue parts of it as "secret material"!

It should be clear that the influences streaming from the Florentine academy of Marsilio Ficino had major impact. There really is very little today of the underlying structure of magic that is different from what was compiled in that time period. Its terminology has been changed and updated, with the inclusion of modern psychological terms, and certain techniques have been refined, but all in all, this magical tradition remains remarkably solid.

There were several later developments that gave the magical tradition further impetus and enrichment. Much of this development came in the formation of several societies that either attracted magical students or overtly promoted magic, at least in some of its forms. One of the more interesting developments has been the further systemization and refinement of magical technique along with the incorporation of initiation rites, which have resulted in various substantial magical systems.

THE EMERGENCE OF THE MAGICAL SOCIETIES

At the beginning of the seventeenth century, two Rosicrucian manifestoes and a short Rosicrucian allegory were published in Germany.

By all accounts, the publication of these documents caused considerable excitement and eventually led to the founding of several Rosicrucian fraternities and societies. Herein we find the beginning of the Rosicrucian movement. These societies practiced a type of mystical Christianity that was augmented by the esoteric arts of Kabbalah, magic, astrology, and alchemy. For the rest of that century and into the next (and still today), Rosicrucian groups would form and dissolve, publish and correspond, and eventually congeal into a distinct tradition.

At the beginning of the eighteenth century, we find that various speculative Masonic lodges were already formed, and interest in them was increasing. In 1717 the English Freemasons formalized their society by organizing into a Grand Lodge system where the once independent lodges were now chartered and sanctioned under the umbrella of a Mother Lodge. Either because of this event or for some other reason, Freemasonry became extremely popular, and it spread to many parts of Europe. Why this is important to the magical tradition may not be apparent, but regardless of one's interpretation of Masonic symbolism, the fact is that it appeals to those involved in magic.

It was not long until new Masonic degrees (rituals) were being introduced and developed. Many of these new degrees began introducing Kabbalistic teachings, chivalric rites, alchemical allusions, Pythagorean numerology, and Egyptian and Rosicrucian symbology into the Masonic milieu. It seems that these inclusions remained only theoretical teachings for the most part; but, there is no doubt that many members of the Masonic fraternity were also members of more practical societies that worked magical rituals and practiced alchemy. It has to be at this point when the blending of magical rituals and initiation rites became much more developed and pronounced.

We find this same trend continuing into the nineteenth century. Yet it is in the latter half of that century that we see the magical tradition receive major impetus, with a variety of strong personalities and influ-

ential societies. At the center we find such personalities as the French-
man Alphonse Louis Constant (1810–1875), best known as Eliphas
Lévi, and Helena P. Blavatsky (1831–1891), born of German parents in
the Ukraine. Madame Blavatsky cofounded the Theosophical Society,
whose members included many who went on to found other mystical
and magical groups. Lévi's writings influenced several occultists who
later founded or joined the "Hermetic Order of the Golden Dawn."

The great accomplishment of the Golden Dawn was a complete
synthesis and systemization of the magical path of spiritual development. This particular society and its derivative groups and members
has had more impact upon today's magical systems than any other. We
can include such writers as William Westcott, S. L. MacGregor Math-
ers, W. B. Yeats, A. E. Waite, Aleister Crowley, Dion Fortune, Paul F.
Case, and Israel Regardie among them. These writers basically defined magical practice and doctrine for the Western world in the
twentieth century.

Today there are several groups who continue the work of the Hermetic Order of the Golden Dawn and the other societies that formed
at the end of the nineteenth century, several of whom were virtually
unheard-of and who had previously worked in a less public fashion.
As we begin the twenty-first century we may very well ask ourselves
what the next stage of magical development might be. In the world in
which we now find ourselves, a world where communication and
transportation have brought the entire globe within easy reach, where
the East and West intermingle as never before, where new discoveries
have brought ancient cultures into better understanding, and new
knowledge of science and nature arises daily, the answer is impossible
to even imagine.

THE UNEXAMINED TAROT

What are the real origins of this mysterious oracle?

Chas S. Clifton

Despite the constant publication of new Tarot decks and books about the Tarot, the Tarot itself remains one of the most influential yet least-examined "texts" of Western esotericism. Most writers on the Tarot are esotericists themselves, and their overall concerns are nonhistorical or even antihistorical. Concerned with the Tarot's eternal aspects, using it to develop systems of divination, self-development, meditation, and qabalistic pathworking, they fail to ask the right questions about its roots, preferring instead to place them in a vague and misty past where robed initiates proceed through torch-lit halls. Nevertheless, the likely historical roots of the Tarot are planted in mystery enough without anyone needing to pile on additional manure. Its story connects the fourteenth century's Black Death and today's New Orleans Mardi Gras parades, and links the game of polo with phallic symbolism.

Unfortunately, this perennial spiritual text with its many manifestations has not received the attention it should from historians of both art and religion, and it is just that sort of interdisciplinary approach that will be needed to understand its several levels. What I would like to do here is merely to outline what the cards are, show the variety of "histories" advanced for them, and suggest what approaches are the most likely to be on target. (Doing so, I am entirely avoiding the subject of divination and the use of Tarot cards as guides to any sort of magical exercise such as "pathworking." Any linkage between one person's mind and the cosmos that makes divination possible can take place regardless of the divination system's history and antiquity. I would only object when someone claims that a spurious history of the Tarot lies behind its employment as a divinatory system.)

When we look at the Tarot for what it apparently is, we look into a mental map of the time when the Italian and French Middle Ages were poised on the cusp of the Renaissance—a time, I would suggest, that is actually stranger and intellectually more foreign to us than we tend to think.

The Tarot's combination of familiarity and "strangeness" is intriguing. It combines the fifty-two playing cards most people know with four more "court cards," the knights, for a total of fifty-six, and then adds twenty-two distinct picture cards, also called the "trumps," "triumphs," or "keys." This second group is frequently called the Major Arcana (or "Big Secrets") by occultists; the other cards by extension are the Minor Arcana. One question that has vexed historians is whether the two developed separately or together; at the present time, informed opinion suggests that the four suits of the Minor Arcana originated in the Islamic world, perhaps in the Muslim kingdoms of northern India or Egypt, while the Major Arcana took shape in Europe.

A large barrier to understanding the Tarot historically is that the decks most commonly encountered today were "improved" by various nineteenth- and twentieth-century occultists such as Eliphas Lévi (Alphonse Louis Constant), Papus (Gérard Encausse), A. E. Waite, Aleister Crowley, Paul Foster Case, and C. C. Zain (Elbert Benjamine).

These in turn followed the lead of Antoine Court de Gébelin, a French Protestant clergyman, who appears to have been the first occultist to see the cards as something more than a medium of gaming and everyday fortune-telling. Around 1781 he pronounced them to be the repository of ancient Egyptian wisdom: intellectuals of the time found Egypt fascinating and mysterious, and the discovery of the Rosetta Stone, which led to the understanding of hieroglyphic writing, was still several years away.

Court de Gébelin's successors, such as Lévi, eager to force-fit the Tarot with astrology, the Hebrew alphabet, or their own personal revelations, redrew and rearranged the cards, emphasizing some aspects and deemphasizing others. Decks showing their influence include the Rider-Waite deck, the Builders of the Adytum and Golden Dawn Tarots, the Aquarian Tarot (drawn by David Palladini), and Crowley's "Book of Thoth." (About the only commonly available traditional Tarot that was not so "improved" is the French "Tarot of Marseilles," designed around 1748 but based on sixteenth-century designs.)

If one's first encounter is with one of the decks just listed, it is easy to miss the familiar elements in favor of the strange. Certainly the cards would appear to express a magicoreligious outlook far different from the West's exoteric Christianity. It is not surprising that some writers have seen the cards as embodying the teachings either of early mystery schools or of later medieval heretics, the quasi-gnostic Cathars always being a favorite possible source.

Aside from the numbered trump cards of the Pope, the Last Judgment, and the Devil, the Tarot seems devoid of Christian imagery. There are no Father, Son, or Holy Spirit, no saints, and no sacraments. Instead, the cards show a mixture of secular rulers (and in some decks, peasants and artisans), abstractions such as Justice and Temperance, and cosmic symbols such as the Sun and the Moon.

Ignoring the mysteries under their feet, some occultists have developed elaborate fantasies about the cards. For example, the astrologer Doris Chase Doane attributed knowledge of the Tarot to the prophets Daniel and Ezekiel and adds (with italics for emphasis in the original), *"whoever wrote the Apocalypse based it all upon the Tarot."* From her predecessor C. C. Zain, founder of the Los Angeles–based Church of Light, she obtained the "hermetic tradition" that underneath the Great Pyramid is a temple of initiation on whose walls hang tablets depicting the same images as the seventy-eight tarot cards, plus another thirty that are more esoteric still.

Zain wished to place the Tarot's origins 35,000 years ago in the mythical lands of Atlantis and Mu. He believed the cards condensed the images of the universal unconscious, which was why they functioned successfully as a medium for divination. His Church of Light issued its own "Egyptian" cards, carrying on the tradition of "improving" the cards.

Another fondly cherished legend tells that in about 1200 a group of leading Arab occult philosophers met in the Moroccan city of Fez and decided to condense all their wisdom into a set of pictures. The ignorant masses would use these for card games and thus ensure their survival until worthy students of the future could absorb their true meanings.

In Tarot history, any connection is fair game. For instance, because there are fifty-six filled-in Aubrey Holes at Stonehenge and fifty-six cards in the Minor Arcana, to an occult commentator such as Stephen Franklin the two not only might be but *must* be connected. (Franklin, who connects the cards with astrological figures in a far-reaching argument based on Pythagorean, Hindu, and Chinese sources, would recoil at being called an occultist, but in the strict sense of the term he is one.)

All of these explanations have one thing in common: they argue by accretion. In other words, the more things they can glue onto the Tarot—Pythagorean numerology, the Hebrew alphabet, particle physics, the hexagrams of the *I Ching,* Mayan pyramids, Egyptian pyramids, Atlantean pyramids, the *Tao Teh Ching,* Stonehenge, the Gypsies, the games of Parcheesi and chess, the lunar asterisms of Hindu astrology—the "truer" and "righter" they are.

This multitude of "histories" was created, I suspect, in response to the Tarot's seeming appearance out of nowhere in late fourteenth-century Europe. Even the Gypsies are easier to trace than the Tarot.

In volume 1 of his *Encyclopedia of Tarot,* Stuart Kaplan, the president of U.S. Games Systems, cites various references to games and gambling from classical Roman, early Christian, and medieval Christian sources to make the point that none of them mention card games—and when it came to denouncing popular gambling games, the Christian polemicists rarely missed a trick, so to speak. Not only that, the fourteenth-century *Arabian Nights* and various early Sanskrit manuscripts on sports and games fail to mention playing cards, Kaplan writes. The prolific fourteenth-century poet and biographer Francesco Petrarch (or Petrarca), who lived from 1304 to 1374 in northern Italy and southern France, wrote a treatise on gambling without mentioning cards. But it may be significant that his last important work was a long allegorical poem called *I Trionfi,* that is to say, "The Triumphs (Trumps)."

The Triumphs celebrated by Petrarch are those of Love, Chastity, Death, Fame, Time, and Eternity, each one seen as having its successive influence on the life of the ideal man. They do not exactly parallel Tarot trumps, but with slight effort could be equated with them, especially as the card called The Lovers in modern decks has also been drawn as "Love." (The other trumps might be Temperance, Death, The Wheel of Fortune, and The World, depending on how one reads them.) More important, this work of the mid-1300s shows how one of the leading Italian literary artists of the time was wedded to the notion of allegory, and how the greater trumps themselves are all allegories. The culture of the time was steeped in allegory as opposed to direct description. (We see this opposition later in the differences between "allegorical" Italian painting and the more detailed works of the Dutch masters.)

Petrarch himself survived one of the watershed events of European history, an event that I believe left its mark on the Tarot: the Black Death. Between the years 1347 and 1351, most areas suffered one or more outbreaks of bubonic plague, a fast-acting bacterial disease spread by flea bites, droplets of saliva from infected persons, and in some cases direct contact between mucous membranes and contaminated body parts such as the fingers. Its nickname came from the purplish-black appearance of many victims after their death from respiratory failure.

Unable to understand where the plague came from or how it spread, Europeans frequently reacted in one of two ways. They either became convinced that it was God's punishment for their sins, or they decided that since life was increasingly uncertain, they would enjoy themselves while they could. The first reaction produced a new kind of religious theater, while the second would have encouraged gambling and other pleasures.

In her history of the fourteenth century, *A Distant Mirror,* Barbara Tuchman notes that under the influence of recurring waves of bubonic plague, a "street sermon" was developed on the theme of Death the Leveler. Groups of the faithful would enact the *danse macabre* (also used as the theme for woodcuts and paintings) showing Death leading away representatives of all classes of society: sturdy farmers, young mothers, proud knights, humble monks, wealthy bishops, and so on. Presentations might also include sermons urging repentance. The plague time six hundred years ago gave us the image of Death as a grinning skeleton, wielding his scythe to "harvest" a field of body parts, the image seen on the thirteenth trump card of most traditional

Tarot decks. (Presumably it is also the ancestor of the semicomic skeleton creations that Mexicans buy for November 1, *El dia de los muertos.*)

This card has also been claimed as an ancestor of the figure of Death drawing a bow that is carved in wood and carried in a cart by the Penitentes, a Hispanic religious brotherhood of northern New Mexico and southern Colorado. Marta Weigle, author of a comprehensive work on the Penitentes, argued that the Tarot trump of Death not only inspired the carven figure but was itself taken from Petrarch's *I Trionfi,* because in the poem and on the cart Death is a female figure (the New Mexicans sometimes referred to her as "Doña Sebastiana"). I think this is an unlikely connection, given the cultural isolation of the area during the early nineteenth century when the Penitente brotherhoods had their major growth; it is more likely that Petrarch, the Tarot's designers, and the founders of Hispanic Catholic lay brotherhoods drew on a common cultural tradition.

Perhaps of all the cards, the image of the Death trump most firmly anchors the Tarot in a definite historical past. Kaplan writes that it is in the postplague decades that references to cards in European documents begin to appear. He refers to various written sermons and city laws that forbid card-playing on moral grounds beginning in the late 1300s. One famous denunciation of playing cards that supposedly gave "a picture of the world" is attributed to Johannes von Rheinfelden, a German monk writing about 1377. Unfortunately, evidence for the date is shaky; the monk's sermon may have been written later, according to Kaplan. But cards are mentioned negatively in a Bernese legal document of 1367, a Florentine decree of 1376, and a Parisian decree of 1397.

It is not always possible to tell whether the cards denounced are the fifty-two-card deck, the fifty-six-card deck, or the trumps. One thing, however, is fairly certain: these documents predate the arrival of the Gypsies in western Europe and they do not mention the cards in any Gypsy connection. The Gypsies, a caste of musicians and metal-workers, migrated westward from India for unknown reasons. They were in Persia in the eleventh century and reached southeastern Europe in the early fourteenth century, according to the *New Encyclopaedia Britannica*. They reached western Europe in the fifteenth century (Paris in 1427, for example), with their leaders carrying forged papal letters that made them out to be Egyptian Christians exiled by the Muslims (hence their name of "Egyptians") and requesting local rulers to aid them. Most likely some medieval Gypsies practiced palmistry or other forms of fortune-telling, but the evidence suggests that they encountered cards in Europe and adopted them then, rather than introducing them from their homeland, as Raymond Buckland argued in a 1990 article. The timing is close enough to be suggestive, but the dates are wrong.

Several Tarot historians have postulated an Egyptian Muslim connection that has nothing to do with Gypsies, however. During the time discussed, Egypt was ruled by the Mameluke dynasties (from the Arabic *mamluk,* or "white [non-African] slave," descendants of slaves converted to Islam who advanced themselves to military and government posts). After successfully revolting against the Arab Ayyubid dynasty, the Mamelukes controlled Egypt from 1250 to 1517, when they were defeated by the Turks; even then they remained provincial rulers and soldiers until they were defeated by Napoleon in 1798 and later massacred or exiled by the resurgent Ottoman Turks.

The Mamelukes (or Mamluks) were known to have playing cards, and several pictorial elements of the Minor Arcana suggest Islamic influence. One is the tendency of early decks to show the suit of swords as the curved scimitars favored by Muslim warriors. In addition, early decks often show the suit of batons or wands as curved sticks. In later decks (such as the Rider-Waite deck) these became straight staves, often with leaves growing from them, and carrying in some interpretations a phallic connotation. The card historian Detlef Hoffman suggested rather that these were originally polo sticks of the type used when the game was first developed by Persian cavalrymen a thousand years ago or more. (Rather than the mallets used today, the first polo sticks were probably curved more like hockey sticks.) Medieval Europeans did not recognize them on playing cards as polo sticks; not until British officers learned to play polo in northeast India in the 1800s did it become popular outside its homeland. Since they had no reason to show curved wands, European artists straightened them and have drawn them that way ever since.

A third minor clue comes from the Visconti-Sforza deck, a gothic-style deck painted in the mid-1400s for a family of Milanese aristocrats and taking the form of fifty-six small cards and twenty-two trumps plus *Il matto,* The Fool. Michael Dummett, author of a book about the Visconti-Sforza Tarot, notes that the *dinari* or coins ("pentacles" in the Waite deck) are painted as gold coins, whereas the *dinari* of the time were copper coins. Gold dinars, however, circulated in the Islamic world; the word "dinar" is Arabic, although with a Latin root.

These historians agree that the trumps are European. Dummett sees them originating in the "romantic, pleasure-seeking d'Este court of Ferrara," a city near Bologna in northern Italy. The ducal family of Este created a Renaissance court noted for its love of literature and learning; one duke founded the University of Ferrara in 1391.

Dealing with the trumps from a historical perspective one by one would take an entire book, so I will discuss only a few of them here. Despite the efforts of occultists such as Crowley to relate their order to the Hebrew alphabet, it is important to realize that the number of trumps in various early packs varied considerably, some running to nearly 100. Besides whatever educational function the trumps may have had, people were using them to play a game called *tarocchi* (plural) or *tarocco* (singular), a game in the same general class as bridge. Dummett says the name was first recorded in 1516, and that the French *tarot* was first spelled *tarau.* Before then, a common Italian term was *carta da trionfi*. This variety is enough, I believe, to disprove the nineteenth-century occultists' predilection for seeing "Tarot" as an anagram of Torah or of the Latin *rota* (wheel).

The original Italian trumps had a less esoteric flavor than those in Waite's or Crowley's decks. What they suggest, rather, is the mixed mental universe of an educated upper-class person of the time: part Christian, part secular European, and partly flavored by the stirrings of interest in Classical Greece and Rome that gave the Renaissance ("rebirth") its name.

Consequently the trumps contain religious notions (Death the Leveler, the Last Judgment) flavored by the medieval concern for the afterlife, secular rulers such as the Emperor and the Empress, astrology in the personified Sun and Moon, and classical pagan virtues: Strength, Temperance, Justice.

Death, Trump 13, may be related to late-medieval piety, but The Wheel of Fortune, Trump 10, recognizes the practical wisdom that "whatever goes up must come down." The Pope is there, but so is the Popess, later occultized to The High Priestess.

The recently printed traditional French "Marseilles" deck plays it both ways: the card, picturing a robed nun wearing the papal triple crown, is labeled "La Papesse/The High Priestess."

She also contains a possible historical anchor point: Dummett and Kaplan both advance the hypothesis that the Popess is Sister Manfreda, a relative of the Visconti family who was elected pope by Guglielmite heretics and burned at the stake around 1300. (These heretics followed Joachim of Flora's teaching that a new "age of the Holy Spirit" was at hand and believed that Manfreda incarnated the Holy Spirit.) The presence of the Popess in the deck was particularly infuriating to the heretic-hunting Dominicans, who denounced the cards in the 1400s.

Other trump cards that have changed over time include The Hermit, originally called *Il vecchio,* "the old man," a Father Time figure holding an hourglass, while The Hanged Man, frequently read as a person undergoing occult initiation (often syncretized with Odin hanging from the cosmic ash tree to gain wisdom) was originally called The Traitor. Hanging executed traitors upside down is an old Italian custom; the corpse of the dictator Benito Mussolini, for example, was hung upside down from a lamppost in Milan after his Fascist government collapsed.

Another significant card in Tarot history is The Chariot, which connects with the whole notion of the Triumphs. Originally a public celebration and parade in honor of a victorious general, a "triumph" in medieval times became part of the pre-Lenten festival (Carnival), with the figure of a fool, king, or general drawn through the streets on a wheeled cart or chariot, noted Bill Butler in *Dictionary of the Tarot*. This directly prefigures today's Mardi Gras processions or any small-town parade, or an event such as a "Blossom Festival." In the late 1400s a German artist, Hans Burgkmair, designed a series of triumphal figures to be used in a public procession honoring the Holy Roman Emperor Maximilian I. Even though the celebration was never carried out as planned, Butler notes correspondences between those designs and the Tarot trumps, saying they originated "in the same legends and customs of medieval times as does the Tarot."

The Fool, often compared by occultists to the "seeker," was sometimes shown more as a madman or as a wild man of the woods, a significant figure in the late-medieval and Renaissance imagination.

To get a feel for the mindscape of the person (or persons) who created the Major Arcana, we could well look at such works as Henry Cornelius Agrippa's book *The Philosophy of Natural Magic* (also called *Of Occult Philosophy*) written around 1530. Tim O'Neill's comment on this connection bears repeating: "[Renaissance Magi] not only literally spoke a different language, but also held a vastly different worldview than obtains today." That worldview was essentially Platonic or Neoplatonic; Agrippa proudly proclaimed himself a follower of Plato. He opened with a Neoplatonic statement of how the cosmos is constructed, a "threefold world" consisting of the Elementary (the four elements of fire, earth, air, and water), the Celestial (the cosmos interpreted through astrology), and the Intellectual (pertaining to divine forces) spheres. A great deal of Agrippa's work involved categorizing (rather than observing) the natural world: assigning, among birds, the swan and pigeon to Venus, for example, and crows, vultures, and raptors generally to Mars. The young lawyer, for so he was then, appears to have been writing an occult encyclopedia chock-full of magical rings, the four humors (temperaments), types of divination, "fascination" and other psychic powers, and of course the Hebrew alphabet. While a great deal of it deals with the natural world, Agrippa's book is not natural history. His birds, beasts, and semiprecious stones are not themselves, but symbols, or counters, in symbolic systems, similar to the way that astrology uses stars and planets not as things in the natural world, but as the hands of a complicated cosmic clock.

As a Renaissance man, Agrippa described his work as "a doctrine of antiquity, by none, I dare say, hitherto attempted to be restored." I believe the Major Arcana, or greater trumps, partake of the same outlook in a less self-conscious way typical of an earlier century. In the mid- or late 1300s someone, whether in Ferrara or elsewhere, was indeed trying to put "the world" into a deck of cards—a world of language, of symbols, of bits and pieces of Christianity, Neoplatonism, and popular outlook. Most probably this person (or persons) was either a lay person or a rather worldly cleric, viewing the world in a philosophical and literary way, conscious of allegory, not impious but no longer orthodox in the medieval way either.

Somehow—and this is another true mystery—the greater trumps became melded with the Minor Arcana, which in Europe was codified into a fourfold division (although some non-European decks had five suits, for example). That fourfold division reflected the exceedingly ancient Indo-European division of society into priests, warrior aristocrats, and stockbreeders/farmers, to which is added the newer class of merchants. In modern Tarot card terms, those are swords (aristocrats), cups (priests), wands (farmers), and coins (merchants).

Certainly the Greater Arcana make up the heart of the Tarot, and I believe that a deeper examination of them in the context of late-medieval or Renaissance Hermeticism would be illuminating. No need to look for imaginary rooms beneath the sphinx of Gaza: there is sufficient mystery closer at hand.

LADDER TO LABYRINTH

THE SPIRITUAL AND PSYCHOLOGICAL
DIMENSIONS OF ASTROLOGY

Do the planets represent forces within us? Are they beneficent administrators of cosmic order or jailers of the psyche? These questions have vexed astrologers since ancient times.

Priscilla Costello

O f all the esoteric studies, astrology is the one least understood and appreciated in our time. Dismissed by science and trivialized by the media, its beauty, depth of wisdom, and value to the modern esotericist are hidden to all but the very few. Yet one cannot fully engage alchemy, ceremonial magic, or Kabbalistic studies without it.

Astrology, which calculates the positions and movements of heavenly bodies and correlates them to events on earth, is probably the oldest study of humankind. But its uses have evolved through the ages. Simply stated, astrology had a spiritual dimension in ancient times and has a mainly psychological character in the twentieth century. The ancients visualized a ladder linking heaven and earth, its main rungs the seven planetary spheres, but in our time the best image is that of a labyrinth. Now one journeys *within* to find the self, encountering archetypal beings or situations that correspond to planetary energies.

THE WORLDVIEW OF THE ANCIENTS

"Ladder" is an apt metaphor, for the spiritual dimension of ancient astrology reflected the worldview of the time. The heavens and the earth were the progressively unfolding work of a creative intelligence whose energy still infused the manifest world. It was natural, then, to read celestial as well as terrestrial events as indicators of divine intention. Just as the universe unfolded from the invisible into the visible dimensions in a great linked chain, so the portents of today foreshadowed the events of tomorrow. Thus omen-based astrology is the most ancient and universal form of the art.

For thousands of years, all known civilizations (in Mesopotamia, India, China, Egypt, Central and South America, Greece, and Rome, among others) have recorded solar, lunar, and planetary cycles. Initially this may have been for agricultural purposes, since the survival of the people depended on the fertility of the land. But astrology may also predate the agricultural revolution of the Neolithic: Alexander Marshack has speculated that patterns of scratches and sequences of marks incised into bone and stone dating back thirty thousand years represent lunar phases and that, far earlier than had previously been thought, human beings were making notations and keeping track of time.[1]

No doubt there was, as there is today, a difference in the response to these observations. The naïve or less educated may have feared an eclipse or the appearance of a comet, but the philosophers understood that they were contemplating the body of God.

Then the purpose shifted and expanded. In Mesopotamia as early as 1800–1750 B.C.E. (possibly earlier) observations were being made to determine the fortunes of the entire tribe or country by the movements of the planets, which were regarded as either abodes of gods and god-desses or as divinities themselves. The earliest compilation of such omens is the *Enuma Anu Enlil,* dating from the middle of the second millennium B.C.E. Observers noted correlations between repeated planetary patterns (such as the extremely regular eight-year Venus cy-cle) and political, economic, or social developments. This type of cor-relation is still done in modern mundane astrology (from the Latin *mundus,* "world"), which uses celestial phenomena such as eclipses, solstices, and equinoxes for prognostication.

The focus shifted again, probably sometime in the mid-first mil-lennium B.C.E., to horoscopic astrology. The primary tool here is a chart cast for a particular moment in time and space. Such a chart may be used to pick favorable times to take action, to answer questions about the future, or to convey information about an individual's life and destiny. This type emerges long after the first, and the precise date, place, and history of its development are controversial. Tradition as-cribes it to the Chaldeans or later Babylonians (c. 600 B.C.E.), and sub-sequently "Chaldean" came to be a rather vague term referring to anyone who was an astrologer.[2]

Though the earliest surviving birth chart, written in cuneiform on clay tablets, dates to April 29, 410 B.C.E.,[3] horoscopic astrology was not fully developed until around the beginning of the Common Era. The place of its synthesis was apparently Hellenistic Egypt, perhaps Alexandria. Like the alchemical vessel in which disparate elements are "cooked," Egypt was the place where Babylonian star and calendrical lore, Greek philosophy, and both old and new indigenous elements (like the fixed stars, the use of zodiacal signs as houses, aspects or an-gular relationships between planets, rulerships, and the "lots") blended.

And what did the people of this period do with this newly birthed astrology? They assessed first the viability and life expectancy of a child (much more in question at that time than now) and indications for the course of its life. One striking difference from earlier practices was that the earliest charts were cast for kings. Now anyone could consult an astrologer and have a chart interpreted. This accords with the new emphasis on the individual that had begun in the Greek classical period.

This type of assessment of the individual's life is not all that different in purpose (though it is substantially different in practice) from modern astrology. But ancient astrologers viewed their art as being embedded in a grand philosophical scheme of the creation, structure, and workings of the entire universe. We find this described in the ancient mysteries, Gnostic writings, early Hermetic material, and Neoplatonism. It surfaces again in the Renaissance, in the works of Cornelius Agrippa and the lovely detailed diagrams of Robert Fludd. It persists still in esoteric ideas about higher planes and spiritual beings.

THE LADDER OF HEAVEN AND EARTH

What constitutes the structure of the ladder? According to this scheme, out of the vast and unfathomable One (the Godhead) emerges a Divinity (God) with a name: Beauty, Truth, Love, Pleroma, *Ain Sof,* or whatever one wishes to call it. And from that Divinity unfolds in sequence the spheres of the fixed stars and the seven planets: Saturn, Jupiter, Mars, the sun, Venus, Mercury, and the moon (arranged in the "Chaldean order," that is, in order of their speed as viewed from the earth). Below the moon we enter the sublunary world, a realm created by the intermixing of the four elements (fire, air, water, and earth), whose unstable combinations account for the changeability of the manifest world.

The soul, divine in nature, descends from the higher realms through the planetary spheres and into embodiment. Consequently the way to illumination or even to complete freedom from incarnation is to climb upward the way one came down. This seems to have been a very ancient teaching. We find it explicitly stated in *The Three Steles of*

Seth, one of a group of Gnostic writings discovered in upper Egypt in 1945: "The way of ascent is the way of descent."[4] But almost exactly the same words appear much earlier in one of the fragmentary aphorisms of Heraclitus, a Greek philosopher of the late sixth and early fifth centuries B.C.E.

This path of ascent was incorporated into some of the ancient mysteries, specifically the Roman mysteries of Mithras. Strongly influenced by the Persian god Mithra, these mysteries came to Rome by way of Phoenician pirates during the first century B.C.E. By the second century C.E., Mithraism was well established. The mysteries, which were open to men only, first subjected the aspirant to ordeals, and then purified, initiated, and feasted him. The Pagan apologist Celsus describes the Mithraic upward way: "There is a ladder with seven gates and at its top an eighth gate. The first of the gates is of lead, the second of tin, the third of bronze, the fourth of iron, the fifth of an alloy, the sixth of silver, and the seventh of gold."[5]

Incidentally, the correspondences Celsus lists among the planetary spheres, gates, and metals are unusual. He inverts the customary sequence, which usually begins with gold or silver, by starting with lead (which corresponds to Saturn). Traditionally the order is silver (the moon), quicksilver (Mercury), copper (Venus), gold (the sun), iron (Mars), tin (Jupiter), and lead (Saturn) in the order of the planetary orbits as viewed from the earth. Magicians and alchemists use these correspondences in the preparation of talismans and amulets, or in laboratory work.

Celsus's description of a ladder with seven gates is supported by archaeological evidence. At one Mithraeum in Ostia, Italy, the floor is laid out with seven stations decorated with appropriate symbols. These represented seven grades of initiation, beginning with *Corax* ("Raven") and ending with *Pater* ("Father"). They were the mundane counterparts to the higher spheres.

The attainment of each of the seven grades certainly implied that one had risen to, and perhaps mastered, the corresponding level. It is not clear whether the Mithraic initiates actually had the mystical experience of these places (as one might today in magical work using the Kabbalistic Tree, for instance). However, there are descriptions of ecstatic journeys through these spheres in Egyptian Gnostic texts, especially *Zostrianos* and *The Discourse on the Eighth and Ninth.*

The *Discourse* is written as a dialogue between a spiritual guide and an aspirant who has already prepared himself for the mystical experience of the highest levels. He begs his teacher: "[My father], yesterday you promised [me that you would bring] my mind into [the] eighth and afterwards you would bring me into the ninth. You said that this is the order of the tradition" (*Discourse* 1:1–7). The aspirant has apparently passed through the lower levels, for he announces: "We have already advanced to the seventh, since we are pious and walk in your law. And your will we fulfill always" (56: 27–9). This certainly sounds as though he has fulfilled the demands of Saturn, the overlord of the seventh level, associated with the cosmic order.

Finally the two do attain to the eighth and ninth, where, beyond the mutability of the lower seven worlds, they perceive the unchanging.

> Rejoice over this! For already from them the power, which is light, is coming to us. For I see! I see indescribable depths. How shall I tell you, my son? . . . How [shall I describe] the universe? . . . I see the one that moves me from pure forgetfulness. You give me power! I see myself! I want to speak! Fear restrains me. I have found the beginning of the power that is above all powers, the one that has no beginning. I see a fountain bubbling with life. . . . I have seen! Language is not able to reveal this. For the entire eighth, my son, and the souls that are in it, and the angels, sing a hymn in silence. And I, Mind, understand. (*Discourse* 57:28–33, 58:1–22)

The eighth sphere, also mentioned in the Mithraic mysteries, is the sphere of the fixed stars. It is analogous to the divine world because of its relatively unchanging nature. The seven levels below, realms of the planets (literally "wanderers"), whose orbits vary and whose movement was now forward and now backward, represent the mutable world. To look up at the star-scattered heavens through which the planets wander is to see the changeable imposed upon the unchanging, a dramatic experience of the paradoxical nature of existence.

We come now to an extremely perplexing problem. The ladder in its idealized form depicts a perfectly unfolding continuum, with successive levels in harmony with the Will of the One and in sympathy with each other. But one has only to look about the world to see that there are aspects of nature ("red in tooth and claw"), types of people (criminals and murderers), and inexplicable events (fires, hurricanes, floods, and famines) that are incompatible with this perfection.

It seems one must decide: Is the world beautiful and good, the creation of a singular and good God? Or is it a place of bondage, corruption, and limitation, dominated by dark powers? If one adopts the former belief, one has to account for the presence of evil, suffering, and death in the world. Is it due to a rupture in creation (like the "breaking of the shells" in Lurianic Kabbalah), which is no one's fault but simply the consequence of the pressure of unfolding energies? Or is it due to some misjudgment of humanity at some point in creation ("original sin")? Or is it, as the Gnostics thought, because the material world is an inferior copy of the divine world, one generated by a second-rate god imitating a higher, more perfect pattern and incapable of getting it right?

The Hermetic writings tell a lovely story to explain this. The perfect Man, bearing the likeness of the Creator, wanted "to make things for his own part also." He broke through the bounding orbits of the planetary spheres, and gazed upon Nature.

And Nature, seeing the beauty of the form of God, smiled with insatiate love of Man, showing the reflection of that most beautiful form in the water, and its shadow on the earth. And he, seeing this form, a form like to his own, in earth and water, loved it, and willed to dwell there. And the deed followed close on the design; and he took up his abode in matter devoid of reason. And Nature, when she had got him with whom she was in love, wrapped him in her clasp, and they were mingled in one; for they were in love with one another.

And that is why man, unlike all other living creatures upon earth, is twofold. He is mortal by reason of his body; he is immortal by reason of the Man of eternal substance. He is immortal, and has all things in his power; yet he suffers the lot of a mortal, being subject to Destiny.[6]

THE ROLE OF THE PLANETS

Aside from being a compelling philosophical question, the problem of evil has important consequences for astrology. The ancient traditions are divided about whether the planetary spirits are malefic or benefic. Are they, as the Gnostics portrayed them, henchmen of the false god or Demiurge who maliciously wish to hinder the soul? Or are they servants of the Most High? The answer depends upon where one places the boundary between the unchanging and changing worlds.

In most of the older teachings, including the Hermetic, the planetary spheres are firmly within the divine bounds. They are described as "seven Administrators, who encompass with their orbits the world perceived by sense; and their administration is called Destiny."[7] That is, they are the agents of Divine Will.

Gnosticism is the main exception to this teaching, and it may be that a negative view of astrology came largely from that tradition. The Gnostics located the planetary directors within the lower or inferior worlds and thus made them the agents of the false god. (It is also true that when Christianity superseded Paganism, the Christian writers disparaged the Pagan gods and goddesses, some of whom had the names of the planets.)

One explanation for evil found in the Gnostic tradition is that given by Isidore, the "son" (whether biological or spiritual is unclear) of the great Gnostic teacher Basilides (early to mid-second century C.E.). In a treatise called *On the Accreted (or Additional) Soul,* Isidore describes how the pure soul descends from the divine world and picks up "appendages" in each of the planetary spheres, so that its innate goodness is overlaid with passions characteristic of each of the planets. These primitive and animalistic desires are what impel the soul to sin. They are progressively left behind as the soul ascends to the higher spheres.

A remarkably similar description turns up in the Hermetic book *Poimandres,* where the specifically negative qualities of each of the planetary spheres are cast off like old suits of clothes on the upward way.

> And therefore the man mounts upward through the structure of the heavens. And to the first zone of heaven [of the moon] he gives up the force which works increase and that which works decrease; to the second zone [of Mercury], the machinations of evil cunning; to the third zone [of Venus], the lust whereby men are deceived; to the fourth zone [of the sun], domineering arrogance; to the fifth zone [of Mars], unholy daring and rash audacity; to the sixth zone [of Jupiter], evil strivings after wealth; and to the seventh zone [of Saturn], the falsehood which lies in wait to work harm. And thereupon, having been stripped of all that was wrought upon him by the structure of the heavens, he ascends to the substance of the eighth sphere, being now possessed of his own proper power.[8]

If the planets are located within the perfect world, however, one either takes on or activates latent positive qualities associated with the planets as one rises. Instead of overcoming the seven deadly sins, one accrues the seven virtues. The *Poimandres* also glorifies the "seven administrators" and reminds us that "Mind the Maker worked together with the Word, and encompassing the orbits of the Administrators, and whirling them round with a rushing movement, set circling the bodies he had made." Man, as the offspring of Mind "who is Life and Light," has "in himself all the working of the Administrators; and the Administrators took delight in him, and each of them gave him a share of his own nature."[9]

INTO THE TWENTIETH CENTURY

Not only is this a positive interpretation of the action of the planetary spheres, but it is also an unusually early psychological interpretation of astrology. Planetary energies are found *within* as well as outside oneself. Although the exoteric astrology of the last two thousand years has sought answers to mundane questions about career, health, and relationships, in the twentieth century, beginning with the work of Dane Rudhyar and Marc Edmund Jones, astrology began to pick up on the swirling intellectual currents of the time and recast its symbolism into the language of depth psychology. It began to develop the seed idea of the planets within.

The particular psychology that best meshes with astrology is that of C. G. Jung.[10] In Jung's psychology, the planets and other cosmic factors become archetypes. The horoscope becomes simultaneously a snapshot of the heavens at the exact moment of birth and a diagrammatic cross-section of one's inner psyche. The chart itself is a type of mandala, a magic circle that contains universal factors (among them the sun, moon, and the planets) but in an arrangement that is absolutely unique to the individual.

In this type of astrology, the planets become most prominent, for they are the carriers of psychic energy. As Jung explained, "Astrology consists of configurations symbolic of the collective unconscious which is the subject matter of psychology; the planets are the gods (and god-desses), symbols of the powers of the unconscious."[11] Interpreted psy-chologically, they are needs or drives that impel one to think, speak, or act in a certain way. In ancient times, one would have spoken of being inspired by a god or goddess.

The planets contain contradictory possibilities within themselves. Mars, for instance, is a primitive energy of aggressive action that may be expressed through sexual desire, anger, or competitiveness. As a primal energy of ego assertion, its nature may be forceful, selfish, and even destructive. Yet properly directed, it provides the ambition neces-sary for accomplishment or the courage to meet and overcome obsta-cles. Its essentially uncivilized quality is revealed by the depiction of Mars as the god of war. He is invariably found on the battlefield, ex-cept in one story where he is dallying with Venus—a true meeting of opposites!

(It's a fascinating aside to note that Sigmund Freud's horoscope fea-tures a triple singleton Mars—the astrologer's way of saying that this energy is extraordinarily emphasized. In Freud's chart, Mars also clashes with Saturn, representing convention and morality. No won-der the theories he developed were centered around primitive and selfish psychic energy, the id, continually checked by the critical, pa-ternalistic superego—a projection of his own inner dilemma.)

One point that Jung returned to again and again is the repeated number symbolism of astrology and its significance. In the round horoscope used after the Renaissance, the prime axes of a chart, the vertical and horizontal lines that intersect in the center, create four sec-tors. Thus there is a rough square within its circumference. Now the "squaring of the circle" was a popular mathematical conundrum from ancient times, a disguise for a philosophical question of some perplex-ity. Since the circle is an immeasurable figure based on pi, one cannot draw a square more than approximately equal to it. As Robert Lawlor writes in *Sacred Geometry,*

Nevertheless the Squaring of the Circle is of great importance to the geometer-cosmologist because for him the circle represents pure, unmanifest spirit-space while the square represents the manifest and comprehensible world. When a near-equality is drawn between the circle and square, the infinite is able to express its dimensions or qualities through the finite.[12]

The chief astrological symbol contains, then, the mystery of the invisible becoming visible. The horoscope is an attempt to represent the unlimited self manifested within a space-time dimension, and as such carries a profoundly spiritual import that is lost on most of those who contemplate it.

From the center of the mandala not only four but also eight or twelve lines can radiate. The number twelve has the greatest prominence in astrology, first because the zodiac is divided into twelve signs, and second because the horoscope is divided into twelve sectors of life experience known as houses. As Jung observed, twelve as a number

> is four times three. I think we have here stumbled again on the axiom of Maria, that peculiar dilemma of three and four, which I have discussed many times before because it plays such a great role in alchemy. I would hazard that we have to do here with a tetrameria (as in Greek alchemy), a transformation process divided into four stages of three parts each, analogous to the twelve transformations of the zodiac, and its division into four.[13]

Jung was right in that the progression of the zodiac from the first sign, Aries, to the last sign, Pisces, encompasses the complete archetypal cycle of human life, from its first appearance as the spark of life to its reimmersion into the cosmic ocean.

The number twelve represents a completion of a process in time, or a totality in general: twelve months in a year, the twelve days of Christmas, twelve people on a jury, and so on. (Perhaps originally one person of each solar type was represented on a jury, so that the full spectrum of human nature was called upon to deliver judgment in a court of law.) The four main sectors of the astrological chart are each divided into three segments, creating an image whose meaning is similar to the Foursquare City, with its twelve gates, described in the Book of Revelation. It is, of course, the City of God.

THE SIGNS OF the zodiac are also archetypes, represented by symbols such as the crab, the bull, the twins, or the two fish swimming in opposite directions. Each portrays a pure personality type, with a number of typical characteristics both positive and negative.

These associations have accrued because every sign is a product of three rhythms superimposed on each other. The first is a double rhythm, that of yang and yin, or positive and negative. Aries is masculine; Taurus, the sign following, is feminine; and so on. The triple rhythm is related to qualities of energy: cardinal or initiating energy, fixed or stabilizing energy, and mutable or changing energy. (Think of these in relation to the seasons. The first month of spring brings the qualities of that season into being; the second month is its fullest flowering; the third sustains that flowering but begins to make a transition to the next.)

The quadruple rhythm is that of the four elements, the basis for the theory of the four humors whose proportions within the human body determined which of four basic temperaments a person would exhibit. Thus each sign is a unique blend of interacting energies, embodying a combination of one, two, three, and four—the fundamental numbers according to Pythagoras.

The sign Gemini, for instance, is yang, mutable, and air—the most active, changeable, and buoyant of all the combinations. Its archetypal expression is the *puer aeternus:* youthful, lighthearted, and mischievous. Its image is two young boys who are twins, and its action likely to be alternating, superficial, and at times even scheming. Its planetary ruler is Mercury, one of whose mythological correspondences is the Trickster.

Gemini also has a counterpart, the sign opposite to it on the zodiacal wheel, which provides its compensatory qualities. Through integrating any of the polarities represented by opposite signs, one comes to balance in the center. Opposite Gemini is the sign of Sagittarius: masculine, mutable, and fiery. While Gemini is superficial, Sagittarius is profound. Gemini signifies the "lower mind," concerned with small talk and social interchange. Sagittarius's province is the "higher mind," given to pondering abstract ideas and searching for ultimate truth.

If Gemini in its quick-wittedness, childlikeness, and curiosity is analogous to the Fool, then Sagittarius's wisdom, maturity, and philosophical nature make it the Sage or Wise Man. And when the Wise Man is seen as the Fool and vice versa, then the two have become one and the marriage of opposites is celebrated. It may be that the card of the Fool—which can be placed both at the beginning and at the end of the Tarot deck—refers first to the unawakened Fool and then to the wise Fool, who now has the life experience represented by the full spectrum of the deck.

Astrology, with its layers of mathematical, mythological, and esoteric meaning, is thus a richer language than psychology. Yet astrology has still another dimension—that of time. One can use a horoscope to generate a timetable of developmental stages in life. While a mandala can have the shape of a cross, a flower, or a wheel, the horoscope is most like a wheel. Its natural movement (were it not a picture frozen at a given moment of time) would be clockwise. Every four minutes of time the daily wheel turns one degree as measured from the horizon.

This turning wheel (which you can now watch almost moment by moment on your computer screen) becomes the wheel of life through such astrological techniques as progressions. In one type of progression, each day after birth corresponds to a year of one's life. The plan-

ets and the four axes of the chart are moved forward, creating new relationships to each other as well as to the original birth chart. In psychological terms, these new configurations correlate with activations
of inner complexes and predictable outer events in life.

Of the four levels of a human being accepted by esotericism (spiritual, mental, emotional, and physical), orthodox psychology focuses
mainly on two: the mental and emotional. It was only Jung and like-
minded thinkers such as Roberto Assagioli and Abraham Maslow
who began to embrace the spiritual.

Both Jung and key figures in the "transpersonal psychology" movement of the 1960s have begun to readdress the realm of spirit or soul,
acknowledging the legitimacy of psychic gifts, higher states of consciousness, and experiences beyond the normal bounds of time and
space. Even so, these forms of psychology do not usually emphasize the
ultimate spiritual purpose conveyed by the image of the ladder—the
soul's return to the Godhead from whence it sprang. Actually, even
transpersonal psychology, like astrology, can only be the proverbial
"finger pointing to the moon." Neither is a religion, nor do they include mystical techniques and rituals for achieving this higher goal.

Psychology continues to evolve toward the spiritual; it remains for
astrology to do the same by rediscovering its spiritual roots. This goal
may receive a tremendous boost from a project called Project Hind-
sight, whose intention is to translate or retranslate all the Greek and a
sizable number of Latin manuscripts on astrology. Spearheaded by a
group that originally included Robert Hand, the Greek translator
Robert Schmidt, and the medieval astrologer Robert Zoller, the project has produced several dozen pamphlets containing the works of
such important early writers as Vettius Valens, Manilius, and Claudius
Ptolemy. The project is not only illuminating traditional Greek and
Roman astrology as it was practiced two thousand years ago, but it is
also revealing similarities (as well as differences) with Hindu astrology.

As a result, the philosophical and spiritual matrix in which ancient astrology was embedded may once again come to light, and the art as we know it may be reborn. The modern labyrinth, with its uncertain geography, may be combined with the ancient ladder, so that the upward and the inward ways conjoin. To "As above, so below" will be wedded "As within, so without." Another image may replace these two, for the metaphor of the ladder unfortunately tends to reinforce a religious bias of the past two thousand years: that up is good and down is bad.

Yet the labyrinth too is one-directional. Perhaps a better figure would be a map depicting both inner and outer territory. Describing the psychic depths traversed in the analytic quest, it simultaneously points to the upward dimensions through which the soul passes. That map is the horoscope itself, which can depict both inner landscape and outer world. It encompasses both ladder and labyrinth. In contemplating it, we stand like "stout Cortes" on the peak in Darien, in awe before the vast cosmos, where the sun, moon, and stars speak their story of our journey into, through, and beyond this world.

10

SOPHIA

GODDESS OF WISDOM

Rediscovering the Divine Feminine in Western spirituality

Caitlín Matthews

The Call of Wisdom

What Wisdom is, and how she came into being, I will relate;
I will conceal no mysteries from you,
But will track her from her first beginnings
And bring the knowledge of her into the open.

— WISDOM OF SOLOMON 6:22

That is how the unknown author of the apocryphal Wisdom of Solomon prefaces his portrait of Lady Wisdom, Sophia. And in truth, she has been too long obscured in the West; it is time to find effective ways to manifest all aspects of this mysterious figure in our world.

Because Sophia has sprung out of a weaving together of Hellenic, Judaic, philosophical, and Gnostic strands, and because, as Lady Wis-

dom, she has long been the preserve of biblical scholarship, there has
been an understandable reluctance to approach her as a practical esoteric archetype. Some have seen Sophia as a kind of feeble or concocted
personification of wisdom, of inferior status to God, who has traded
under the aspects and attributes of many pagan goddesses.

However, the need to attain a common language and symbology
with which to speak about and understand the Goddess is one of the
major struggles occupying us at present. For the last two thousand
years in the Western world, God has been imaged and referred to as a
masculine deity. And although, prior to this time, both gods and goddesses existed alongside each other in numerous religions, as they still
do in other parts of the world today, in the West we have lost the facil-
ity to operate in a bi-deistic sense. It will be many decades, if not centuries, before group consciousness accepts the Divine Feminine.

However, the reemergence of the Goddess in the twentieth century
has begun to break down the conceptual barriers erected by orthodox
religion and social conservatism. For the first time in two millennia,
the idea of a goddess as the central pivot of creation is finding a welcome response. But although the figure of the Goddess has been in
eclipse until this century, she has not been inactive. She has been working away like yeast within the chewy dough of daily bread. The foundation mysteries of the Goddess underlie later spiritual developments
that are generally associated with the esoteric streams of orthodox religions. It is especially within the figure of the Goddess of Wisdom that
these mysteries were transmitted into our own time, taking many
strange and unexpected routes.

Significantly, the major mystics of all faiths have perceived the
Lady Wisdom as the bridge between everyday life and the world of
the eternal, often entering into deep accord with her purpose. But although such mystics as the medieval abbess Hildegard of Bingen or
the Sufi Ibn ʿArabi are hardly considered to be "goddess-worshippers"
in the feminist sense, they nevertheless show that the channels to the

Divine Feminine have been kept open and mediated by many so-called patriarchal faiths in some quite surprising ways.

I believe that Sophia or Wisdom combines both the practical and transcendent form of the Divine Feminine—the Goddess herself. (In this article, I have used Sophia and Wisdom interchangeably, regardless of Sophia's particular biblical and Gnostic heritage.) This view is at variance with all other studies of Wisdom that see her as an allegorical or subsidiary figure to the Divine Masculine—God. We need to learn that Wisdom is not *part* of any deistic schema, she is *central* to our understanding of spirituality. And while she may be invoked by many for purposes as various as the creation of a female priesthood within Christianity or as the inspiration of feminists in search of a broader view of the Goddess, Sophia is, at the last, her own self: the leaven that permeates creation, life's creative impetus and completion.

The greatest strength of Sophia is that she transcends the dualism that has bedeviled our Western society since the fading of the prehistoric and Classical eras when the Goddess was last manifest as a powerful entity of wholeness. Yet, ironically, Sophia herself, in nearly every culture, has appeared under two polarized archetypes: as a dispossessed daughter of God, wandering the roads in tatters, or else as a transcendently lovely virgin whose highway is the stars. Yet in whatever form she has appeared, her call has gone forth to practice again the compassionate wisdom by which life should be lived. How humanity has answered her call is a story of great complexity and wonder.

THE BLACK GODDESS

Wisdom is close at hand, always busy about her work. But the Western world has been so busy about its affairs that only a few unusual people have had time to comment on her existence. Sophia has been appropriated by scholars, clerics, and philosophers who have chosen to robe her in such overblown esoteric language that she is hardly recognizable. Wisdom trades under impossible titles: Mother of the Philosophers, *das Ewige Wiebliche* (the Eternal Feminine), *Sedes Sapientiae,* and other such nominations do not inspire confidence. Such beings are impossibly remote: they sit about all day in courts of law or in palaces, on intensive committees and government boards. They are scarcely approachable in these forms.

And yet, we have the dichotomy that Wisdom is most appreciated by the very simple and unlearned, who turn to her as naturally as to their own mothers, for she really helps them in ways that philosophy and other arcane studies do not. They feel at home with Wisdom because she has seen and heard it all before; she has the same kind of battered face as her petitioners, for she offers real wisdom, not the kind offered by Lady Bountifuls who are all mouth and no sense.

This is aptly borne out in C. S. Lewis's masterly retelling of the Psyche story *Til We Have Faces.* Here, Psyche's hard sister, Queen Orual, has gone to the temple of the goddess Ungit, where she has been responsible for installing a brand-new statue of the goddess. She witnesses a peasant woman cast herself down in front of the ancient stone that was formerly the only representation of the goddess.

> "Has Ungit comforted you, child?" I asked.
>
> "Oh yes, Queen," said the woman, her face almost brightening, "oh yes. Ungit has given me great comfort. There's no goddess like Ungit."
>
> "Do you always pray to *that* Ungit," said I (nodding toward the shapeless stone) "and not to *that*?" Here I nodded towards our new image, standing tall and straight in her robes . . . the loveliest thing our land has ever seen.
>
> "Oh always this, Queen," said she. "That other, the Greek Ungit, she wouldn't understand my speech. She's only for nobles and learned men. There's no comfort in her."[1]

We need to go down to the roots of the Goddess of Wisdom and reveal her many guises, whether it be her transcendent, starry face or her workaday, primeval one. The blackened old stones once venerated as goddesses and the crystalline virgins of esoteric spirituality are not so dissimilar, for they both represent Sophia at the archetypal extremities of her appearance. Neither image is better or more achieved than the other; Sophia is not interested in qualitative judgments, but in what works. Accordingly, she adopts the form most near to our heart.

The Goddess of Wisdom appears in nearly every culture and society. She is clearly distinguished by unique qualities and symbolic representations: she is concerned with the survival and maturation of all creation. She is distinguishable from many popular forms of the Divine Feminine by the fact that she frequently appears as the Black Goddess. She is black because she is primal, and, like Isis, she keeps her glory veiled. She often takes the appearance of a hag, an aged widow, or a dispossessed woman. But she is primarily the keeper of earthly and heavenly wisdom and the guardian of its laws. At the other end of the archetype, Wisdom as Sophia is gloriously beautiful, ageless, eternal, mediating transcendent spirituality.

These polarized appearances—as Hag or Queen of Heaven—are the two sides of one coin, one archetypal power. Just as coal and diamond are both carbon—that basic substance of life—so does the Goddess of Wisdom manifest her power through seemingly opposing appearances. The Goddess of Wisdom is seeded within us all.

The first personification of the Divine Feminine is as land-feature, as the earth itself. The primal earth-mothers of prehistory, the mountain mothers who sculpt the land, the black meteorites venerated as goddesses—it is in these forms that the primal wisdom of the Goddess of the Land was first known by our race. The earth that is our home and dwelling place becomes, in Sophiology, a prime mythic symbol of Sophia's presence—exampled by her manifestation as the Shekinah, the holy dwelling of the Divine upon earth. She is the guardian of all that is made, because she helped make it, appearing in Proverbs as the cocreator of the universe, ever at God's side as a busy work-woman.

Sophia has kept open the channels of communication between the Divine and earthly realms, possibly as a result of her dual manifestation, for she is both transcendent Goddess and incarnate messenger of the spiritual realm. The Goddess of Wisdom has also played a great part in the work of justice: "Behind each law, mercy is concealed," is a Jewish saying that is borne out in Sophia's many guises. As the Zoroastrian Daena, she appears to the soul newly arrived in the afterlife: standing upon the çinvat bridge she challenges the soul by appearing as the sum of its deeds. If the soul is fraught with evil deeds, she appears as an ugly woman who drags the soul over the bridge down to hell. If the soul's deeds have been good, then she appears as a beautiful maiden saying, "I am thine own Daena. I was loved, thou hast made me still more loved. I was beautiful, thou hast made me still more beautiful." And the two pass over into paradise. This mirroring of the soul is significant: Sophia thus always appears to remind the soul of its divine origins. The Egyptian Maat, whose feather weighs the soul in the afterlife, is similarly one of Sophia's many personas.

The pre-Islamic streams of Wisdom stem from Mazdaen, Zoroastrian, and Manichaean sources; they subtly survive in the mystical traditions of Islam, notably Sufism. One of its prime mystics, Ibn 'Arabi, had a vision of Sophia while he was in pilgrimage at the Kaaba in Mecca. The black meteorite housed within the Kaaba by Muhammad was traditionally supposed to have once been worshipped as the Goddess. It is around this black stone that modern pilgrims to Mecca still circumambulate—a thought that gives us another insight into the nature of Sophia as Black Goddess.

But it is Judaism—both its orthodox and mystical streams—that has given us the most familiar image of Sophia as the Shekinah: the

Spirit of God that accompanies the Israelites as Pillar of Cloud and Fire. She was, according to some traditions, self-exiled from Paradise in order to accompany the generations of Adam and Eve: her brief sojourn in the Temple before its destruction was a honeymoon before the Shekinah had to be borne within the individual soul of each pious Jew. The glorious restoration of the Temple and its present desacralized state are deep images within the Jewish psyche of the two faces of Sophia, as well as the state of the human soul.

A greater part of the myths surrounding Sophia concern her continual quest to be reunited with her consort. She is Bride of God or of the Logos. The Christian myth of the Assumption of the Virgin into Heaven is a prefiguring of Sophia's prophesied entry into the Pleroma with her spouse, the Logos, for the Blessed Virgin is mystically understood to be the Bride of her Son, just as Sophia is similarly understood, according to some myths, to be the Bride of her Father. Orthodox Judaism observes this very union between God and his Shekinah on the Sabbath eve, when pious Jewish couples make love. This pairing of God with Goddess is part of the earthly, homely religions of the ancient Middle East, when the tribal ruler conjoined with the Goddess of the Land, usually represented by her priestess, in a mystical wedding ritual whose echoes are still discernible within the erotic poem of the Song of Solomon.

One of Sophia's roles, as Black Goddess, is to accompany the soul and bring it into alignment with the light of the spirit, whose messenger and manifestation she is. Sophia is the familiar touchstone, the *prima materia* that will change to gold if we exercise the alchemy of the soul. While she is exiled from us, she can reflect our sad condition: when she is united with us she can burnish our spiritual aspirations until we reflect her transcendent beauty.

QUEEN OF THE WEST

Sophia is really the uncrowned, unrecognized Queen of the West. She has crosstracked all spiritual systems in one form or another, from Gnosticism to the Shaker movement. She has both pagan and orthodox forms—Christian, Judaic, and Islamic. She is a saint, as the Eastern Orthodox Saint Sophia, and a sinner, in Gnostic tradition being frequently represented by Mary Magdalene.

Present in philosophic traditions as far apart as Plato, where she is the World-Soul, and Goethe, where she is the Eternal Feminine, Sophia emerges fully in the writings of Philo of Alexandria, the Hellenized Jew who stood in the headwaters of the Sophianic tradition, the blending of Middle Eastern, Egyptian, Jewish, Christian, and Hermetic streams. Due to Philo's genius, we may discern in Sophia the features of Isis, whose name recurs throughout the history of the Western Way as the Savior Goddess, the alchemical queen, the "Lady of the Perfect Black."

But it is perhaps in Gnostic tradition that Sophia is best known, although there are various traditions recounting her story. In most Gnostic cults, Sophia was divided into two: the transcendent, Upper Sophia, and the fallen, Lower Sophia—sometimes called Barbelo or Achamoth. While having dual form, Sophia does not naturally lend herself to dualism—in the sense of a polarization of good and evil. Yet, in the text "Thunder-Perfect Mind," Sophia speaks of herself in an extensive list of antithetic epithets that take into account the misunderstandings that may arise in the person of dualistic mind:

It is I who have been hated everywhere
And who have been loved everywhere.
It is I who am called life:

And whom you have called death.
It is I who am called law:
And whom you have called lawlessness.
It is I whom you have chased:
And it is I whom you have restrained.[2]

In the Secret Gospel of John, Sophia begets Ialtabaoth, the First
Aeon, who drew upon the power of his mother to beget the archons
and to form the world. When Sophia noticed the loss of her power,
"she grew darker, for her consort had not come into harmony with
her." As ever, the recurrent themes of darkness or blackness and of her
lost consort surround Sophia. This consort, within Gnosticism, is
properly the Logos or Christ. But, as in mystical Judaism, where the
Shekinah, the Bride of God, remains exiled from paradise until the
end of all things, it is not until the *Apocatastasis,* the great Return to
the Pleroma (the fullness of heaven), that Sophia and her consort may
conjoin.

The testimony of the Church Fathers, particularly Saint Epiphanius, speaks continually of the Gnostics' search for the lost power of
their mother, conceived by the Gnostics, says Epiphanius, to reside in
male and female emissions of sperm and menstrual blood. However
true his accusations of their "partaking of their own filthiness," it becomes clear that the Gnostics understood the intrinsically spiritual nature of creation; as it says in the lost Gospel of Eve:

It is I who am you and it is you who are me.
And wherever you are, I am there.
And I am sown in all: and you collect me from wherever you wish.
And when you collect me, it is your own self that you collect.[3]

All that is made bears Sophia's likeness. Her stamp is on everything,
so recognizing the features of Wisdom is the name of the game. The

Gospel of Philip also speaks of Sophia as the salt that makes the offering acceptable: it is a compelling parallel to Christ's saying (Mark 9:50), "Have salt in yourselves and be at peace with one another." Without the savor of Wisdom, all religion, philosophy, or spirituality is flavorless.

Sophia passed from the syncretistic melting pot of Alexandria and found a home in many hearts. Christianity subsumed Sophia and her Logos in one being. The chief architect of this construct was Saint Paul, who, following the lead of Philo, put the rational, masculine power of the Logos (the Word) and the intuitive, feminine power of Sophia (Wisdom) into the person of Christ. A similar kind of action can be paralleled in the conflation of the Chinese goddess Kwan Yin with the male Buddhist god Avalokitesvara. This kind of thing was happening all the time within certain Gnostic cults whose texts spoke of "the masculine virgin, Barbelo." But attempts to appropriate female imagery and attributes to a male being are never very successful.

For example, Sophia has begun to play a significant part in Christian feminism, some of whose proponents look to the Christo-Sophia—a kind of androgynous being whose potentialities do not seem, to me at least, to be very promising. Certain parts of the Gospels are regarded by biblical scholars to be partial interpolations of Sophia's voice. Thus, when Christ is mourning over Jerusalem in Luke 13:34 "O Jerusalem . . . how often would I have gathered your children together as a hen gathers her brood under her wings and you would not," we are to hear the voice of Sophia breaking through in subtextual and prophetic tones. This ground seems to me to be more fruitful for exploring the Christian feminist position. Either Sophia is sufficiently charismatic to effect a change in our fragmented culture *in her own person,* or she is a wisp of straw in the wind, a mere shadow of former goddessly greatness whose passing should not be mourned. Such a view is hardly tolerable to non-Christian feminists, who generally like their goddess to be female and unattached. Yet, despite them, Sophia expresses a propensity for acquiring consorts or for androgyny.

Sophia's words have also been, perhaps more logically, appropriated
to the feasts of Mary, whose feast-day antiphons and readings are
nearly all from the apocryphal Books of Wisdom. The papal encyclical
that announced Mary's Assumption into Heaven, the subject of Jung's
Answer to Job, has established for all time the shared theme between
Mary and Sophia: "Mary as bride is united with the Son in the heavenly bridal chamber."[4] It is said that, had Pius XII lived, he would
have declared Mary Co-Redemptrix with Christ—an even more earth-
shattering declaration than that of the Assumption. If such a doctrine
were to be proclaimed in the next few decades, the future of Sophia as
a major figure of spiritual redemption would be established for all
time within Christianity, for Mary perfectly comprehends the mystical
role and attributes of Sophia.

Throughout medieval Christian mysticism Sophia keeps appearing. The works of the prodigious medieval abbess Hildegard of Bingen are particularly rich in references to Sophia as Sapientia, whom
she sometimes also identifies with both Ecclesia, the Church, and with
Mary.

The Hermetic and alchemical currents were a powerful force in
Sophia's survival. It was, strangely, in the post-Reformation period
that Sophia found a new lease on life that was to have profound effects
on nonconformist Protestant and Russian Orthodox persuasions alike.
The prime messenger of Sophia during this era was Jacob Boehme,
who, in his self-educated and mystical way, expounded a doctrine of
the Virgin Wisdom that swept across Europe. Boehme had read
widely in both Hermetic and Kabbalistic areas; the clues to his doctrine lay dormant in these esoteric books. His doctrine influenced the
Behemists, a British mystical group under the leadership of Dr. John
Pordage, including its main amanuensis, Jane Leade, an almost forgotten female nonconformist mystic; it eventually influenced William
Blake, in whose visionary poem "Jerusalem" Jerusalem herself appears

in dual form as the transcendent spouse of Christ and as the fallen Vala, the consort of Albion.

Another figure influenced by the Behemists was Mother Anne Lee of the Shakers—perhaps not the most promising of Sophiologists at first sight, yet she founded her sect on an angelic ideal of celibate men and women, confirming her belief in the androgyny of the Godhead, as propounded by Boehme, instanced in this Shaker hymn:

The Father's high eternal throne
Was never fill'd by one alone:
There Wisdom holds the mother's seat,
And is the father's helper-meet.[5]

Sophia probably finds a more individual persona in Eastern Orthodoxy, where she is often iconographically depicted as a crowned, red-winged angel seated upon a throne with the world at her feet: Mary and John the Baptist stand either side of her as Theotokes (Mother of God) and Forerunner, while Christ appears above her head in a roundel, signifying his immanent descent to the throne of Wisdom. Orthodoxy receives the stream of Wisdom via the early Christian links of the Church Fathers, on the one hand, and on the other, from elements of Altaic shamanism, which shares similar Sophianic myths, as well as from the esoteric school of Boehme. The nineteenth-century Russian school of Sophiology represented by Vladimir Soloviev and his followers, Father Paul Florensky and Sergius Bulgakov, is deeply mystical. Soloviev, perhaps the most passionately dedicated to Sophia's cause, directly addressed the very heart of Mother Russia. He speaks here of Sophia:

She herself will descend to you.
Then you will no longer in mortal slavery

Entice the laughing sunrise
In your wretched and humble aspect.

She and you form one law,
One behest of a Higher Will.
You are not eternally condemned
To a despairing and mortal anguish.[6]

Boehme's most recent adherent, Rudolf Steiner, drew greatly from his work. The theme of Sophia is deeply woven through Anthroposophy, which had claimed Wisdom for itself.

The track of Sophia is found now in the new Gnosticism that arises from the work of Jung and his followers, and from the rippling effect of esoteric work the world over: Wisdom is busy about her work once more. And it is surely in the West that Sophia is most needed and least appreciated.

The esotericist and mystic have long been friends with Sophia and known that wisdom is "a gift and sacrament of God and a divine matter, which deeply and in diverse manners was veiled in images by the wise."[7] This alchemical treatise, *Aurora Consurgens,* perfectly describes the manner in which Sophia has acted as both the veil and that which the veil conceals: esotericism's best vanishing trick. She signifies the esoteric and Gnostic current that hides itself and that, like the philosopher's stone itself, is both prized and despised.

The rediscovery of the Gnostic Scriptures at Nag Hammadi in the 1940s has fueled a great resurgence of interest in alternative forms of Christian belief. Many esotericists will find obvious parallels between these texts and those of the Corpus Hermeticum. We have already seen the active formation of Gnostic churches in California; whether we will also see the growth of a neo-Gnostic magical system will be very interesting. But there is one further consideration: What are the potentialities of Sophia for those who give central place to the Divine

Feminine, whether as independent goddess or as the feminine face of
the Godhead sharing her power with a consort?

THE PASSION OF SOPHIA

The return of the Virgin Wisdom as Díke (Justice) is prophesied by
Virgil in his Fourth Eclogue. It is one of the many themes that threads
Sophia's mythos, wherein the Savior Goddess comes, withdraws, and
is found again. As it says in both the Book of Enoch and in the apocryphal Books of Wisdom, "Wisdom found no place where she might
dwell."[8] Just as the Shekinah is said to find a home in the soul of pious
Jews, so now does Sophia, as Goddess of Wisdom, find her dwelling in
the hearts of all who seek practical ways to bring the healing wisdom
of the Goddess to the world. Sophia speaks about her second coming
in the Gnostic text "The First Thought in Three Forms" (*Trimorphic
Protennoia*):

> And I came, for a second time, in the manner of a woman;
>   and I spoke with them.
> And I shall instruct them about the coming end of the realm
> And I shall instruct them about the beginning of the coming realm
>   which does not experience change,
>   and in which our appearance will change.[9]

With such a prophecy before us, we must be alert to the signs of the
times, which certainly begin to speak of Sophia's leavening of the world.

It has been a long night and a slow dawning for those who look to
the Goddess for their spiritual inspiration. The second coming of the
Goddess has proved of inestimable value to people everywhere, for it
has provided them with a new mythic pattern, a saving story to live by.
Sophia, as the inheritor of major attributes of goddesses such as Isis,
and of the mystical aspects of the Divine Feminine within Christianity

and Judaism, stands in a unique place to offer a new paradigm for our age.

In many ways, the Passion of Sophia is also our struggle, as women and men of goodwill who seek peace and the harmonious integration of the Divine Feminine. For women, in particular, Sophia brings a message of hope and glory. The solution of Sophia to the problems of ill-treatment, captivity, and abuse of all kinds has been, according to all her stories, to walk away and find another home, ever exiled, ever searching, ever mourning the loss. But hers is not a victim mentality; rather it is an earnest striving after justice and completion. For she ever returns to the places of imprisonment and misery, finding ways to redress and heal. This continual visiting and withdrawal of Wisdom can be likened to the processes of the soul, with which we are sometimes aligned and sometimes disconnected.

The anger of many feminists, especially in the early days of consciousness-raising, has resulted in many women walking away from imprisoning relationships and no-win situations into richer areas of life, where their gifts can be utilized to the fullest. In others, the challenge has been recognized but not yet acted upon. The ability to leave behind our initial anger and find in ourselves the fount of compassion, which will heal even those who have hurt us, is the true mark of Sophia in her sister- and fellow-workers. For the leaven of Sophia still works in the most intractable circumstances. Sophia's Passion is a daily, ongoing affair for many people who miraculously find the skillful means to cope with misery, despair, poverty, abuse, racism, and the rest of humanity's self-imposed problems.

What are the effects of cooperating with Sophia? According to the Gnostic tradition, we are all part of Sophia's family. "Kinship with Wisdom brings immortality,"[10] we are told: the empowerment and enrichment of spirit that all mystics and esotericists strive for. She is the silent companion who stands at our elbows as we toil to attain the Great Work, whether that be in magical operation, mystical union with the Divine, or the daily grappling with humanity's problems, our striving to reflect the light of the spirit in our world. By virtue of her own passion, Sophia is a liberator from outworn modes of thought that keep us captive.

For all, the Goddess of Wisdom reaches down to the depths of our need. She is the skillful means by which we may be realized. Like the black, abiding earth, her simple being is so vastly present that we have not noticed it. Indeed, perhaps we have not known the depths of our need or that any assuaging wisdom was near at hand. If we act *as if* Sophia were present and call upon her in faith, we might find the strength of her assistance. To be adopted consciously into her family, we need to acknowledge and clarify our spiritual condition: this is the true Gnosis—for to know ourselves is to find our spiritual likeness in her features.

Gnosis, like Sophia herself, has been scattered to the four winds. If we can catch some small fragment and actualize it in our lives, more of Sophia's wonderful story will become known. As Steiner wrote of Isis-Sophia: "We must give form to this legend, for it sets forth the truth of our times. We must speak of the dead and lost Isis, the divine Sophia, even as the Egyptians spoke of the dead and lost Osiris."[11] Indeed, at times, reclaiming the pieces of this passion narrative is as arduous as Isis's own search for parts of her consort. But it is a task in which we must persist. For Sophia says: "I love those who love me, and those who seek me diligently find me."[12]

EXPLAINING WICCA

An overview of the teachings of today's

predominant form of Neopaganism

Judy Harrow

At the Parliament of the World's Religions, held in Chicago in 1993, people were trying very hard to be respectful and inclusive. The opening ceremony featured brief greetings from many leaders of the world's major religions. Almost all of them said the same thing, in very nearly the same words: "We all worship the same *one God,* although we call *Him* by many different names."

Four times as many people came to the Parliament as had been expected, so there was no way all of us could fit into the main assembly hall. The ceremony was carried throughout the hotel on closed-circuit television. Many of the Wiccans present gathered in the Covenant of the Goddess hospitality suite to watch the ceremony. ("Wicca" is the Old English root of the modern English word "witchcraft." These days many of us have adopted the older word as an end run around centuries of hostile stereotyping. In this new usage, "Wiccan" is equivalent to "Witch.") We were visibly present at a major interfaith gathering for the first time, and not at all sure of our welcome.

As each leader repeated the basic statement, we winced and groaned. We certainly didn't, and still don't, want to make unnecessary waves. But our faith is not just one more form of male monotheism. To honestly gain a seat at the table, we will have to make this understood.

Some of us think we follow a new religion. Others believe our religion is ancient, although newly emerged from centuries underground. Either way, only a very few of us were raised in this faith. It is new in *our* lives. We are just learning—or reconstructing—the ways of European Pagan nature mysticism. We really don't yet have enough of an experiential base to reflect upon, nor have we had time yet to develop a well-articulated theology. Many of us are also diffident because we lack formal theological education and the analytical and descriptive skills that it might provide.

How can we begin to explain our religion to a curious and sometimes suspicious world? Using such standard theological terms as "theodicy," "eschatology," and "salvation" will not work. These arise from biblical worldviews. We are different, different way down to the roots. Yet the questions that open-minded and sincere neighbors ask me are most often guided, consciously or not, by these categories.

Real communication has to start with something as basic as our understanding of the word "religion" itself. Leonard Swidler, professor of Catholic thought and interreligious dialogue at Temple University in Philadelphia, describes religion as "an explanation of the ultimate meaning of life, based on a notion of the Transcendent, and how to live accordingly." He goes on to define the transcendent as "that which goes beyond the everyday, the ordinary, the surface experience of reality. It can mean spirits, gods, a Personal God, an Impersonal God, Emptiness, etc., etc."[1] That's a good beginning.

The Latin root of the word "religion" means "reconnection." I understand "religion" to mean activity of many different kinds that is intended to restore the connection between humankind and the sacred (a more theologically neutral term than "transcendent"). Through religious activity we work toward clarifying our understanding of the sacred, developing conscious contact and living our lives in growing accordance with that deeply felt connection. In the simpler and more poetic words from the musical *Godspell,* we seek "to see You more clearly, love You more dearly, follow You more nearly day by day."

Swidler suggests that religions normally contain four components: creed, cult, code, and community, which he calls the "four c's." These certainly can be described in contemporary Wicca.

Our community is so diverse and decentralized that nobody can or should speak for all of us. After twenty years as a Wiccan initiate and seventeen as a working High Priestess, I offer myself and the coven I lead as typical examples.

CREED

"Creed" refers to a religion's concepts of the sacred, its values, its general worldview. For me, this would also include the stories, symbols, myths, and metaphors used to convey this understanding.

Wicca is not a religion of the book. No one sacred scripture defines Wicca or Neopaganism. Instead we are free to choose among a kaleidoscopic array of poetry, stories, and symbols. More important, we are taught that it is within ourselves that we will ultimately find what we seek. Lived experience is the base upon which our inherited structure of written and oral traditions is built and the standard against which those teachings are continually tested.

I'm wary of making descriptive statements about the sacred, since I believe it to be a Reality far beyond human comprehension. Like most Wiccans, however, I relate to the sacred as primarily immanent rather than transcendent. If the concept of transcendence means anything to me, it is that the whole is greater than the parts, perhaps even greater than the sum of all the parts. So as the wave does not presume to define the ocean, I make no attempt to define the infinite and ineffable. I can only speak of my own experience and perceptions and of those of my community.

We might be mistaken. At best our understanding is necessarily partial. In all humility, we must hold our concepts and metaphors lightly. Neither our understanding of our Gods nor our sense of appropriate behavior should ever become reified and static. Instead we hope and work for lifelong personal growth and continuing development of our traditions across the generations.

From the perspective of immanence, I experience the sacred as a very present Source, the life within my every living moment, rather than as a Creator from long ago and far away. I neither perceive nor acknowledge any kind of division between the Creator and Creation. Instead my quest is to perceive power and beauty, meaning and value within the everyday and the ordinary—in these bodies, on this Earth, here and now.

I am also a polytheist. This is not because I presume to define the sacred as either plural or singular, but because of my understanding of the human religious imagination.

Pure monotheism is all inclusive. Since it leaves no one out, it does not oppress anyone. Yet history shows that only a few gifted individuals have ever been able to sustain that pure consciousness of an abstract all-pervasive Divinity. Most of us, in order to relate to the sacred, need to stick a face onto God.

Once we do so, the all-inclusive God usually devolves into one face and one model. Whichever face you choose—stern, white-bearded Father; loving, giving Mother; or any other—most of us are left out. This was quite recently demonstrated when Pope John Paul II explicitly cited exclusively male models for Divinity as a rationale for refusing to ordain gifted and dedicated women. Practically speaking, monotheism is exclusive rather than inclusive and just about always oppressive.

My Pagan faith, on the other hand, honors the diversity of Divinity and the Divinity of diversity. Our many Gods, or, if you prefer, many models of the sacred, show us an inclusive holiness that crosses all lines, including gender, age, and occupation. Balance and integration are also important to us, and we often use marriage myths to model the reconciliation of apparent opposites into dynamic complementarity. This multivalent model of Divinity is very different from simplistic dualism, which views good and evil as an absolute dichotomy without shading or nuance and personifies them accordingly.

Although Witches have for centuries been depicted as devil worshippers, in truth we do not even acknowledge a God of absolute evil, let alone worship one. We do not invert the values and symbols of biblical religion, nor are we primarily motivated by rebellion against the traditions into which most of us were born. We do not understand or define ourselves in contradistinction to any other faith. Instead we reach back to older and simpler forms, those we believe to be the ancient shamanic ways of tribal Europe, rooted in the living Earth.

I worship the Goddess. Generally Wiccans offer their primary devotion to the Earth Mother. This is not in any way to deny the existence or power of other Deities, and in fact we address Them when we feel the need. But we are born of Mother Earth, nourished throughout our lives from Her bosom, and return to Her in death just as the leaves return to the forest floor. Embracing Her as our primary contact with the sacred emphasizes the interpenetration of Deity with ordinary everyday life.

Some Witches worship the Goddess exclusively; most also worship Her consort, the wild, free God of animal life, most widely known as

Pan. Some covens and groups of covens concentrate on a particular ethnic pantheon, such as the Celtic, Greek, or Egyptian. Others, like my own, are more eclectic in their practice. Overall, though, it's fair to describe most Wiccans as immanence-based polytheists who offer primary devotion to the Goddess, Mother Earth.

In addition to our understanding of Deity, most Wiccan covens use two major symbolic systems to represent the wholeness of life. These are the Quartered Circle and the Wheel of the Year.

The Quartered Circle represents wholeness in terms of space—the four cardinal directions onto which we map seasons, human developmental stages, and many other things. To me, the most important of these are four aspects of human function: knowledge, passion, wisdom, and skill. We try to place ourselves at the balance point, in the center, and draw on these capacities as needed.

The eight-spoked Wheel of the Year represents wholeness in terms of time—the interacting cycles of Earth and Sun, which produce the seasons of the land. We use this as a metaphor for the endless rhythm of dreaming, doing, harvesting, and letting go that moves through the great and small changes of our lives. This is the pulse of day and night, summer and winter, life and death. We aspire to dance gracefully within that rhythm.

CULT

"Cult" is not used here in its recent pejorative sense. Instead it means ritual, spiritual practices, prayer, ceremony—all those activities that nurture the participants' relationship with the sacred and empower them to live their lives accordingly. This is the two-way path between belief and behavior that passes through the worshipper's deep mind.

The Wheel of the Year forms the basis for our Wiccan ritual calendar. There are eight festivals, which we call Sabbats, in our year. The equinoxes and solstices represent the cycles of the Sun. The four cross-quarter days of Samhain, Oimelc, Beltane, and Lunasa, the mid-points of each season in the old British agricultural calendar, are more closely Earth-related. Taken together, these festivals connect us with all nature through the ever-turning seasons that directly affect all living things; they also serve as symbols for human life stages: birth, adolescence, marriage, death.

Witches also celebrate the rhythms of the Moon, Earth's lovely daughter, bringer of dreams and poetic inspiration. Traditionally, the eight Sabbats are times for community-wide celebration and attunement with natural cycles, the exoteric aspects of our religion, whereas the Moons—celebrated when the Moon is full—are for more intensive personal and small-group focus on inner work and conscious contact with the sacred.

One thing that outsiders find most fascinating about us is that we believe in (and practice) magic. That is, we believe that the inner work we do may well result in outer-world changes: healings, job magic, hearth magic. This should not startle those who accept the efficacy of prayer.

Our ways of worship may seem very different, but underlying them is the same basic desire—to bring our lives into alignment with our Gods. Although perfection may be forever beyond us, we may reasonably expect to deepen our understanding and develop some wisdom. These insights can guide our everyday actions, helping us to live more authentically. When we live from our core values and see how they play out in the world, we have a basis for deeper reflection and clearer insight. Belief and behavior are mutually reinforcing and mutually correcting. Ritual helps keep them connected, to the benefit of both.

CODE

"Code" means the behavioral guidance that all religions provide for both ethics and etiquette. I believe that the central purpose of religion is to sustain, amplify, and clarify the connection between our everyday lives and our core values, thus nurturing our conscious contact with the sacred. Lacking a concern for ethics, ritual becomes at best a feel-good exercise, a cheap, safe, and legal high—or, at worst, an excuse for blasphemous hypocrisy.

Typically, religions have some core ethical statement, some "golden rule" that summarizes their sense of appropriate conduct. Wicca is no exception. We call ours the "Wiccan Rede." ("Rede" is an archaic word, derived from the Middle English *reden,* which means "to guide or direct." "An" is an archaic equivalent of "if.")

> *Eight words the Wiccan Rede fulfill:*
> *An it harm none, do what you will!*

This is a simple, powerful statement of situational ethics and radical freedom. Witches accept no arbitrary restraints on our freedom of choice. We have no universally applicable set of "thou shalts" and "thou shalt nots." Any harmless behavior is permissible to us. For us, the term "victimless crime" is an offensive oxymoron. Neither does our religion seek to regulate the minutiae of our daily lives in order to maintain our collective sense of identity. We follow a "high-choice" ethic.

This may seem like permissiveness, but in fact our way is far more demanding than the most stringent set of commandments. Without rules, the burden falls on each of us to ensure that our actions do as little harm as possible. Without any absolute standard of good and evil, we are each required to think and feel our way through all the complexities, weigh all the probable results and implications of our choices. In the crises and choice points in our personal lives and in our responses to community and social issues, no authority figure directs us. We are on our own.

We have no "orthodox" rulings on marriage, sexuality, divorce, military service, assisted suicide, and the like, although certainly we think and talk about such subjects. When I as a priestess am asked for counsel, my role is to make sure that the inquirers have considered many perspectives and used both their minds and their hearts in coming to a conscientious choice. Ultimately each of us must take our own responsibility and experience the outcomes of our actions. In a world of cause and effect, there is no need for contrived retribution.

Some of us believe that cause and effect, which we call karma, can play itself out over many lifetimes. Others understand reincarnation as a metaphor for all the cycles and changes within this life, each felt as a little death or a small rebirth. We are also taught the principle of "threefold return"—that whatever we do, good or bad, will come back to us threefold. Some of us take this quantity literally; others understand this as a metaphor pointing to the reality that whatever goes around comes around amplified, and in utterly unpredictable ways. These differences of detail aside, Wiccans understand that we ourselves will reap the rewards, and bear the consequences, of both our actions and our omissions.

The Rede is basic, a common starting point. First, do no harm. Second, tolerate no restrictions unless the behavior they seek to proscribe is demonstrably harmful. Third, when you see harm done, take what action you can to protect and heal while respecting the free will of those you would aid. These good rules offer us maximal freedom and full responsibility, but little guidance for personal growth and development.

And here is where polytheism gets really interesting. Each of us is a unique individual with a special set of potentials to develop, gifts from the God/dess for us to bring to the community and the world. We also go through some very different developmental phases during our lives.

So we typically work with one, or a very few, God/desses at a time, those whose energies, stories, and symbols seem related to the current stretch of our growth path. We seek Their guidance through ritual invocation and apply it in our daily lives. So one would expect to see very different types of behavior from priestesses of Athena, Aphrodite, or Hestia. This might very well extend to symbolic trivia, like our choices in clothing or food, as reinforcers for the particular changes we are trying to make in ourselves. None of these is seen as holier or more ethical than the other, simply different. Through all our stages and phases, we live by the Rede.

Our code is clearly not the same as some others, but we have a code. Live in accord with your own core values. Be careful about what energies you call into your life. Take heed of the voices on the wind. An it harm none, do what you will!

COMMUNITY

"Community" means the whole web of human relationships, large and small, intimate and extended, formal and informal, all the ways in which we connect with people of like mind and common interest. Here we are specifically discussing religious community, the human context for each person's spiritual growth.

Let's start by clearing up one common misconception. In the first place, contrary to popular belief, male Witches exist. Mother Earth surely has sons as well as daughters. Male Witches are often extraordinary men, strong and confident enough to give up long-accustomed gender privilege. There is no gender-specific word for our men; we are all called Witches.

There is a debate about whether Wicca is a religion in its own right, one of the growing family of Neopagan religions, or whether Neo-

paganism is our religion and Wicca is one of several dedicated religious orders within that larger whole. I tend to the latter view. In my
experience, when we say that every Witch is a priest or priestess, we
are not alluding to a Protestant-style "priesthood of all believers" but
to a more intense level of dedication and commitment. For most of us,
this is a major part of our lives, a source of inspiration and an outlet for
creative self-expression. We conduct the rites, and we also engage in
religious scholarship, arts, and counseling. We are among those who
are actively making the Pagan renascence happen.

Most of us, most of the time, work in covens. A coven is a small, intimate Wiccan group that works intensely together over a long period
of time. Traditionally covens have no more than thirteen members.
Covens may be all female, all male, or mixed. Some have leaders, an
individual or a couple; others are nonhierarchical collectives. All of
them are intimate support groups in which people learn, work, worship, and grow together. They are comparable to Christian base communities and Jewish *chavurot*.

Probably the majority of North American covens are bootstrap operations. A group of friends becomes interested in the Old Ways of
Nature. They begin to research and study and pool their knowledge.
Eventually this knowledge flows into the creation of rituals that work
for the members. The process of study and experimentation becomes
self-reinforcing, and the members eventually reach the point where
they feel comfortable calling themselves priests and priestesses. That's
all it takes.

Other covens—my own happily included—grow out of traditions
and lineages. The term "tradition" means to us much the same thing
as "denomination" means to a Protestant: a subdivision of our faith, a
group with its own theological interpretation or ritual style. "Lineage"
refers to the direct historical relationship between covens. Sometimes
an experienced member of a coven wants to try some innovations.
Sometimes covens just get too large for comfort. When either (or,

more often, both) of these things happens, a "daughter coven" forms. We call this process "hiving off."

Traditions and lineages serve as support systems for some covens. In addition, Wiccans have developed several other community-wide systems of support.

There are literally hundreds of small, amateur magazines, where information, recipes, rituals, and poetry can be shared. Many yearly gatherings and festivals, regional and national, give us the opportunity to meet one another, worship together, and share information through formal workshops and informal conversations. And, of course, there are informal networks. In some localities there are even peer support groups for coven leaders.

There are also some institutional supports. Organizations such as Covenant of the Goddess exist to secure us the legal benefits enjoyed by other churches. They also engage in interfaith outreach and public education, hoping to dispel the old images and help our neighbors understand us better.

On the other hand, solitary Witches exist. Most of us work in covens, to be sure, but some find occasional solitary phases to be important to their growth, and still others feel called to be lifelong solitaries. Wicca is a faith that offers many choices and honors many paths.

What we don't have, and don't want, is a unitary, pyramidal structure that centralizes authority and distances people from the sacred. What we don't have, and don't want, is a religious bureaucracy that would divert our financial and human resources toward its own self-perpetuation. What we don't have, and most certainly don't want, is anyone daring to try to intervene or mediate between us and our Gods.

I'M A PRIESTESS, deeply involved in this emerging religion, and so I wonder: Why, after nearly two millennia of brutal suppression, are the

Old Gods and the Old Ways now coming so rapidly and so exuberantly back to life? Why now? Why us? What can we contribute that the others still lack?

These are just my personal speculations: There is conversation going on in our culture among religions, with everyone else listening in. This ongoing religious conversation gives society an important part of its guidance and values. All the well-known religions have a place at the table, and some of the newer ones are gradually beginning to gain places as well.

Some of the voices at the table argue for repressive and retrogressive actions. A few even call for the establishment of a theocracy in our land. Others, like the much-mourned Martin Luther King, sound a more gracious note. But the conversation is still incomplete. Perhaps there are many voices, many views still left out. The omission that appalls and terrifies me is this: Who at this table speaks for Mother Earth?

Religion connects our everyday behavior with the sacred in many different ways. Since at least the time of the great biblical prophets, one way has been to offer correction, to "speak truth to power." So through centuries of history, religion has been the cry of the oppressed, the soul of a soulless situation, the heart of a heartless world. That has not changed, nor should it. What has changed is the terrifying scope of the present crisis.

Modern industrial society, having lost its heart and soul, now turns to devour its own body. Blind, psychotic greed, directed against the Earth Herself, throws Her into a life-threatening crisis. She needs Her guardians, advocates, companions, and healers. She needs us right now. She calls us to Her. As all our lives depend on Hers, so this need must be met. We must learn what we forgot: to see Her once again as a sacred living thing. We must share this knowledge with others, not to change the way anyone worships, but to change the way we all live. As Charlie Murphy puts it in his song "The Burning Times":

Now the Earth is a Witch, and the greedy burn Her
   stripping Her down with mining and poisoning Her skies.
But to us the Earth is a healer, our teacher, our Mother,
   the weaver of the web of life that keeps us all alive.
She gives us the vision to see through the chaos.
She gives us the courage. It is our will to survive.

ESOTERIC
BROTHERHOODS

12

THE HIDDEN SAGES AND
THE KNIGHTS TEMPLAR

Has the unseen guidance of secret orders been a force

for human progress? This millenia-spanning

mythic overview argues that it has.

Robert Richardson

To students of history, religion, or the occult, a pattern of individual names and esoteric movements appears on the canvas
of time like a sudden flash of light, then just as quickly vanishes. A group of disparate people—sometimes famous, sometimes obscure, sometimes solitary, sometimes united, but always engaged in
some amorphous activity—spontaneously surfaces. Just as suddenly
their traces evaporate, their true purpose and the scope of their actions
never comprehended. Understanding their reality seems to be beyond
our grasp. Further study may grudgingly yield information—but it is
inconclusive, incomplete, perplexing. Their nature and purpose seems
to forever remain a mystery. The search for a solution only leads to
speculations, not genuine answers.

For us to intellectually apprehend how and why esoteric groups
work and influence the world requires a different type of thinking, a

thought process that sees these organizations and their activities as an ebb and flow of an ideal. Most of us have approached the inquiry into the nature of how esoteric groups actually work and influence history by studying the limited and grossly distorted documentation available about them, like an investment analyst abstractly examining from afar the sterile financial structure of a multinational corporation. But for us to understand the nature of historical esoteric groups, we should first attempt to find their underlying purposes. If we approach their study through that avenue, we may be able to understand why and how they work to achieve their purposes.

All of the positive esoterically tinged movements that have influenced history share one common characteristic. They seek to positively impact and alter, in a transformational way, the entire structure and direction of society. Their impetus is to interject into day-to-day living a transcendent awareness and communion with the spiritual element of life, to give a spiritual orientation and focus to the material activities of day-to-day living—to, in effect, spiritualize the material. The reason for this direction is to correctly align man with the necessary spiritual path to fulfill his spiritual destiny. Their motives are highly altruistic, despite the wildly imaginative suspicions and innuendoes of many writers and even some church leaders. The methods employed by many powerful Western spiritual movements are always entirely in keeping with these goals.

The best known of these movements have manifested at key transitional points in Western history. The Rosicrucian movement on continental Europe. The less obvious but equally influential Hermetic academies in Renaissance Italy and England. The Cathars in southern France. The Essenes at the dawn of the Christian era. And the best known, and by far the most misunderstood, of these groups, the Order of the Poor Knights of Christ and the Temple of Solomon—the Knights Templar. Each of these groups formed, existed, and survived a certain duration to accomplish a particular mission, then vanished.

Through their actions, each of them positively influenced society as we know it today.

Historians and spiritual writers have expended a great deal of ink unsuccessfully trying to explain what these groups were about and what they believed. Each of these groups encountered considerable opposition and conflict and, seemingly, was superseded by rival groups. History is invariably altered by the victors to suit their goals and needs. Most of the existing works about esoteric groups have been based on deliberately distorted records left by the supposed victors. For example, as has been very aptly stated, attempting to draw an accurate picture of the activities of the Knights Templar by studying the records of the Inquisition is like trying to get an accurate picture of the activities of the wartime French resistance solely by studying the records of the Gestapo.[1]

However, one unaltered stream runs through each of these groups. It is their operational procedure. Each group has several common yet contradictory characteristics. Their organizational structure is both hierarchical and independent. It is at once interdependent and self-sustaining. In other words, it is a cell-like structure, organized around a belief system, designed to be able to function without need for a central governing body, yet still maintaining dutiful fealty and responsibility to the doctrine that the overall body represents. To cite one case, most people, ignorant of the actual working nature of the Essenes, assume that the Qumram monastery was the only Essene entity. In fact, many Essenes lived in the day-to-day society. The Qumram community was a centralized training base. Essene headquarters were on Mount Carmel. The Essenes, like the Cathars, the Templars, and the Hermetic academies, could function independently if cut off from their supposed core. The Rosicrucian groups are the best recognized model of this structure. This system later became the basis for intelligence organizations and underground resistance movements. They were consciously organized like the esoteric societies, designed to continue functioning without support or contact from the main body, yet incapable of revealing the heart or details of the structure of the entire organism if penetrated or compromised by opposing forces.

Similarly, each of the esoteric groups has other definite organizational characteristics: some sort of unified command-and-reporting structure that always appears vague and mysterious to outsiders. A highly disciplined internal training system. A firm code of conduct. An adherence to a canon of basic beliefs not fully comprehended by outsiders. The unwavering concept of individual personal responsibility and personal accountability. And the invariable but gracefully unstated implication of leadership by example.

These traits do not define a belief system per se, but something far more important and exceptionally relevant to our society today. They define a principle-centered existence that is applied in day-to-day affairs. They define very clearly a specific way of living one's life. This way of life is lived in accordance with the knowledge and principles that have been carefully and selectively handed down orally through generations of initiates, and have as their basis the essential principles of the universe and the knowledge of the origin and purpose of man. This orally transmitted information is referred to as "The Tradition," and sometimes, when collected in a preserved body of wisdom, "The Temple."

Before examining more closely how this system has impacted us, it will benefit us to review the Western model for the public visibility of this system. The model was long established in the West. It entered into a decline. Its adherents transferred the model to other bases, perpetrated it, and preserved it for transmission into the future. The model was the Egyptian Temple system.

All of Egyptian society was organized along an esoteric and an exoteric basis. The exoteric structure centered around the pharaonic system of government, with which academic students of this civilization have occupied themselves in an effort to comprehend why this society lasted so long and so successfully. Their studies have not seen much successful fruit, because they have failed to comprehend that it was the esoteric structure that sustained the entire basis of the Egyptian dynasties and the surrounding society for so many centuries.[2]

This esoteric structure has had little effective study in academic circles, like most of man's genuine history. It was organized around the Temple system. The Temple system was based on the gradual instruction of an increasingly elite group. This study took many decades. It involved intensive personal discipline. It began with a period of self-purification. It entailed physical, mental, and spiritual training. It worked on all aspects of the being.

The successful candidate was gradually culled away from his peers. The less capable aspirants were weeded out. The more fortunate were advanced progressively and carefully through the system over many years. They studied the physical and spiritual aspects of man, his origin, purpose, and relationship with the Divine, becoming true physicians who could heal not just the physical being. Through increasingly progressive steps, they ultimately advanced to a series of tests. Some of these tests proved fatal to the aspirant. One objective of the training was an induced out-of-body experience in the Great Pyramid. To return the aspirant to this plane required the efforts of a high priest with twelve disciples. The priests were not always able to return the aspirant, and the death of the aspirant was not uncommon. When the aspirant did return to this plane, he consciously saw the world differently, as one who has been reborn with new knowledge and a new perspective. This is the origin of the phrase now so popular with fundamentalist Christians, "born again." In the end, a handful of carefully trained and highly developed individuals were advanced into an elite priesthood that, through its adherence to spiritual principles, maintained a balance that facilitated the functioning of Egyptian society. Their point of view had by now changed. They no longer worked on spiritual progress for their own sake, but for the benefit of the upward evolution of mankind. And from their inner core, they were dispatched to different corners of the known world to indirectly help the lesser developed advance themselves, thereby assisting in the progress of humanity.

The Temple replicated the structure and spiritual principles of the universe. The outer society replicated the Temple and its spiritual principles, but in a form not articulated to the common people, who were not sufficiently developed to consciously understand, honor, and fulfill its reality. Instead, by replicating the principles in society, the average person was able to live in rhythm with the principles and to become positively influenced by them, growing through this process without making the total dedication and sacrifice required of the elite core group.

The Egyptian pharaonic concept represents the embodiment in the person of pharaoh of the highest principles and aspirations of the society. The pharaoh was the outward representative of the Temple principles and of the life of the entire society. He was supposed to live life in the material world in compliance with the inner laws of which the populace remained only vaguely conversant. The pharaoh was supported and aided in this role by the inner and most highly developed elite of the Temple priesthood. His dictums were executed by a separate administrative arm.

It is difficult if not impossible for any group, no matter how dedicated, to indefinitely sustain itself in accordance with spiritual principles. Such organizations have a period of life in which they create an expression suited to the times, accomplish the mission, and disappear, to be succeeded in another time and place by a successor organization suited to the expression of its times. During the existence of any group, as individuals successively replace each other from generation to generation, changes occur. Some are more able than others, some less able than those who precede or follow them. Human frailty sets in. Slight changes in even a highly disciplined Temple system can have vast implications over time. Alterations in the focus and dedication of those holding the pharaonic throne could divert the course of events. Embodying the weather vane of a society or group is neither easy nor sustainable. Gradually, systems and principles can deteriorate.

But over that same time period, the seeds of the future can also be planted. Non-Egyptians were allowed to enter the Temple system. Some advanced through the full training. Some returned back to their own countries. This is the origin of the system called the Mysteries, which arose in the Mediterranean pre-Christian era as Egyptian culture declined. The Mysteries appeared in a different form but followed the same lines as the Temple system. It was the same message, simply put into a different bottle, a bottle styled for the people of Greece and the Mediterranean world. Similarly, the Egyptian Temple system is undeniably the training ground for the great Pythagoras and the system of knowledge that he spread through ancient Greece and southern Europe.

The teachings of Pythagoras appeared differently as well. Styled in a more modern form, they followed the same line as the Temple, but less rigid. Still, they entailed an academy: a gradual system in which the candidate advanced degree by degree toward a higher level of mental and spiritual development—and an outward aspect as well, a concern with the nature and direction of humanity, just as in the Temple system. Metaphorically, the superiority of the system of knowledge that he represented is expressed by the parable of his dying of starvation on the steps of the Temples of the Muses.

While the Temple system was being disseminated to the north and east of Egypt by Pythagoras, another Temple-trained initiate followed a similar path of preserving the initiatic knowledge. His name is known to history as Moses. He aligned with an obscure people and reconstituted their societal structure and belief system around the Temple principles. By restructuring an entire ethnic people, he ensured that aspects of the Temple system would be preserved by this insular group for generations, until its next reconstitution was necessary in a form applicable to the requirements of that time.

Moses reconstituted the Temple system among the Jewish people in a manner styled after the Egyptian model. A specific caste of priests was physically organized around a Temple. The entire twelve-tribe system—itself a mystical anagram—focused on the Temple, and the life of the nation centered on it, on their faith, and on a specific identity as a people set apart, unique in God's eyes, and held together under a pharaoh-like king. Even the mystical Tree of Life of the Kabbalah directly corresponds to the Egyptian Neters. The focus on their religion as the core of their existence gave the Jewish people their unique identity and enabled them to survive the cultural annihilation experienced by others. But it did not give rise to the powerful spiritual current Moses had hoped for. This vacuum gave rise to the mission of the Essenes.

The Essenes, like the Templars, are a widely misunderstood spiritual group. Subdivided into different groups and having members active both in their monastic training ground at Qumram and throughout the Jewish community in day-to-day living, from their headquarters at Mount Carmel they were directed toward one specific goal—the preparation of an entity sufficiently advanced to bear the higher consciousness that would incarnate in the man known as Jesus. This particular mission extended far beyond the concept of the messiah, which may be loosely defined as the priest-king. In the concept of the messiah is the return of the pharaoh, the embodiment of the spiritual governing principle in the day-to-day affairs of the state, but in the Essene case it involves a particularly advanced consciousness carrying an impulse to revive the spiritual facets of mankind. The pharaonic ideal also appeared throughout Europe, degenerating over time into the present concept of royalty. Interestingly, all prophetic Jewish literature, except one book, foretells and focuses on the coming of a messiah.

For the Essenes, the mission was consuming. In an occult sense, the entire organization focused on the incarnation of a spiritual being who would alter humanity through the implantation of a spiritual impulse. The documents of their training base at Qumram denote the discipline that was expected to be extended in daily life. There is little in the aspects of daily training in these documents that is not in other spiritual schools. Their nature has assumed a special character, given that those men and women in the modern world who are primarily responsible for studying these documents do not understand the rudiments of the way in which individuals are trained to live in society and reflect spiritual values, nor can they apprehend a methodology so broad that it intends through deliberately indirect actions the reformation of the entire society.

The name Essene has many interpretations. One of the most interesting is "trowel," the tool with which a mason works with stone and mortar to create a building. The Essenes were masons, building the house of God in themselves. By doing this, they were working to help advance mankind. Ultimately, the mission of creating the vessels adequate to sustain the spiritual capacity necessary for the reformation of society was successful. The Essenes, their mission completed, disappeared from history, most traces of their existence obliterated by the different Jewish sects that opposed them.

The start of the Christian era marked a singular turning point. Prior to this time, many conflicting religious expressions of the same ideals existed side by side. The Greek Mysteries are allegorical representations of the Egyptian system. The rise of various cults such as Sol Invictus, Mithras, and the Roman system of gods are all representations of the same group of principles. This mass confusion was consolidated in the early years of the Christian era as the Roman church proclaimed itself supreme and systematically absorbed or annihilated its opposition, driving these movements into extinction. But by these

actions, the Church created a widespread common vocabulary and belief structure.

During this time, Pythagorean thought assumed an academic and
philosophical character and resurfaced later in Neoplatonic ideals.
Plato's ideals, often seen as observations derived from Athenian society
or a philosophical treatise, are really esoteric principles expressed as
the restoration of a balanced and spiritual order. As opposed to blind
obedience, man functions in an intellectual manner driven by principles. But the outcome is still the same dream the sages have held for
centuries.

The manifestation of the esoteric movements took a different form
in the south of France in the eleventh century with the group called
the Cathars. Before reviewing the Cathars, it is important to hold
everything preceding them in perspective to understand the change in
direction that begins its implementation with the Cathars and the
Templars. In Egypt, a highly structured elite imposed a regimented
society based on spiritual principles on a less enlightened humanity
to evolve their awareness. In Israel, an elite group worked to effect a
top-down solution to promulgating spiritual principles, but without
rigidly structuring society. In the Pythagorean and Platonic systems, a
small group worked for the good of humanity, but without rigidly
structuring society, and emphasizing the value of individual intellectual reasoning capacity. Each of these directions represented gradual
steps toward the realization of the development of human potential
and individual freedom. Centuries later, humanity would realize the
benefits from the seeds planted by these groups.

The appearance of the Cathar movement is viewed by historians as
the rise of a new religion that jousted with Christianity for supremacy
and, like so many groups that have struggled with the Roman church,
lost. The Cathars are primarily known to us by relatively recent works
that interpret their story in light of our limited knowledge of their activities. The Cathars are usually traced back to the Bogomils and other

groups. The Cathars are, in fact, only the same principles, appearing again in the guise of the message of the times. The Cathar priesthood, the Parfaits, were noted for their unimpeachable conduct, purity, and dedication. They contrasted so sharply with the corrupt Roman church that people flocked to them, especially in the south of France. However, it is by their conduct that we must see what they really are. They seek by conduct to show men how to change their daily lives. They do not proselytize. They do not impair individual freedom. In fact, by standing in contradistinction to the prevailing power of the predominate secular authority of the time that imposed its will from top down, the Roman church, the Cathar parfaits encouraged among the common people the freedom of individual choice. It is expressed by principles lived in action by an elite priestly core that maintains focused spiritual values.

What survives of the Cathars today is distorted by people who think the incomplete remnants of the misunderstood Cathar belief system is the key. The key was their code of conduct. That is what attracted followers, that is what made believers, that is what they promulgated. Persecuted for forty years in the very first crusade, hunted down, killed, and driven underground, they were succeeded by three distinct movements, the Troubadours, the trade guilds, and the orders of knighthood, particularly the Knights Templar.

The Troubadours were a means through which the sages deliberately intended to imbue man with an orientation toward putting spiritual principles in action. Traveling minstrels, harmless singers of songs, tellers of poetry, the Troubadours offered no overt threat to the established power structure. They moved through all levels of society, from royal courts to common taverns. Through their actions and their travels the Troubadours began the seeds of the first popular literature, of the beginning of a common popular consciousness. They were the first to move ideals on a widespread basis into the popular imagination. Through them, the legends of the Grail and high spiritual ideals

lived in action came into popular consciousness. They became the vehicle for inspiring the popular imagination.

The trade guilds held a simple task. They inspired a code of conduct in daily living for the common people. A harmonious order was
established. That order was constituted around discipline and respect
within the guild for members and for their work. Work itself became
a noble ethic to be valued. And because of the protection of the Knights
Templar, the guilds were spared from oppression by the nobility.
Under the unseen guidance of the secret orders, the road up from slavery and serfdom had begun for the common people.

Before turning to an overview of the Templars it is significant to
note how key turning points have occurred in the transmission of the
esoteric spiritual message. It was first transmitted to an elite in societies. The populace was given a highly simplified version. After the
consolidation of much of the West by Rome, it was transmitted
through role models. After the suppression of the Cathars, it was
spread through the means of ordinary society, not just to sustain an
elite, but in disguise, through and to every man. It reached into their
lives in songs, it touched their imaginations with inspiring stories, and
became principles in the lives of working men and the foundation of
the guilds. And all these principles were based on one unifying ideal—
the impulsion of proper spiritual principles and their use in focusing
day-to-day living to uplift the consciousness of man so that he could
evolve and fulfill his purpose and destiny.

The Knights Templar remain today the single greatest force for
turning the spiritual mind of the West. Many prominent occultists
have contended over the years that the beginning of the decline of the
West and of its spiritual dark age—the age of Kali Yuga—started
with the suppression of the Templars. Today it is fashionable for writers and historians working from records left by the Inquisition to
charitably agree with the Inquisition that the Templars had become

corrupt, that they had fallen from principles, and to tacitly agree with some of the charges against them. These conclusions are the reiteration of falsehoods promulgated by the only keeper of information in its time, the Roman church, to cover up its own actions against the Templars, actions motivated by the Church's and French leaders' greed for the Templars' wealth.

To review how the Templars worked in the world is not possible within the confines of this space. But a summary of a handful of their accomplishments clearly reveals its purposes and the workings of a genuine esoteric organization. Like the Essenes and every other genuine group, a core inner order actually provided the Templars with their spiritual impetus and direction. But by bridging all worlds of their time—spiritual and material, nobility and common man, religious and military, commerce and contemplation, Christian, Jewish, and Islamic—the Templars moved the entire course of history. These activities marked another turning point in history. While their inner order worked esoterically on spiritual self-development, everything they did was an action in the world of its time directed at impacting the day-to-day lives of people in a positive and transformative way. Their goal and mission was the transformation of all of society, and nothing less. But their method was to work through the key aspects influencing the society of their time in order to inject spiritual principles in daily life and plant the seeds for future change.

The best description written of the activities of the Templars remains as follows.

> The mission of the Knights Templar was two-fold. Firstly, to inject a certain spiritual idealism into the world of their time through a number of concrete actions. Secondly, to insure the continuity of the Spiritual Tradition of the Temple by seeking out the sacred esoteric heritage of mankind wherever it was to be found, to reunite it, and to present to a certain spiritual elite a

synthesis of the Tradition adapted to the Western mentality of the Middle Ages.[3]

The Templars' mode of action was uniquely suited to their times. It moved at one and the same time on multiple levels because it was practical, pragmatic, and designed to create immediate effects. But it also created an atmosphere that carefully sowed the seeds for long-term future changes on material and spiritual levels. In this regard a few concrete actions of the Templars are particularly worth noting.

The Templars sponsored the building of churches, chapels, and great cathedrals across Europe. Templar churches embodied in them certain esoteric geometric and mathematical principles that create a transformative effect on worshippers. The effect subliminally led more people to experience the value of the spiritual on their everyday lives. At the same time, cathedral building had a positive economic impact on the overpopulated and impoverished European society. Churches and cathedrals dedicated to the Templar patron, the Virgin, promoted the feminine principle of spirituality, and, again subliminally, raised the oppressed status of women in society by providing a female role model for veneration.

The Templars created a new class in society. They raised up the common man by protecting the working masons and sponsoring the first genuine, independent movement of the trade guilds, the Compagnons de Saint Devoir (the Companions of the Rule of Holy Duty), who built the Templar-sponsored churches and cathedrals. These trade groups, formally placed under Templar protection some time around 1145, created an internal hierarchy, taught codes of personal conduct and ethical values to the illiterate craftsmen, provided sources of income, protected widows and orphans of members, and created through the graded craftsman system a hierarchy similar to the discipline in an esoteric order. In a network of houses in various parts of every country through which apprentices traveled and worked, common manners and fair play were instilled, and a sense of common, shared interests was developed. From their contacts with the Eastern initiates and esoteric schools of the Middle East, the Templars imparted to the master tradesmen certain secrets of geometry and mathematics for incorporation into the cathedrals, thereby raising the consciousness of the trade class.

The guild houses eventually evolved into the Masonic lodge systems, and the shared sense of values created the concept of a unified society of the working man. In addition to creating a sense of self-worth among the individual members, this system was the beginning of the first principles of equal rights for all. After the suppression of the Templars, the Compagnons were persecuted for many centuries. But when the plague swept through Europe and decimated the population, the longer-term impact was the elimination of European overpopulation that had created a surplus of labor and resultant poverty. By protecting the guilds from oppression by the nobility and the Church, the Templars left in place a mechanism that ensured both a cohesive structure within the plague-decimated common society and a body that spoke on behalf of the common people. It allowed the standard of living to rise and the basis for a new way of life to begin. The feudal system waned, replaced by new centers of power. And, indirectly, the course of society and the evolution of consciousness expanded. Principled but indirect stimuli often have far-reaching results. As the modern writer and statesman Vaclav Havel noted during his own seemingly impossible struggle against Communist authoritarianism, "even a purely moral act that has no hope of any immediate and visible political effect can gradually and indirectly, over time, gain in political influence."[4]

The umbrella of Templar action extended beyond the working tradesmen. The Templars were originally said to be founded to protect travelers on their way to Jerusalem. The protection of travelers to the holy place was a metaphor for providing the spiritual means to higher knowledge. But one reason the Templars became widely venerated by the common people was because their network of European commandaries actually did make travel on the roads safer for the peasants. Heretofore, the common people enjoyed no protection from ubiquitous road bandits or pillaging nobility. The protection of the European roadways not only facilitated the safe movement of commerce. It was the first truly widespread societal benefit enjoyed by all classes of society. For the first time, a commoner enjoyed the same protection as nobility. Once a seed of equality is planted and assumed as a given by any society as a whole, the process of eventual transformation is assured. By becoming an independent force on which every part of society could depend, the Templars sowed the seeds for the concept of common standards for all in society and governance.

Much has been made of the fact that the Templars virtually invented international banking when they became a repository of royal treasuries, the executors of wills, and the financiers of kingdoms, and became fabulously wealthy as a result. Seen in a different light, it has never been noted that for the first time there existed through the Templars a common source of trust and justice. Royalty could be assured their treasuries would not be pillaged. They could travel safely from location to location without fear of robbery and knew that they could secure funds at any Templar preceptory along the way. They could be assured that heirs would not deprive each other of their inheritance, because the Templars would enforce will provisions fairly. And commoners with possessions could be assured that Templars would execute their wills justly, prevent their possessions from being usurped by the nobles, or even care for their children in the event of their deaths. Again, this was the first widespread standard of unimpeachable fairness available to all levels of society, a singular force on which people from all walks of life could depend. From these actions eventually grew the ideal that justice could be fair and serve all.

The Templars also impacted the concept of government. They

were both advisors to kings and adversaries of the tyrannical use of royal power. One of the most famous encounters between royalty and the Templars occurred when English king Henry III attempted to upbraid the Master of the Temple in England and was instead bluntly countered, in modern terms: "Be careful what you say, King. For if you cease to rule with justice, you will cease to be King." What royalty and the Church, and later historians, would decry in this exchange as Templar arrogance was in fact an assertion of the rights of society against the abusive power of royalty. The Master of the Temple in England would later be witness to the signing of the Magna Carta and a behind-the-scenes force in its creation and execution. Similarly, by fighting for the freedom of the small border kingdoms of Aragon, Navarre, and Mallorca from Muslim forces and aligning with those kingdoms, the Templars ensured the existence of smaller independent and more liberal states.

Lastly, the Templars provided a covert bridge that had not previously existed to other faiths. Generations of historians have failed to comprehend that the accusations of Templar familiarity with Islamic and Jewish sects represented not the religious "corruption and betrayal" of which their enemies accused them, but rather the specific mission of attempting to regenerate a commonality of knowledge and respect of beliefs—which happens to be characteristic of modern religious tolerance. By their very existence, the orders of chivalry, and specifically the Templars, paved the way for the Renaissance—thus the ideals stirred by the Troubadours became physically embodied by the orders of knighthood. Through the orders of chivalry, the idealized Troubadour poetry became a manifest reality. It demonstrated that the highest ideals that inspired men could in fact become a living reality, that the concept of the Grail quest could become a genuine, worldly search for the spiritual and a way of life.

By the start of the fourteenth century the secret orders had moved from working with a small spiritual elite to a hidden vanguard that worked quietly in society. The emphasis each esoteric group made in their life-cycles of approximately two hundred years foreshadowed the next major step in human progress and evolution. The ideals and energy put into motion by the orders of knighthood soon came to flower in the Renaissance.

In Italy the influence of the esoteric on many of the leading noble families became a primary motivation for the explosion of learning and culture that became known as the Renaissance. Through the sponsorship of families like the Medicis, learning—new modes of thought and the rediscovery of ancient wisdom—returned to become a valued world distinctly apart from the province of the Church, as in ancient Greece.

In the Renaissance, the ideal of the Platonic reformation of society took root. Through the wealth of key Renaissance families, art was sponsored, books rediscovered, and esoteric principles applied in the cultural aspects of life, from creating a rich fabric of meaning in a garden to promoting the translation of the *Corpus Hermeticum*. For the first time, the implementation of esoteric ideals was openly carried out through the medium of families who remained fully engaged in everyday life. They sponsored activities influencing mundane existence. They injected the concept of beauty and harmony into their residences and surroundings. Architecture and music again became important and vital. Even gardens (e.g. the Boboli Gardens) became expressions of the esoteric ideals of beauty, harmony, and balance, inspiring the Renaissance and infusing society. The esoteric mission of the Templars to bring a moribund society back to life with new ideas and spiritual principles finally flourished, 180 years after their demise.

Cultural figures took the lead in this revival. Marsilio Ficino strongly influenced the rebirth of Platonic and esoteric ideals and teachings. At Villa Carreggi, outside Florence, Ficino actually started a Platonic academy under the sponsorship of Cosimo de Medici. However, it was Giorgio Gemistos, long forgotten to history, who was the hidden hand moving the Renaissance to fruition by providing the inspiration for Cosimo's actions. An occultist and sage council, Gemistos met de Medici in 1437 when Gemistos attended the ecumenical council of Florence/Ferrara as the unofficial advisor to the Greek delegation. During this council he spent time with de Medici. His inspired vision of transforming religion and culture through a spiritual revival led de Medici to redirect his own life. He began a fervent pursuit of the translation and introduction of classical texts and metaphysical ideas to vivify every aspect of life. The objective of this work was nothing less than the transformation of the life of man and its orientation toward a spiritual way of living through inspiring the cultural elements of society. From the Platonic academy and the esoteric lodges of Italy, waves of creativity and new expressions surged across Europe, imbuing all levels of society with new ideas and planting the seeds for future changes.

In England, in the light of the Renaissance and inspired by esoteric orders spanning the English Channel and connecting Britain and the Continent, an academy called "The Temple" arose at Gorhambury, becoming an influence on the future course of the West.[5] Originally under the direction of Sir Nicholas Bacon, along with another esoteric academy founded at Mortlake by John Dee, it became focused around his adopted son, Francis, trained from youth for his work and initiated and trained in an esoteric lodge in France. The full impact of Bacon and the lodge that worked around him has not yet been fully realized.

Together with a group of men representing all key facets of the society of his time, Bacon wrote the plays attributed to Shakespeare and took the interesting multidimensional symbol of Pallas Athena, the spear-shaker, as an image in works published under his own name. The entire structure of the Shakespearean plays are based on principles in esoteric teachings. This is why they have had such an enduring appeal. They were a message styled to the common man. Even the design of the Globe Theatre was an embodiment of the esoteric principles. Bacon and his group sought to reintroduce the proper use of the intellect in reasoning through his essays and attempts to reform institutions, to redirect the ancient dialectic methods to a tool that could be, like the plays, accessed by anyone. Of equal and often overlooked importance, the group introduced the reformation of the English language as a vehicle for the transmission of esoteric and cultural concepts. They firmly planted a series of ideals in English culture that eventually, through England's global colonies, began a far-reaching transformation beyond the confines of Europe.[6]

Attempts during this era to establish a republic such as the Palatinate in Bohemia, and the little-studied activities of John Dee in Bohemia to reform religious activities, did not meet with success. But the ideals widely established through these activities and the concurrent issuance of Rosicrucian pamphlets fired a wide imagination in society and, according to some academic sources, very probably led to the period known as the Enlightenment.[7]

Throughout history, slowly, step by step, the process of transforming humanity has been gradually aided by the activities of positive esoteric societies. The actions of positive groups have resulted in benefits realized sometimes generations later in society. Most interestingly, to the students of these groups and of the ebb and flow of history, they seem to be acting in anticipation of the next advancement necessary in human evolution. For some time now, the activities of these organizations have appeared quiet, depending perhaps on the fruition of past efforts to create a positive movement in humanity or awaiting a new impetus from their own core.

The trend of worldwide culture for the last two hundred years has inexorably been moving toward the enhanced concept of individual freedom. Today, with some exceptions, we live in a world in which individual freedom is often taken for granted. The options of free will and choice by individuals are becoming a driving force. Now, even commerce and technology have joined to accelerate this evolutionary step as free market economies, the Internet, and broadband technologies will soon bring to people across the globe previously undreamed-of options for working, learning, communicating, and participating.

Yet, in this time, the stakes in the essential struggle of the spirit have become higher than ever. The conflict between light and dark is more subtle, the struggle less overt, but the future consequences of our personal actions will be higher than ever because of the variety of choices and the possibility to exercise self-indulgence through the vehicles of technology and commerce without restraint or discernment. The outcome of this struggle, to determine whether or not man will sink into self-indulgent materialism or rise above it to create a truly better world, is far from certain. It no longer depends on others, but on ourselves. We can actively work to become more spiritual, thereby transforming ourselves and the material world and successfully realizing what generations of initiates have dreamed of and worked toward, or we can choose to work to materialize and dull the spiritual aspect of man into haziness until it is ultimately lost. The choice of which future we actively wish to create is now man's individual responsibility, and the result of that choice and of our actions will ultimately be our legacy to future generations.

THE ROSICRUCIAN DREAM

The Rosicrucian vision of a better world suddenly burst upon
seventeenth-century Europe, and its impact is still felt today.

Christopher McIntosh

The word "Rosicrucian" is one that most readers will have
heard many times. Yet if I were to ask for a definition of the
word I would probably be given a wide variety of different
answers. I might be told that it has something to do with esoteric
Christianity, with reincarnation, with alchemy, or with Kabbalah. All
of these things are part of the answer, but not the whole answer. So
what is Rosicrucianism? For the time being let us call it a current of
thought and ideas that has been flowing through history for at least
three and a half centuries and probably quite a bit longer, sometimes
underground, sometimes coming to the surface, but always pushing
human beings toward certain goals. I say that we can trace the current
back three and a half centuries because that was when it first came to
the surface. So let us go back to that moment in history.

The opening scene is Germany at the beginning of the seventeenth century. The Reformation had taken place just over a hundred years earlier. Now part of Germany was Protestant, part was still Catholic. The two sides had not yet reached any proper *modus vivendi,* and the tension between them was soon to erupt into the Thirty Years' War, which was to prove one of the most disastrous wars in European history. So there was an expectation of coming calamity. And there was a feeling that European civilization in general had somehow gone wrong. Now it was at this time that strange things began to happen in a certain part of Germany.

We now focus on the town of Kassel. It was here, in 1614 and 1615, that there appeared two mysterious manifestoes of unknown authorship. The first was in German, but its title was a mixture of German and Latin. It was called *Fama Fraternitatis dess Löblichen Ordens des Rosenkreutzes,* which means: *The Fame (or Proclamation) of the Praiseworthy Order of the Rosy Cross.* The second was called the *Confession Fraternitatis,* the *Confessio of the Fraternity.*

These documents told a curious story. They told of somebody called Christian Rosenkreutz who was born in the year 1378. As a boy of sixteen he traveled to the Middle East and spent some time at Damcar in Arabia, where there evidently existed some kind of utopian community. As the *Confessio* puts it, "those who dwell in the City of Damcar in Arabia . . . have a far different political order from the other Arabians. For there do govern only wise and understanding men, who by the King's permission make particular laws." At Damcar, Rosenkreutz learned Arabic and received scientific and occult teaching and came into contact with a mysterious book, referred to simply as "the Book M," which he translated into Latin.

After three years at Damcar he was directed to go, via Egypt, to Fez in Morocco, which was, and still is, one of the holy cities of Islam and the site of one of the oldest universities in the world. So at the time Rosenkreutz is said to have gone there it would already have been a great center of learning for many centuries. This is how the *Fama* describes his experience at Fez: "At Fez he did get acquaintance with those which are commonly called the Elementary Inhabitants, who revealed to him many of their secrets." (Possibly what is meant by Elementary Inhabitants are the "Elemental Spirits" of magic.)

After two years at Fez he went to Spain hoping to impart his new-found knowledge but met only with hostility and mockery. And this experience was evidently repeated in other countries. So he returned to Germany and eventually gathered about him a small group of men who shared his ideals, and this was the beginning of the Fraternity of the Rosy Cross. The Fraternity had, as its headquarters, a building called the House of the Holy Spirit. The brothers dedicated themselves to studying and spreading the ancient wisdom and also traveled around doing good work such as healing the sick. One of them, it is said, went to England, where he cured the young earl of Norfolk of leprosy. Christian Rosenkreutz himself lived for 106 years, dying in 1484.

After his death the brotherhood was continued by his successors. Then in 1604 the brethren were carrying out some rebuilding in their headquarters when they came across a hidden door on which was written in Latin: "After 120 years I shall open." Behind the door they found a seven-sided vault illuminated by an artificial sun placed in the middle of the ceiling. The floor, walls, and ceiling of the vault were covered in symbolic figures, and there were also chests containing books and ritual objects. In the middle of the vault was an altar, and beneath the altar was a coffin containing the perfectly preserved body of Christian Rosenkreutz.

This description of the vault was to capture many people's imaginations. Two and a half centuries later the English occult society, the Golden Dawn, actually made a vault corresponding to the description in the Fama. One of the key rituals of the order, the Adeptus Minor initiation ritual, was a reenactment of the discovery of Rosenkreutz's body.

The discovery of the vault was taken by the brethren as a sign that the time was ripe for the society to declare its existence publicly and to invite people of learning and goodwill to participate in the society's aims and ideals. What were those aims and ideals? We don't get a very clear idea from the manifestoes, but it appears that the brethren believed in a system of universal knowledge incorporating theology, philosophy, mathematics, astrology, and so on. They were firm believers in Christ and the scriptures. Furthermore, they claimed to have access to an ancient and secret body of wisdom that enabled them to interpret the scriptures correctly. What they appear to be referring to here is Kabbalah, which is, among other things, a means of decoding the Bible. They talk about being able to understand certain characters and letters that form the basis of all creation. Again, this seems to refer to the Kabbalistic notion that the universe is actually made up of the letters of the Hebrew alphabet in different combinations.

Their beliefs can perhaps best be summed up in the word "Gnosticism." By "Gnosticism" I mean the ancient belief that man's spirit is imprisoned in matter by a mischievous creator. Man is, as it were, living underwater, not realizing that up above is light and air and that if only he could swim to the surface he could get back to his true element. In the Gnostic view this predicament is not entirely hopeless because there are some people who possess *Gnosis,* that is, knowledge or wisdom that enables them to swim up and to teach this to others. (This Gnosis, this lifebelt of wisdom, is very often represented by a female figure. The Greeks called her Sophia.) This is the essence of Gnosticism, and this is, I believe, what lies behind Rosicrucianism.

The Rosicrucians also knew about alchemy, in the sense of a dual process, physical and spiritual, in which the spiritual part was the more important. The early Rosicrucians clearly belonged to the Protestant rather than the Catholic camp. (There are some very contemptuous references to the pope in the manifestoes.) But they felt that all of Christendom was in need of a new impulse. They believed that

Europe was on the threshold of a new age in which spiritual, intellectual, and political enlightenment and brotherly love would flourish, and they saw their role as being able to help usher in this new age.

That essentially was the message of the first two manifestoes, but, of course, what is not clear is whether the brotherhood existed at all or whether it was a deliberately created myth.

In 1616 appeared a third Rosicrucian document published at Strasbourg, in German, under the title *Die Chymische Hochzeit Christiani Rosenkreutz* (The Chemical Wedding of Christian Rosenkreutz). The title is slightly misleading because it is not about the wedding of Rosenkreutz himself but purports to be an account by him of his experiences as a guest at the wedding of a king and queen. The wedding takes place in a castle that Rosenkreutz reaches after an arduous journey.

The story is full of occult imagery. For example, on the fifth day of the celebrations, the guests are taken to an island in seven ships flying flags bearing the symbols of the planets. On the island an alchemical operation is conducted in a seven-storied tower, in which two homunculi are created from the bodies of six people who have been killed. In the roof of the tower is a hole through which two souls descend and enter the homunculi. Finally, the company returns to the castle, this time in twelve ships flying flags of the zodiacal signs.

The author of this document was a nineteen-year-old man, Johann Valentin Andreae. Andreae was in fact a very important figure. He was a Protestant pastor and theologian, immensely influential in the German Protestant movement—in fact almost a kind of Luther of his day. And the strange thing about him is that in some of his later writings he referred very contemptuously to the Rosicrucian movement. In his autobiography, for example, he called it a "jest"—and this had led some people to say that the *Chemical Wedding* was in fact an attempt to debunk Rosicrucianism. I don't believe this myself. I believe Andreae was—at least when he wrote the *Chemical Wedding*—very deeply involved with the whole Rosicrucian movement. So these three manifestoes are the basis of the Rosicrucian movement as we know it.

The effect of the three manifestoes was astonishing. They stirred up a tremendous controversy in Europe. Many people wrote to the brotherhood hoping to be admitted. If any received replies they remain unrecorded. Other people attacked the brotherhood. Others claimed to be members of it. And in due course many societies were set up imitating the one that is described in the original manifestoes—which, as I say, may or may not have existed. So what you ended up with was a core of mystery, with huge ramifications, emanating out from these publications.

Part of the appeal of the Rosicrucian movement lies in the richness of the Rose Cross symbol. It is possible to interpret this in all sorts of different ways. Both the cross and the rose are very ancient motifs. The cross appears in many religions and mythologies and seems to indicate a universal tendency for man's inner consciousness to seek four-fold patterns: you have four points of the compass, four seasons, four elements, four worlds in the Kabbalah, and so on. The cross also suggests masculinity, and—in the Christian tradition—suffering, sacrifice, and death.

As for the rose, this can also be seen in many different ways. One of the things that the rose stands for is secrecy. The sign over Roman taverns signified that anything said in drunkenness would not be repeated—hence the expression *sub rosa,* meaning confidential. On another level the rose can be seen as the Western form of the lotus. Now the lotus, in Hindu mythology, represents the female life principle and is the symbol of the *yoni* or female sexual organs. So we have lotus/rose as female, cross as male.

And if we look at ancient Egyptian mythology we find that Osiris, the god of the underworld who died and came to life again, is often shown wearing a crown of lotus flowers. So here we have another possible interpretation: lotus/rose is resurrection, cross is death. In other

words, the Rose Cross represents the balance between a series of polarities: death and resurrection, male and female, sacrifice and the reward of sacrifice.

It is an elusive symbol, but a very suggestive and powerful one. And
it is typical of the great inner wisdom tradition of which Rosicrucianism is part to use these shorthand emblems that carry deep layers of
meaning. Many examples can be found in the emblem books of the
sixteenth, seventeenth, and eighteenth centuries—for example, the famous image of the dolphin curled around an anchor, with the motto
Festina lente ("Hasten slowly"). These emblems serve as a secret code
through which those in touch with the inner traditions can communicate their ideas, but they also work at a deeper level than a message
that is framed in straightforward words.

So did the Rosicrucian plan misfire? I think not, because this is an
interesting example of what happens when you plant a mystery in the
collective mind of society. It's like dropping a stone into a pond: the
ripples go on and on. And, in this case, the initial impact was so strong
that the ripples are still going today.

And this, I believe, is exactly what the authors of the manifestoes intended. They took the view that if you wanted to bring about a new
age, the way to do it was to frame your ideals in the form of a legend,
to cloak the legend in mystery, and then to launch it in such a way that
it was bound to create endless debate and controversy.

Well, how successful was this ploy? Did those men who launched
the manifestoes succeed in bringing about any of the reforms that they
desired? You may well say—looking at the state of Western civilization—that they failed. But before we judge, let's look a bit more closely
at some of the repercussions of the manifestoes.

Now, although the Rosicrucian philosophy was presented as a
total package of religion, science, and so on, it tended to divide into
three different streams: first, there was the scientific, philosophical

stream; second, the social and political stream; third, the Hermetic-Kabbalistic-alchemical stream.

Now there is evidence that the first of these two streams gave rise to a number of learned institutions in various parts of Europe, including the Royal Society in England, which of course was, and still is, one of the most important scientific bodies in the world. Many of the inventions and discoveries that have shaped our environment have come out of the Royal Society. I shall not go in detail into the connection between the Rosicrucian movement and the Royal Society, but one link, for example, is through an interesting man called Comenius: a Bohemian refugee, a member of the Andreae circle, interested in Utopian ideas, who envisaged an ideal state in which science and religion would flourish side by side and in which men of all creeds and races would be respected. Comenius came to England in about the 1640s, and he knew the leading scientists of the time. And furthermore, it is clear that scientists such as Robert Boyle and John Wilkins knew all about the Rosicrucian movement. When the Royal Society was founded in 1660 it is very likely that it was in some sense an attempt to realize the scientific and philosophical side of the Rosicrucian ideal.

It is also possible that Rosicrucian influences were behind the creation of speculative Masonry. For example, there is a Scottish poem of the year 1638, which contains the lines:

For we be brethren of the Rosie Cross
We have the Mason's word and second sight.[1]

So clearly there is at least some connection between Rosicrucianism and the early history of Masonry. And in Masonry we see really a combination of all three of the streams that I mentioned: the philosophical, the social, and the esoteric. Here again there may be a link with Comenius, as he also knew many of the men who were behind the formation of the Grand Lodge of London.

Now think for a moment of the influence of Masonry: the fact that a large proportion of the signatories of the American Declaration of Independence were Masons, the fact that Masons played a large part in the French Revolution, and so on. We are talking about a colossal influence.

Let me give you another example of the influence of Rosicrucianism in history. I mentioned earlier that many societies and fraternities have adopted the Rosicrucian label. One of the most important was a German fringe Masonic group called the Order of the Golden and Rosy Cross. This Golden and Rosy Cross was a remarkable phenomenon. It was a kind of Golden Dawn of its day, bringing together many different elements and fusing them together in the same way that the Golden Dawn did. In fact the Golden Dawn adopted the grade system used by the Golden and Rosy Cross.

The aim of the order was described as follows: "to make effective the hidden forces of nature, to release nature's light which has become deeply buried beneath the dross resulting from the curse, and thereby to light within every brother a torch by whose light he will be able better to recognize the hidden God . . . and thereby become more closely united with the original source of light."[2]

That passage is pure Gnosticism, and it confirms what I was saying earlier about the Gnostic character of the whole Rosicrucian movement.

The Golden and Rosy Cross was founded in about 1757, and it soon had lodges all over the German-speaking world. There was, for example, a very active lodge in the duchy of Sulzbach. And it is no coincidence that Sulzbach at the time was a tremendous center of Hermetic and Kabbalistic studies. There was even a Hebrew press there.

But the real heyday of the order came when one of its members became king of Prussia in 1786. This was King Frederick-William II,

successor to Frederick the Great. During his reign the court and government were dominated by a Rosicrucian clique led by the king's two
Rosicrucian mentors, Johann Christoph Wöllner and Johann Rudolf
von Bischoffswerder. Wöllner was something of a fanatic, and there is
a story that on one occasion he wrote to a fellow member of the order
telling him to stop doubting that adepts of the eighth degree had the
ability to hatch chickens out of hard-boiled eggs.

Under Frederick-William II Prussia became for a time virtually a
Rosicrucian state. Unfortunately it all collapsed because Wöllner and
Bischoffswerder pursued thoroughly reactionary policies, made themselves very unpopular, and were eventually turfed out when the king
died and his son came to the throne. So the Rosicrucians—like any
other body of men—sometimes failed.

There are many other examples I could give you of the practical influence of Rosicrucianism. I could point to the mystical community of
German settlers in Pennsylvania that was influenced by Rosicrucian
ideas. I could point to the Golden Dawn and the enormous ramifications that has had. I could point to the vast amount of literature, art,
even music, inspired by Rosicrucianism.

So it begins to look as though those early Rosicrucians did achieve
something after all.

When we look at something like Rosicrucianism, or at the Templars or at Freemasonry or at the legends of the Holy Grail, we are
looking at the tip of an iceberg. I believe that behind these phenomena
lies a very ancient current. What precise form it takes I know not, but
I believe that every so often in human history this current comes to the
surface. It can emerge in the obvious form of an esoteric movement. It
can also come out in more subtle ways. It can come out in the arts or in
science; in architecture, in garden design, in craftwork, in typography.
But one usually recognizes it when one sees it because it has a certain
stamp of yearning for eternal beauty and truth.

And at this point I should like to mention a piece of fiction that

struck me as being a remarkable allegory of the Rosicrucian movement. It comes in a short story by Jorge Luis Borges called *Tlön, Uqbar,
Orbis Tertius.* The essence of the story is this: you are asked to imagine
a group of people who come together and decide that they will invent
a fictitious country. They then decide that they cannot invent a country in isolation so they must invent an entire planet. And this is what
they do. Furthermore they produce an encyclopedia of forty volumes
all about this planet, which they call Tlön. The encyclopedia contains
minutely detailed descriptions of every aspect of this imaginary world:
its geography, history, folklore, religions, languages and their gram-
mar, literature, and so on. Then they surreptitiously leak out clues
about the imaginary world—at first just little things such as religious
objects. Then they plant a copy of the encyclopedia in a library, and
gradually this mysterious world starts to capture people's imaginations
to such an extent that the real world starts to imitate it. And toward
the end of the story Borges writes: "A scattered dynasty of solitary men
has changed the face of the world. Their task continues." That could
equally well describe the men who launched the Rosicrucian movement.

In conclusion let me address the question: What is the relevance of
all this to us today? In the first place, it is possible to draw certain parallels between the age of the Rosicrucian manifestoes and the present
day. There was the same feeling then, as there is today, that the world
was in chaos and needed a change of direction. And there was the
same expectation of a coming New Age. The Rosicrucians linked it
with certain astrological indications. Likewise we link it with the Age
of Aquarius.

The Rosicrucian vision of the New Age is one that makes a lot of
sense today. I mentioned the Rosicrucian emphasis on universality.
One aspect of this is the need to draw together religion and science, so
that the scientist always works in a spirit of service to God, as the alchemists did. Today we are seeing a renewed striving to reconcile science and spirituality. Furthermore this holistic vision has begun to

embrace not just religion and science but many other areas of our culture including art, architecture, technology, politics, and ecology.

I think perhaps the most important thing about the relevance of the Rosicrucian path for us today is that it involves not only personal enlightenment but also service in the widest sense. We are talking about a complete vision, a dream of what humankind and the world could be like. If you want to have a dream, the Rosicrucian one is still alive.

14

MASONIC CIVILIZATION

The origin of Freemasonry remains a much-argued mystery, but

modern civilization is in many ways a Masonic project.

Richard Smoley

M asonry. To some, the word connotes sinister conspiracies, an underground cabal that, through means unknown and scarcely imaginable to ordinary mortals, topples governments and manipulates currencies.

To others, more adept at observation than imagination, it evokes images of small-town America, of solid citizens in cheap suits congregating at the lodge on the second story of a shabby Main Street commercial building.

In either case, today's seekers may wonder why Masonry should interest them. While some grain of esoteric knowledge may be buried in those peculiar rituals, how powerful could it be? The Masons we know—a father or an uncle, perhaps—so far from being mystic masters, usually blend unobtrusively into the background of middle-class life.

Personally I am not a Mason. I know no more of this tradition than can be found in books. Yet from the small amount of reading I've done, I'm convinced that every spiritual seeker today owes an incalculable debt to Freemasonry. You could even say that ours is fundamentally a Masonic civilization. (Freemasonry and Masonry, by the way, are more or less interchangeable terms; "the Craft" is a common nickname for it.)

To understand why Masonry is so important, it's helpful to look at its origins—at least as far as we can glimpse them. The oldest known Masonic text, the "Old Charges," which dates at least as far back as 1400, sets out a legendary heritage that begins with the antediluvian patriarch Jabal, who discovered geometry ("the which Science is called Massonrie") and wrote down his findings on pillars of stone. After Noah's Flood destroyed all human civilization, the Egyptian sage Hermes Trismegistus rediscovered this knowledge and passed it on in a lineage that includes Nimrod, Abraham, Euclid, and the eighty-thousand masons who were said to have worked on Solomon's Temple.[1]

Like many branches of the Western inner traditions, Masonry thus claims to go back to ancient Egypt and Israel. But most scholars today—including many Masons—would say there is no evidence of any such link. Hence most opt for one of two theories of Masonic origins.

The first one holds that Masonry evolved from the medieval stonemasons' guilds. The medieval guild, a combination of trade union and regulated monopoly, had the responsibility of inducting trainees and preserving trade secrets; this was the origin of the famous Masonic passwords and secret handgrips. And because medieval civilization was steeped in religion, spiritual and ethical instruction was included in the apprentices' training, giving rise to the lessons imparted in the Masonic degrees.

In the early modern period, the guild system began to break down; as it did, the associations of practicing stoneworkers—what is known as "operative Masonry"—began to evolve into the "speculative Masonry" of today's lodges. Here the old symbolism of plumb and square, compass and gauge, for moral and ethical virtues was retained, but now purely symbolically. Eventually the "operative" side was lost altogether, and Masons were drawn chiefly from the nobility and bourgeoisie.

Such is the first theory. It is semiofficially promulgated by many Masonic organizations and books, and is the more-or-less standard account. It does have some major problems, however. As Christopher Knight notes, it doesn't explain why Freemasonry seems to have originated in Scotland, where there were few if any stonemasons' guilds, rather than on the Continent, where there were many. It also fails to explain why, in an age where nothing was more of a blot on one's social standing than any kind of connection with work that soiled one's hands, the gentry and intelligentsia suddenly became interested in the knowledge embodied in a craft guild. It is as if a socialite today went to the union local in search of esoteric knowledge. Finally, the religious sentiments in the surviving guild texts are strongly Christian. Yet explicitly Christian motifs are almost completely absent from Masonry.

The second theory is far more romantic (which can be a disadvantage if it is being judged by historians who pride themselves on caution and sobriety). It says that Freemasonry is a reformulation of the knowledge possessed by that mysterious medieval order known as the Knights Templar. Some scholars, notably the amateur historian John J. Robinson, argue convincingly for this view. I tend to agree with them. Here's why.

The Templars reached the zenith of their might in the thirteenth century, when they wielded great power not only in the Holy Land but in Europe. But when Palestine fell back into Muslim hands in 1291, the Templars lost their apparent reason for existence, and various powers, including the pope, made plans to consolidate them with their rival order, the Knights Hospitallers. The Templars, perhaps overconfident of their prestige, did not maneuver very capably in this situation. Many were rounded up, tortured, and executed.

Not all the Templars fell into their enemies' hands. Many of the knights were never caught, and a large Templar fleet consisting of eighteen ships at the French harbor of La Rochelle vanished before they could be seized. No one knows what happened to them.[2]

After this many Templars seem to have taken refuge in Scotland, whose king, Robert the Bruce, was at that time under excommunication by Rome and was also fighting to keep his country free from English rule. The Scottish cause was not faring well; the English had set up strongholds throughout much of Scotland, and it seemed only a matter of time before the nation fell under England's sway.

But in 1314 the tide turned decisively. At the celebrated Battle of Bannockburn, Robert the Bruce routed English forces two and a half times the size of his own, guaranteeing Scotland's independence for the next three hundred years. Oddly enough, even here the battle seemed to be going against the Scots when at the last moment a mysterious force came to their aid. Accounts of this event are garbled; the best known version says the camp followers of the Scottish army entered the fray, blowing horns and waving homemade flags. Mistaking them for real reinforcements, the English panicked and fled.[3]

You don't have to read many accounts of battles to understand how the tide can be turned by such flukes. Even so, it's strange to think that the proud English knights could have been routed by a seedy brigade of whores and scullery lads.

Another explanation, favored by Michael Baigent and Richard Leigh, those tireless champions of alternative history, says that the mysterious force was a detachment of Templar knights, and that the legend of the camp followers' attack was a story cooked up to boost Scottish national pride while disguising the real source of Robert's help.[4] At any rate, by the time the ban of excommunication was lifted from Scotland in 1328, the Templars would have had plenty of occasions to find cover.

There is some evidence for Templar survivals in the British Isles after their suppression. Robinson argues that the Peasants' Revolt in England in 1381 was not a spontaneous uprising but an event carefully orchestrated by heirs to the Templar lineage. He notes, for example, that the rioting mobs often went far out of their way to sack properties belonging to the Knights Hospitallers, who had taken over the Templar holdings in England. Robinson also notes that the leader of the revolt was one Wat Tyler—and every good Mason knows that the "Tyler" is a lodge function: he is the one who stands guard outside the meeting.[5]

Robinson also points to a curious allusion in the initiation rite of the third degree, that of the Master Mason. Here the candidate is told that the initiation "will make you brother to pirates and corsairs."[6] Is this a recollection of the vanished Templar ships that (we may speculate) turned to piracy to avenge themselves on the perfidious European powers? The connection becomes more plausible if you remember that one of the symbols associated with the Master Mason's degree is the skull and crossbones on a black background—the Jolly Roger familiar to every schoolboy.

Finally, there is the matter of the "blood oaths." The Masonic rituals allude to a number of blood-curdling punishments that the initiate invokes upon himself if ever he violates the secret. In the second, Fellowcraft degree, for example, the candidate binds himself to his oath "under no less penalty than to have my left breast torn open and my heart and vitals taken from thence and thrown over my left shoulder and carried into the valley of Jehosaphat."[7]

As Robinson points out, such oaths are mystifying if it is a matter of stonecutters' trade secrets—but quite understandable for Templars on the run, who, if they were handed over to the Inquisition, would have suffered torments far more excruciating than these.

The evidence for a Templar connection is more compendious and more intricate than I can really do justice to here, but if we accept this hypothesis, we might ask how the Templars turned into the Freemasons. To have a sense of this, we must look at a small and quirky chapel a few miles south of Edinburgh, known as Rosslyn. It is on the estate of the St. Clair, or Sinclair, family and was built between 1441 and 1486. Though ostensibly the private chapel of an aristocratic family, it has never served as such; the St. Clair's chapel is in their house.

Moreover Rosslyn seems to possess an enormous number of non-Christian motifs. "The figure that occurs most frequently," write Baigent and Leigh, "is the 'Green Man'—a human head with vines issuing from its mouth and sometimes its ears, then spreading wildly, in tangled proliferation, over the walls."[8] Is this "Green Man" connected with "Baphomet," the bearded head that the Templars' enemies accused them of worshipping?

Christopher Knight and his coauthor Robert Lomas suggest in their book *The Hiram Key* that Rosslyn was built as a replica of Herod's Temple, on which the Templars had conducted excavations during their time in the Holy Land. Rosslyn even has two pillars, "the apprentice's pillar" and "the Mason's pillar," which, according to Knight and Lomas, correspond to the two pillars, Jachin and Boaz, of the Jerusalem Temple—and of the Masonic lodge.

But one of the most intriguing pieces of evidence is a carving on a wall at Rosslyn. Knight claims that it portrays the astonishing scene of a first-degree Masonic initiation—conducted by a figure in Templar garb. Knight and Lomas conclude:

> Many modern Freemasons believe that their organization is descended from the semi-literate working-class ritual practices of the medieval guilds of stonemasons. It is an origin theory that is riddled with problems, yet it did seem to explain the well-documented references to the early operative lodges of Scotland.

The true reason is more the reverse: it was speculative masons (Templars) who adopted operative masons (stoneworkers) and introduced them to lower-level secrets concerning Solomon's Temple.[9]

By the early seventeenth century, Masonry begins to enter the public scene, and we encounter records of lodge meetings in several Scottish towns. Depending on who you believe, Masonry at this point began to be permeated by the esoteric currents that Frances Yates has dubbed "the Rosicrucian enlightenment," or, alternatively, these esoteric dimensions simply became better known. By 1638 a Scottish poet named Henry Adamson could write:

For what we do presage is not in grosse,
For we be brethren of the Rosie Crosse;
We have the Mason word, *and second sight;*
Things for to come we can foretell aright . . .[10]

It might be overinterpreting to say that Adamson was specifically connecting the Masons with the Rosicrucians (the mysterious order that was the subject of several celebrated pamphlets written around 1614); he may simply have been playing with associated ideas, just as a satirist today might lump Shirley MacLaine together with crystals and Atlantis without believing they necessarily have anything to do with one another.[11]

But there is other evidence for a Masonic-Rosicrucian link. One of the most influential of the seventeenth-century speculative Masons was an Englishman named Elias Ashmole, who was initiated in 1646. Ashmole, a noted antiquarian (his collection forms the nucleus of Oxford's Ashmolean Museum), was also one of the founders of the Royal Society, the first modern organization for scientific investigation. Before its formal establishment in 1660, the group's members, meeting informally, called themselves "the Invisible College"—a term taken from the Rosicrucian manifestoes. Nearly all of the Royal Society's first members were Masons.[12]

Henceforth Masonic history becomes more a matter of record and less of conjecture. After the Grand Lodge of England was formed in 1717, Masonic history enters into the spotlight. Some of the most significant participants in the American Revolution were Masons, and Freemasonry was at least as important in forming a unified modern Italy as it was in influencing our own Founding Fathers.

Thus, if the Templar theory holds true, then the betrayal of the Templars by king and pope was amply repaid, for Freemasonry has been one of the chief sponsors of republican government against monarchism and of rational, scientific investigation as opposed to ecclesiastical dogma. But is this all it comes to? Was the rise of modern science and democracy just a long, drawn-out act of revenge? And does this make the Masons the enemies of Catholicism, as many Catholics—and not a few Masons—seem to believe? I think not. It's worth trying to understand why.

Western civilization, for all its greatness, has never entirely succeeded in reconciling the sacred with the secular. Christianity, persecuted both by the Jewish and the Roman authorities, hardly had a healthy relationship with the worldly powers in its formative years. When it almost accidentally became the state religion of the Roman Empire in the fourth century A.D., the Christian church was more or less unprepared for the role. In later centuries Eastern Orthodoxy would turn into an arm of the Byzantine state, while Catholicism, stepping into the vacuum created by the collapse of the Western empire, began to intrude into the realm of secular power.

By the thirteenth century, popes like Innocent IV were not only temporal lords (ruling most of central Italy) but were even claiming universal sovereignty; they regarded secular monarchs like the Holy Roman Emperor as mere henchmen. (The emperors themselves, of course, never quite saw things this way, leading to some of the greatest political struggles of the Middle Ages.)

It was in this atmosphere that the Templars were dissolved. The popes and bishops were alternately manipulating, and manipulated by, the kings and emperors of Europe, and corruption flourished on a scale that makes our furors over Whitewater and Newt Gingrich's finances look puny. Whatever truth there may have been to the idea of Templar heresies, the chief motive for their dissolution was probably the authorities' greed for their wealth.

Friday the thirteenth of October, 1307, was the day the sacred and secular powers chose to descend upon the Templars, and for Western civilization it was a very unlucky day indeed. For the Templar dissolution seemed to be final proof that, despite the considerable spiritual power the Church possessed and continues to possess, it could not be trusted in matters secular.

Since that time, if you grant the Templar-Masonic link, the heirs to the Templar lineage in both Europe and America have fought to separate secular from sacred authority, culminating in achievements like the First Amendment of our own Constitution. This struggle was not won in a day or even a century; religious tolerance was a distant dream for many centuries after the Templars were jailed.

Masonry does not, as far as I can see, dispute the spiritual teachings of the Church; its requirement of a belief in a Supreme Being and a life after death are perfectly consistent with Catholicism. But by its insistence on respect for all religions, Freemasonry does challenge Catholic (and all other) claims to an exclusive monopoly on spiritual truth; only in the sense that it undercuts the doctrine *Extra ecclesiam nulla salus* ("No salvation outside the Church") can it be called anti-Catholic. For similar reasons it frightens many Protestant fundamentalists.

Given that both modern science and modern democracy have Masonic origins, it's not entirely specious to contend that ours is a Masonic civilization. This is not to say that it is free from abuses of its own. Like the medieval Christian civilization that preceded it, the modern "Masonic" civilization presents its own problems: representative government is prone to abuses too, while scientism has turned into a new form of bigotry. These excesses, if they go unchecked, may call for a response from the "conscious circle of humanity" much like the one that turned the Templars into the Masons. Most probably, though, Masonic civilization is, like its predecessors, only one stage in an enormous program of constructing a grand Temple of human experience, whose nature and goal we today can barely guess at.

To address another question, is there a Masonic conspiracy juggling world events behind the scenes? I, of course, have no way of knowing, but to all appearances, Masonry is less influential than it was a century ago. I suspect that there are circles in which Masonic affiliation may help as a means to advancement—but that's a far cry from saying it's a dark web of international evil. Connections in the "old boys'" network and what sociologist C. Wright Mills called the "power elite" are probably far more influential in personal advancement than Masonic rings or secret handshakes—as they probably are in global political and business decisions.

But let's turn away from these grand perspectives and ask what Masonry offers in a spiritual sense. There are many interpretations of Masonic rites, symbols, and degrees; some are more plausible and authoritative than others, but none is taken as an absolute within Masonry itself. This suggests not only that Masonry has tried to avoid slavery to creeds and formulations, but that the ultimate meaning of its rituals lies in the rites themselves. That is to say, their import is not some kind of implicit verbal message, but rather the effect they have on the being of the candidate. Carried out properly, the rites should leave their own distinct mark on the individual on both conscious and unconscious levels. As Thomas Worrel has noted in an article on the Masonic degrees, the process may resemble C. G. Jung's picture of individuation.[13]

For me, the most fascinating of the Masonic mysteries has to do with the Master Mason ritual, which recounts the story of the death of Hiram Abiff (sometimes Adoniram, "the lord Hiram").

In this legend, Hiram works as the chief architect of Solomon's Temple.[14] Three "ruffians" conspire to extract the secret of the Master Mason from him. One day as Hiram tries to leave the site of the unfinished Temple through the south entrance, he is stopped by the first ruffian. Armed with a rule, the ruffian demands the secret. Hiram refuses, and the ruffian strikes him with the rule on his right temple. He sinks down onto his left knee.

Hiram then rushes to the west gate, where he is accosted by the second ruffian, who holds a level. Confronted with the same request, Hiram again refuses and is struck on the left temple with this tool. He falls onto his right knee.

Now Hiram, faint and bleeding, staggers to the east entrance, where the third ruffian is posted. Being refused as well, he hits Hiram on the forehead with a heavy stone maul, which finally kills him.

The ruffians bury Hiram in "the rubbish of the Temple," later exhuming him to give him a more permanent burial under an acacia tree to the west of the site. King Solomon and another Hiram, king of Tyre, dispatch a search for the lost master. A group of workmen find him, and Solomon gives Hiram Abiff his third and final burial near the Holy of Holies of the uncompleted Temple. Solomon raises a monument to him in the form of a virgin weeping over a broken column and holding a sprig of acacia; behind her is the figure of Time with a scythe; he holds a snake to her head. With Hiram dead, the Temple will remain unfinished until one who knows the "Master's Word" can complete it.[15]

What could this strange tale possibly mean? I will try to give one interpretation here. It is not meant to be definitive; indeed, as I've said, such a thing is probably impossible. What I'm about to say owes a great deal to an account in Harold W. Percival's fascinating and compendious 1946 work *Thinking and Destiny,*[16] but it is not identical to Percival's account.

Hiram is consciousness. The Temple that he is building is the true Self, the complete and integrated human being. The three ruffians are the three ordinary functions that operate in man, frequently described as thinking, feeling, and doing. Now these functions, the three ruffians, work together at least well enough to plot against Hiram. But because they are unintegrated and unconscious themselves, they cannot attain their goal. In fact they only end up "killing" the consciousness, that is, making it descend into the oblivion of ordinary life.

There are also higher functions in man, symbolized by Solomon and Hiram of Tyre. They do not have the secret of consciousness either. But they can at least set up a memorial—that is, a reminder that something has been lost. Until it is found, man is subject to the forces of time and delusion (symbolized by the serpent).

Interestingly, the three ruffians are named Jubelo, Jubela, and Jubelum. The first part of the names is obviously akin to Jabal, discoverer of "the Science called Massonrie," while the suffixes resemble the Latin masculine, feminine, and neuter endings. But as Percival notes, there is another dimension to these endings. If you put them together, you have "Aoum," or the sacred syllable "Om," which Percival equates with the true Mason's word. That is to say, the three ruffians, the inferior functions of man, possess part of the secret of consciousness. But they do not have the secret of integrating them and bringing them to the higher level symbolized by the Temple.

If Masonry is a true initiatic tradition, it contains within its rites and teachings and symbols the means to restore this lost word and bring the Temple to perfection. (I am told that this is part of the Royal Arch ritual, one of the many higher degrees of Masonry.)

I personally do not have the experience to say whether Masonry, now or ever, has possessed the secret of restoring the "lost word" of consciousness. But the Masonic tradition has been a prime inspiration for many of the modern paths of esotericism. H. P. Blavatsky was greatly indebted to it; the founders of the Hermetic Order of the Golden Dawn were all high-degree Masons; even Gardnerian Wicca, with its three degrees of initiation, is believed to have been inspired by the first three degrees of Freemasonry.

This leads us back, perhaps, to the notion of conspiracy; paranoids may shriek that here is more evidence of some grand plot to lure humankind toward the lairs of Satan. For my part I can see no such thing; indeed if there is a worldwide conspiracy to increase consciousness and promote tolerance, scientific inquiry, and representative government, I can only regret that it has not proved stronger.

MYSTICS
AND TEACHERS

HEAVENS AND HELLS
THE INNER WORLDS
OF EMANUEL SWEDENBORG

In his many spiritual journeys, the Swedish visionary saw heaven

and hell as places where our "true affections" come to light.

Gary Lachman

B y orthodox standards, the idea that the everyday world is not the *only* world is a strange, fantastic notion. This materialist view, which declares that reality is what we perceive through our senses, enjoys almost universal acceptance; it is, however, really only a very recent notion. Earlier races and cultures did not believe that reality was limited to what we could see, hear, touch, taste, or smell. Indeed they felt as confident about the reality of an unseen spiritual world as we do about the physical world. To someone of the Middle Ages, it was as obvious that a spirit world really existed as that a tree or house did. Perhaps it was even more obvious, as his religion told him that the physical world was relatively unimportant, but that his eternal destiny lay in the worlds beyond.

Although the "one world" view of reality—described by William Blake as the "single vision and Newton's sleep"—has held sway in our culture for the last few centuries, there has always been a current of thought in the West that has kept alive the notion of other worlds. In recent times these two notions of reality have entered into a curious dialectic. While neuroscientists close in on the purportedly physical basis of the mind, a movement in popular culture to embrace other worlds has arisen on a wider scale than ever before in modern times. Channelers, psychics, mystics, and visionaries of all kinds crowd the spiritual marketplace, some offering profitable insights, others making profit of a more dubious character.

In *The Doors of Perception and Heaven and Hell* Aldous Huxley wrote: "Like the earth of a hundred years ago, our mind still has its darkest Africas, its unmapped Borneos and Amazonian basins."[1] In these words we see at once the attraction of other worlds and the problems involved in exploring them. It is easy to lose our way in unknown regions, and without some sense of the terrain it is difficult to judge the claims of those who say they have journeyed there. We *could* plunge in and take our chances, accepting the extravagant reports of others, although we have no way of verifying them. But a better way would be to find a reliable guide.

One of the most systematic and internally consistent guides to other worlds in the modern era is the Swedish visionary philosopher Emanuel Swedenborg. One suspects that in naming his book on visionary states *Heaven and Hell,* Huxley was paying tribute to Swedenborg, whose own work of that title is one of the most fascinating guides to other worlds in the Western spiritual canon. In 1745, at the age of fifty-seven, Swedenborg underwent a profound spiritual crisis. The result was a cartography of the inner realms that is unsurpassed and has rarely been equaled by any voyager to these other worlds before or since.

PSYCHIC POWERS

Emanuel Swedenborg—or, as his family was called until it became ennobled, Swedberg—was born on January 29, 1688, in Stockholm,

Sweden, and died in London on March 29, 1772. Even in regard to his own death, the man who spent over twenty years recording conversations with angels and spirits gave proof of his ability to pierce the barriers between this world and those beyond. In the last month of his life, Swedenborg discovered through the spirit world that John Wesley, the founder of Methodism, wished to meet him. Although Wesley *did* wish to meet Swedenborg, he had mentioned his desire to no one. A few days before he was to set out on an extensive speaking tour, Wesley received a letter from Swedenborg saying that he, Swedenborg, had been "informed in the world of spirits that you have a strong desire to converse with me."[2]

Wesley was astonished and wrote back, regretting that he would have to put off a visit for several months, but would be grateful for an audience on his return to London. Swedenborg replied that this would be impossible, as he was to die on the twenty-ninth of the next month, which he did.

Swedenborg's prediction of the date of his own death is only one example of his remarkable psychic powers. Reports of his gifts have been documented in the many books on his life, and this account of Swedenborg's psychic abilities could be extended considerably. Fascinating as they are, however, these "minor miracles"—as the psychologist Wilson Van Dusen calls them[3]—are hardly the stuff to have given Swedenborg an immense spiritual influence on their own. But figures as notable as Goethe, William Blake, Henry James Sr., Samuel Taylor Coleridge, Honoré de Balzac, W. B. Yeats, and August Strindberg were profoundly influenced by Swedenborg's writings on other worlds. For Ralph Waldo Emerson, Swedenborg was "one of the mastodons of literature . . . not to be measured by whole colleges of ordinary scholars."[4] And for Helen Keller, herself, in a different way, an inhabitant of an unseen world, her "large Braille volumes containing Swedenborg's teachings" were "full of secrets of the spiritual world."[5]

Why should Swedenborg have such powerful appeal for these and

thousands of others who follow his teachings, either in their own way
or as members of the Swedenborgian Church? Essentially the answer
is this: Swedenborg had been to heaven and hell and had come back to
tell about both in painstaking detail.

THE JOURNEY INWARD

For the greater part of his life, Swedenborg did not concern himself
with inner worlds but with the scientific study of the outer one. His intellect was insatiable. By the time of his spiritual crisis, he was already
a respected figure in Sweden, both as the author of an immense number of scientific studies on everything from metallurgy to the anatomy
of the brain and as a statesman and assessor of Swedish mines. He was
also an inventor of considerable talent: when given the task of trans-
porting several ships inland across mountains, he managed it successfully ahead of schedule. Swedenborg, then, was no vague mystic, and
his practical, step-by-step approach to mapping the inner worlds lends
his reports of heaven and hell a consistency lacking in those of less
meticulous voyagers.

As Wilson Van Dusen writes, "The result of the journey within is a
fundamental broadening of the individual's values and perspectives
that takes account of what used to be habitually overlooked and dis-
counted."[6] Although he had mastered the scientific and philosophical
knowledge of his time, Swedenborg had paid scant attention to his inner life, to the world of feelings. His highest aim at the time of his crisis was, curiously enough, to find the seat of the soul in the human brain,
a goal contemporary neuroscientists continue to pursue. Swedenborg
was to discover that his scientific search for the soul was not only hopeless but led away from the true house of the soul: the inner reaches of
the human mind.

This truth was brought home to him in a series of shattering visions, recorded in his *Journal of Dreams*.[7] In the culmination of this ini-

tiation, Christ in a dream asked Swedenborg if he had "a bill of health"—a reference to an incident in Swedenborg's life when he was almost killed because he was suspected of carrying plague. Swedenborg answered, "Lord, thou knowest better than I," to which Christ replied, "Well, then do." Swedenborg understood this to mean he was to go further into the spirit world.

SWEDENBORG'S CRISIS LED to his basic insight: the deeper we go into the mind, the closer we draw to the spiritual worlds. As he was to write in *Heaven and Hell,* "the individual is in touch with the heavens as far as his more inward reaches are concerned."[8] One of Swedenborg's most valuable assets in his inner explorations was a remarkable ability to remain for several hours in that curious threshold between waking and sleeping known as the hypnagogic state.[9] Like C. G. Jung, Swedenborg discovered that in this liminal state the mind remains alert and *can watch inner processes at work,* can even enter into conversations with them. Jung called this process "active imagination"; Swedenborg thought of it as speaking with angels and spirits.

Whether inner psychological processes and spiritual beings are the same or different things is an open question. Swedenborg didn't bother about these distinctions. For him the inner and the spiritual were one. According to his doctrine of correspondence, the human mind is a reflection of the higher worlds, just as the physical world is a reflection of the human mind. He writes in *The Universal Human:*

> There is a spiritual world that is distinct from the world of nature, [and] correspondences occur between spiritual phenomena and natural ones; . . . things from spiritual sources that come into being in natural phenomena are representations. They are correspondences because they are responsive, and representations because they portray.[10]

For Swedenborg, the whole of reality corresponds on various levels to the One Reality, which is the source of all: what he calls the Lord's Divine.[11]

Swedenborg's study of the curious visions and voices we see and hear as we drift off into sleep convinced him of their autosymbolic character.[12] In the hypnagogic mode, the psyche represents its current state in symbolic form; hence it is an excellent method of acquiring knowledge of one's "self," otherwise obscured by the deceptions and distortions of the conscious ego. Our conscious egos may lie about our attitudes and motivations, but in the hypnagogic state, the psyche spontaneously expresses the truth about ourselves. And although the same symbols occur in hypnagogic states as in dreams, the consciousness retained in the hypnagogic state allows us to communicate with inner processes—or spiritual beings—in a way that is extremely difficult in dreams. Describing the hypnagogic, Swedenborg wrote: "There is a kind of vision which comes . . . between the time of sleep and the time of wakefulness, when man is waking up. . . . This is the sweetest of all, for then heaven operates into his rational mind with the utmost tranquillity."[13]

If Swedenborg had stopped here, he would be remembered today as an early explorer of a fascinating method of self-analysis. But his curious ability to remain in the hypnagogic state for extended periods allowed him to continue his inward journey to realms rarely visited by living human beings.

HEAVEN, HELL, AND THE SPIRIT WORLD

Swedenborg's visions of the inner worlds are profoundly Christian, although not in any orthodox sense. Heaven, hell, and the intermediary sphere Swedenborg called the Spirit World (similar to what Catholicism knows as purgatory) are not "places" one goes to after death, as one might go from London to Paris. They are states of being. Our final destination in heaven or hell is not determined by the will of a patriarchal deity, but by what Swedenborg called our "true affections."

Swedenborg's descriptions of the inner worlds are scattered throughout his work. Many of his writings, like the mammoth twelve-volume *Arcana Coelestia,* the six-volume *Apocalypse Explained,* and various shorter works, deal with biblical symbology. For Swedenborg, the Bible is written in a symbolic code based on the doctrine of correspondence and depicts truths about the spiritual worlds. His five-volume *Spiritual Diary,* maintained over a period of nearly twenty years, is a day-to-day record of his experiences on the inner planes. Throughout its more than two thousand pages are insights on everything from "The Food and Drink of Spirits" to "The Purification of Societies after the Last Judgment."[14] Entries begin with statements like "I conversed with angels about the Lord, saying that His Divine was from Eternity" or "When hypocrites ascend into heaven . . . they appear in the eyes of the angels there of a hideous countenance." But the absolutely necessary work for understanding Swedenborg's vision of the worlds beyond is his magnificent *Heaven and Hell.*

What first strikes a reader of *Heaven and Hell* is that this is no work of airy speculation. Swedenborg has seen and heard.

> Today's churchman knows almost nothing about heaven, hell, or his own life after death. . . . Many people born in the church deny these things and ask in their hearts, "Has anyone come back and told us so?" To prevent so negative an attitude from infecting and corrupting people of simple heart and simple faith, it has been made possible for me to be right with angels and to talk with them person to person. I have also been allowed to see what heaven is like and what hell is like; this has been going on for thirteen years.[15]

Swedenborg was appalled at the ideas of heaven and angels held by the learned of his time—their notions of an invisible abstract realm and of insubstantial creatures, Blake's "allegorical abode where existence hath never come."[16] In keeping with the doctrine of correspondence, Swedenborg's heaven is a place where angels live in houses, belong to communities, eat and drink, perform tasks, speak, have governments, wear clothes—in short, do everything that we do here on earth, but in an atmosphere of beauty and transfigured meaning that far surpasses our mundane sphere. It was this "concrete" aspect of Swedenborg's heaven—along with his claim to have direct experience of it—that the theologians of his time railed against, to the point of trying to have him declared insane.

In Swedenborg's view, the world to which the soul awakens after death is very much like the one it has just left—so much so that many spirits do not know they are dead. Van Dusen suggests that the terrifying hallucinations suffered by individuals diagnosed as schizophrenic may be the work of these unfortunate souls.[17] They may also be caused by lower spirits. Swedenborg taught that throughout our lives we interact with a hierarchy of spirits. Though most often disturbing, many of the hallucinations Van Dusen's patients reported were of a helpful, guiding, higher nature, suggesting that higher spirits—angels—were also present in human experience. Ordinarily we are unconscious of their presence; in the schizophrenic the barrier between the worlds has cracked. It's up for debate whether today's channelers are in touch with higher spirits or lower ones.

After death, to get to heaven—or, as the case may be, to hell—souls must first pass through an intermediary state, the Spirit World. Here one comes to terms with one's "true affections." As Swedenborg says, "the world of spirits is neither heaven nor hell. . . . It is where a person first arrives after death, being, after some time has passed, either raised into heaven or cast into hell, depending on his life in the world."[18]

After this initial self-confrontation, souls are "opened to their internals" and begin to drift toward their real nature. For Swedenborg, human beings are essentially made of two qualities, or powers: intention and discernment, or love and reason. What is true of a person is what he thinks from intention and actually does, not merely what he "knows." As Swedenborg writes, "a person is a person by virtue of his intention and his resulting understanding, not from understanding apart from intention."[19]

As the inner worlds are states of being, deceit is impossible there. Although on earth we can say one thing while thinking another, in the Spirit World we are forced to experience who and what we truly are: "Absolutely everyone there [in the Spirit World] is resolved into a state in which he speaks the way he thinks, and displays in his expression and gestures what his intentions are."[20]

A healthy existential dictum: what we really are depends on what we really feel, not on outward learning. Many believe they are on their way to heaven, convinced they have led a good life by adhering to the law and by following in outward deed the mandates of the church. But outward deeds do not determine one's place in the worlds beyond. If our true affection shows a real love of others and a desire to transcend the self, we are on our way to heaven. But if our true affection is centered on self-love and all that this entails—greed, envy, licentiousness, desire for power over others—then, regardless of outward appearance, we sink downward into hell.

SWEDENBORG'S HELL IS an unremittingly revolting state, and at times his account of it reads like some nightmarish blend of Hieronymus Bosch and William S. Burroughs. Ordure and vomit, unspeakable stenches, insatiable desires, gnawing hungers, interminable darkness, and the constant harangue of bickering souls surround its inhabitants. As in heaven, souls in hell live in houses and cities. But if heavenly dwellings are of supernal beauty, hellish ones are quite different.

> In some hells, one can see something like the rubble of homes or cities after a great fire. . . . In milder hells, one sees tumble-down huts, crowded together. . . . Within the houses are hellish spirits, constant brawls, hostilities, beatings. . . . There are robberies and hold-ups in the streets. . . . In some hells there are nothing but brothels that look disgusting and are full of all kinds of filth and excrement.[21]

There are other hells: arid wastes, dank caves, thick forests filled with dangerous beasts. One's presence here is not a punishment meted out by a judgmental deity, but the result of one's inner nature and the choices made in life. Heaven and hell are the poles between which the human spirit quivers in the tension of freedom. Without the temptation of the lower spheres, our spiritual growth would lack rigor and challenge. For Swedenborg, there can be no salvation unless we free ourselves of evil through our own free will.[22]

In any case, souls who find themselves in hell actually enjoy it. After death we journey to the world of our making. Those who find themselves in the hellish depths have paved their way through self-centeredness, which tears apart the fundamental unity of the cosmos. The essence of Swedenborg's doctrine can be found in the saying of the Chinese philosopher Mencius: "Those who follow the part of themselves that is great will become great men; those who follow the part of themselves that is small will become small men."[23] Swedenborg might paraphrase it thus: Those who follow the part of themselves that transcends self will choose heaven; those who follow the part of themselves that is centered on self will choose hell. In hell the reality of one's inner niggardliness is apparent, whatever one's station in life. Swedenborg often hobnobbed with bishops there.

If Swedenborg's hell is an unappetizing prospect, his heaven is a state of almost unimaginable fulfillment. Yet Swedenborg's determination that heaven and angels are substantial has polarized his readers. Some find this notion attractive: the higher worlds are not totally "other," and as far as our own lives are directed toward the good and the true, we participate in them now, on the earthly plane. For others, Swedenborg's depiction of angelic homes, parks, clothes, meals, and sexual relations are simple-minded transferences of earthly things into a heavenly setting, where everything is just as it is here, only better.

I believe the key to understanding Swedenborg's vision is his teaching that the essence of the One Reality is human. It is through our own humanness that we have access to the Divine. Our human experience corresponds to spiritual reality. Hence nothing human falls outside the realm of spirit, just as spiritual realities are not totally different from human ones. Our lives on earth reflect spiritual meanings, and the worlds beyond contain the latent potential of our experience.

For Swedenborg, this idea was represented in his vision of the universe as the Great Man. The doctrine of correspondence demands this. We are as we are because the Divine is human, and the worlds, spiritual and physical, represent this fact. Just as we can perceive aspects of our own being in contemplating natural phenomena, we find evidence of the Divine by looking into ourselves. Reality for Swedenborg is a reflection, in all its myriad parts, of the Divine Human at the center of things.

Yet if heaven greets us with familiar surroundings, conditions there are very different than on earth. Time and space are not as we know them. Swedenborg taught that time in heaven is not counted in days, weeks, years, but in changes of state, anticipating by more than a century Henri Bergson's belief that we grasp the true nature of time by direct intuition. Space is likewise different: in heaven distances are measured not by physical location but by degrees of empathy. Spirits of like mind are "near" each other in heaven, whatever their "location" (an arrangement for which global communication networks seem to be striving).

The essence of this teaching is that the true reality lies in our mental states, not in their physical reflection. Just as the sun is the center and source of our part of the physical universe, in heaven the Lord's Divine, the One Reality, is the source of heavenly warmth and light: love and truth. Whichever way angels turn, they look east and see the Lord. Angels also speak to each other, but their language is of such compactness and significance that in one word they can communicate more than we can in volumes.

There are in fact three heavens: the celestial, the spiritual, and the natural, each successively at a further distance from the Lord's Divine, each participating to a greater or lesser degree in Divine truth and love. The celestial heaven is the most ineffable, participating directly in the will or intention of the Divine. The spiritual heaven participates less in this, but takes part fully in the Divine understanding, or discernment. The natural heaven shares less in Divine discernment, and, by heavenly standards, is far from Divine intention.

This arrangement parallels the structure of our mental life. Our rational consciousness is concerned with the natural, physical world; in dreams and hypnagogic states we seem to enter a realm outside time and space, where we begin to understand the nature of the spiritual worlds; and in deep meditative trances we become aware of the One Reality, whose essence, Swedenborg and many other mystics tell us, is love.

Swedenborg's description of heaven is rich in detail and precludes a brief summary. Following the doctrine of correspondences, he relates each aspect of angelic life, from the architecture of heaven to celestial apparel to its spiritual significance. The overall effect is that of a vibrant, radiant, complex world whose parts infinitely reflect each other. Swedenborg's heaven is no static perfection; it unfolds with the pulse of the divine will. The images are breathtaking. Heaven itself, Swedenborg tells us, is made of angels, each angel belonging to a society of like "true affections," the whole host of them forming the body of the Great Man.

Swedenborg's heaven is on par with the visions of Dante, yet the essence of life there is summed up in his homely maxim "Do the good that you know." The good, for Swedenborg, is no abstract philosophical concept, but always the matter at hand, like washing the dishes or taking out the trash. No one in heaven is idle. Every angel has his uses. Swedenborg rejected the idea that in heaven one amuses oneself for eternity, with angelic choirs or otherwise. "Such a life would not be active," he wrote, "but idle . . . there is no happiness in life apart from activity."[24] In heaven every angel has work to do according to his "true affection."

In fact the joy of heaven comes from pursuing one's true affection and being of use to others. This quasi-Victorian notion of utility is related to Swedenborg's teachings on the knowledge of angels. The knowledge of angels consists in what they *do*—a basic existential ethic. Angels only learn what they can act on. Knowledge that merely instructs, without directly invigorating their activity, is useless to them. What is important in heaven is not outward show, but inner reality. Intention is everything.

It may seem anticlimactic to arrive at so unpretentious a doctrine after a guided tour of heaven and hell, but the profound effect of Swedenborg's teachings on the souls who have encountered him suggests otherwise. Although Swedenborg journeyed to "other worlds," his central concern was how we lived in this one. Unlike later inner voyagers like H. P. Blavatsky and Rudolf Steiner, Swedenborg's teachings did not include reincarnation. Like conventional Christianity, Swedenborg regarded our stay on earth as limited, and he believed that what we do here matters immensely. Yet Swedenborg does not share the profound anxiety that another Scandinavian Christian thinker, Søren Kierkegaard, felt when confronted with the terrible responsibility of freedom. Swedenborg's vision is essentially one of exuberance and health—and that is a doctrine well suited to this world or any other.

16

BLAVATSKY
AND HER MASTERS

Who were Madame Blavatsky's mysterious Masters?
Secret teachers hidden in Tibet? Figments of her
imagination? Research suggests that they were real
people whose identities she carefully concealed.

K. Paul Johnson

The Russian esotericist Helena Petrovna Blavatsky (1831–1891) is increasingly recognized as the central figure in the occult revival of the nineteenth century, with an influence that has been felt in fields as diverse as poetry, politics, and astrology. Blavatsky is best known, however, as the founder of the modern Theosophical movement, which is based on teachings she claimed to have received from living men she called "adepts," "Masters," or "Mahatmas."

Although in the past century many derivative organizations have incorporated these Masters into their beliefs, the historical reality of Blavatsky's hidden sponsors has never been seriously investigated. This may be partly due to a false assumption on which all accounts have been based—that Blavatsky's assertions about her Masters must be accepted or rejected wholesale. Yet there is another possibility, which I believe to be true: that the Masters were real persons systematically fictionalized in Blavatsky's accounts. Blavatsky's alleged Masters changed within a few years from John King of Spiritualist fame[1] to Tuitit and Serapis Bey of the Egyptian Brotherhood of Luxor and finally to Indian Mahatmas or "great souls." Under their alleged inspiration, Blavatsky (often known as HPB), her associate Henry Steel Olcott, and others established the Theosophical Society (or TS) in New York in 1875. Three years later, the adepts directed Blavatsky and Olcott to India, which marked the beginning of a period in which the Mahatmas' existence was widely debated.

In India the Society grew rapidly, largely because of the travels of its founders and the success of their magazine *The Theosophist.* The two Mahatmas most involved with the Theosophical Society during HPB's Indian years were Morya and Koot Hoomi (or Kuthumi), who were alleged to perform wondrous psychic feats through her. She insisted that she had spent years studying occultism with them in Tibet, where these Indian-born adepts resided.

Correspondence with Morya and Koot Hoomi was instrumental in attracting prominent Anglo-Indians to Theosophy. Most notable of these converts was the newspaper editor A. P. Sinnett, who wrote two books, *The Occult World* and *Esoteric Buddhism,* based on the Mahatmas' letters. These letters often arrived in peculiar ways. In the fall of 1880, HPB went to visit Sinnett and his wife in Simla; during her visit the Sinnetts were astounded by occult phenomena HPB performed with the Masters' alleged assistance. First Mrs. Sinnett received a note from Koot Hoomi found high up in the branches of a tree. A few days later, a cup and a saucer materialized under a bush for an unexpected picnic guest in the morning, and a missing brooch miraculously appeared for another guest at supper. Before HPB left Simla, a note from Koot Hoomi, along with another brooch, materialized inside a pillow belonging to Mrs. Sinnett. After the TS headquarters moved to Adyar in 1882, Mahatma letters were frequently received in a cabinet called the "Shrine," located in the "Occult Room" adjacent to HPB's bedroom. They also fell from the ceiling in various places and appeared in the margins of sealed correspondence.

By 1884, Theosophy had acquired many Indian disciples and was beginning to attract Europeans in large numbers. But that year two disgruntled employees, Alexis and Emma Coulomb, made charges of fraud against Blavatsky, claiming that they had participated in faking psychic phenomena aimed at proving the Mahatmas' existence. Among the Coulombs' charges were that the Shrine was designed to allow letters to be inserted through a sliding panel in the back, making them appear to have materialized paranormally. Their accusations led to an investigation by Richard Hodgson, who was sent to India by the British Society for Psychical Research. Hodgson concluded that the Masters did not exist and that all their alleged manifestations were fraudulent. Theosophists rejected his report as being based on lies by the Coulombs.

For the past century, opinion on the Hodgson report has been polarized between those who regard it as definitive proof of fraud and those who reject it as totally unjust. A century later, in 1986, the Society for Psychical Research published a critique by the handwriting expert Vernon Harrison that discredited crucial elements of Hodgson's case against Blavatsky. But Theosophists have overinterpreted this as complete vindication, when in fact many questions raised by Hodgson remain unanswered.

Although there were indeed real Masters directing HPB at the time, the Koot Hoomi correspondence was at least partly fraudulent, as is proven by letters received by Olcott in June 1883 giving instructions for forging letters to Sinnett. First Morya wrote, "Unless you put your shoulder to the wheel yourself Kuthumi Lal Singh will have to disappear off the stage this fall. Easy enough for you."[2] This was reiterated two weeks later, when another adept conveyed Morya's request that "you . . . put your whole soul in answer to A.P.S. from K.H. Upon this letter are hinged the fruits of the future. Let it be one that can be shown with honour to everyone."[3] Finally, a second letter from Morya closed with the reminder, "Be careful about letter to Sinnett. Must be a really *Adeptic* letter."[4] Although Hodgson was wrong to trust the Coulombs as reliable witnesses, he was justified in suspecting that the Mahatma letters were not quite what they seemed.

In the spring of 1885 Blavatsky left India forever. During the next two years she stayed in various places in Europe, working on her magnum opus *The Secret Doctrine.* In 1887 she went to London, where she spent the last four years of her life surrounded by adoring disciples. During this period she published *The Secret Doctrine, The Key to Theosophy,* and *The Voice of the Silence,* as well as many periodical articles in English and French. She died on May 8, 1891, leaving a legacy of bitterly divided opinions on her Masters, her occult phenomena, and her Theosophical doctrines.

Many subsequent occultists have incorporated Blavatsky's Masters into their teachings. Her direct spiritual descendants include such figures as Gottfried de Purucker, Charles W. Leadbeater, Alice Bailey, and Elizabeth Clare Prophet, all of whom have claimed communication from HPB's Mahatmas. More indirectly, Rudolf Steiner's Anthroposophical Society, H. Spencer Lewis's Ancient and Mystical Order of Rosae Crucis (AMORC), and Max Heindel's Rosicrucian Fellowship all claim that their founders were instructed by adepts reminiscent of those described by Blavatsky. The Secret Chiefs of the Hermetic Order of the Golden Dawn and the Ordo Templi Orientis are clearly akin to the Theosophical Masters. The Caucasian Greek teacher G.I. Gurdjieff claimed that his teachings emanated from the "conscious circle of humanity," which also resembled HPB's brotherhood of adepts. In the most extreme cases, the Masters are seen as the Great White Lodge, the inner government of the world. Secret rulers of the planet, they are opposed by evil black magicians who are always seeking to undo their benevolent plans.

This doctrine of endless magical war between opposing lodges gives rise to equally endless paranoid fantasies. Among the standard variations are delusions of grandeur ("I am the true agent of the Masters"), persecution ("The Black Lodge is out to get me"), influence (events are controlled by the Masters or their opponents), and reference (messages from the Masters appear in unexpected form). Such paranoia has understandably given the Masters a reputation as a fantasy of unbalanced minds. But unlike all her twentieth-century successors, Blavatsky left abundant clues to the historical identities of her real teachers, although they have gone largely unexplored.

In order to delve into these mysteries, it has been necessary to look behind the occult myth that has prevented serious examination of the subject. My years of research into the identities of HPB's sponsors have yielded a surprising volume of solid information about her hidden allies. By juxtaposing her tales of the Masters with historical records, it is possible to determine that she did indeed work in secret concord with a succession of spiritual and political leaders. Much remains unclear, and some of the identifications of the adepts I have proposed are quite speculative, but often they are obvious and simply "hidden in plain sight."

Blavatsky's fascination with Tibet as home of the Masters was rooted in her childhood experience of the Kalmuck tribe, which practiced Tibetan Buddhism in a region near Astrakhan in southern Russia. (Her maternal grandfather was the administrator appointed by the tsarist government for the Kalmuck and German settlers in the area.) As an adolescent, HPB became familiar with the Rosicrucian Masonry practiced by her great-grandfather, Prince Paul Dolgorouki, in whose large occult library she spent many hours. Prince Paul had belonged to the Rite of the Strict Observance, founded in Germany around 1754, which claimed to emanate from a worldwide network of Unknown Superiors, and he was rumored to have met the celebrated eighteenth-century mages known as the counts Cagliostro and Saint Germain. The "Count Alessandro di Cagliostro," as he styled himself, had promulgated his Egyptian Rite of Masonry in late eighteenth-century Europe, attracting great interest from the aristocracy with his magical feats and grandiose claims. As the last victim of the Inquisition, he became a Masonic martyr whose memory was a rallying point for later opponents of monarchy and the Catholic Church.

Two generations later, the Italian revolutionary leaders Giuseppe Mazzini and Giuseppe Garibaldi were heroes to radicals throughout Europe. They exercised their influence partly through the leadership of societies like the Carbonari and the Masonic Rites of Memphis and Misraim, which preserved Cagliostro's heritage. As a young adult, after leaving her husband (a middle-aged man she had impetuously married at age seventeen), HPB traveled extensively in the company of Albert Rawson, an American artist, and later of Agardi Metrovitch, a Hungarian opera singer. Both were political radicals affiliated with Cagliostro's Egyptian Masonry and Rosicrucianism. Blavatsky seems to have been associated with the exiled Mazzini in London in the 1850s. She admitted accompanying Metrovitch to Italy in 1867 to fight with Garibaldi against papal forces in the battle of Mentana, where she was seriously wounded.

During the 1850s and 1860s, HPB became familiar with Sufism, Kabbalah, the Druze, and Coptic Christianity. Paolos Metamon, a Copt magician, taught her and Rawson in Cairo in the 1850s and was still her mentor there twenty years later; he is apparently the original of her Master "Serapis Bey." In the early 1870s in Cairo, she was also associated with several other esotericists. It is likely that among them was Jamal ad-Din al-Afghani, a political reformer, Sufi teacher, and Freemason who later went to India around the same time as HPB and Olcott. Other Cairo figures from whom she derived inspiration were Louis Bimstein, a Polish Jew who later became "Max Theon," teacher of the Cosmic Philosophy,[5] and the British vice-consul and Masonic leader Raphael Borg. Blavatsky, Metamon, and Bimstein tried to establish an occult society in Cairo in 1871, but the effort failed.

After moving to New York in 1873, HPB was reunited with Rawson and met his Masonic and Rosicrucian associates, most importantly Charles Sotheran, who became a cofounder of the TS. Sotheran belonged to the Societas Rosicruciana in Anglia and the Masonic Rite of Memphis, which honored Cagliostro. The Theosophical Society was also linked with a mysterious Brotherhood of Luxor based in Egypt, with which Bimstein was affiliated. Shortly before the founding of the TS, HPB noted in her scrapbook that she had been ordered to found a "secret society like the Rosicrucian lodge."[6] As late as 1878, HPB and Olcott were considering making the TS a Masonic order, as advised by Sotheran and others. Thus it would be hard to overestimate the influence of secret societies in the early years of the history of Theosophy.

After her 1879 arrival in India, however, new forces behind the scenes became far more important influences on Blavatsky. Initially she and Olcott honored Swami Dayananda Sarasvati, founder of the reform group known as the Arya Samaj, as their Indian guru. Dayananda denounced all Hindu practices and doctrines from the post-Vedic period, and wished to remake Indian society on the basis of his interpretation of the Vedas. From Olcott's memoirs it is clear that at first HPB insisted the swami was one of her Masters; later, after a falling-out due to his religious intolerance, he was supplanted by other Indian Mahatmas.

When the flow of Mahatma letters was at its greatest, in the early 1880s, the TS was affiliated with a Sikh reform organization, the Singh Sabha, and a network of Sikh and Hindu maharajahs in a secret coalition opposing Christian missionaries. Thakar Singh Sandhanwalia, the founding president of the Amritsar Singh Sabha, corresponds in intriguing ways to clues about Koot Hoomi's identity in the

writings of Olcott and HPB. His Singh Sabha, which emphasized revival of Sikh scholarship and literature, promoted reform ideals similar to those of the Arya Samaj, and was especially effective in improving
education in the Punjab. The TS was also linked with other reform
organizations, such as the Indian Association and the Indian National
Congress, that were devoted to the revival of Indian culture and the
attainment of national self-determination.

Maharajah Ranbir Singh of Kashmir corresponds in many ways
to Morya as described by HPB, and was indubitably a supporter of
her work in India. Because his subjects included Muslims, Buddhists,
Christians, and Sikhs, Ranbir Singh was deeply committed to promoting religious brotherhood. He was a Hindu devoted to the Vedanta
philosophy, but supported translation and publication of scriptures of
all faiths represented in his kingdom. Several other maharajahs, including those of Indore, Faridkot, and Benares, either joined the TS
or lent it support.

Although much of HPB's portrayals of Morya and Koot Hoomi
was designed to mislead, she included enough accurate information to
make a persuasive case for their identities as these historical figures. In
1880, the Mahatmas' letters were full of geographical references to Punjab and Kashmir. But in the next few years, a cover story about their
residence in a Tibetan ashram was promoted, and a number of false
testimonies were concocted as a diversionary tactic. Mahatma letters
gave instructions for this deception, for example, telling HPB's young
Indian disciple Mohini Chatterji to "make it as strong as you can, and
have all the witnesses at Darjeeling and Dehra."[7]

Blavatsky did indeed have connections in Tibet; the Bengali explorer Sarat Chandra Das, who spent more than a year there, was on
intimate terms with Olcott. Under the authorization of the Panchen
Lama's prime minister, Das obtained a large number of authentic
texts, which he seems to have forwarded to HPB through Olcott for

use in her writings. But this rather indirect link to the Panchen Lama's court (situated in Shigatse in southern Tibet) had nothing to do with Morya and Koot Hoomi, although HPB made elaborate efforts to portray her Indian Mahatmas as residents of Shigatse.

Yet in 1883, in the midst of this mythmaking, Olcott and some companions journeyed to Amritsar, Lahore, and Jammu, allegedly directed by Morya and Koot Hoomi, who met them in those places. The historical record shows that they were welcomed to Lahore by Singh Sabha leaders and to Jammu by Ranbir Singh. But improbable claims about Tibet were such successful diversionary tactics that neither the investigator Hodgson nor subsequent writers looked elsewhere for the Mahatmas. While Hodgson's suspicion that HPB and the supposed *chelas* (disciples) of the Masters were engaged in deception was indeed justified, he went further than this. He erroneously concluded that the Masters did not exist and that Blavatsky's mission was to advance Russian interests.

For HPB, Hodgson's denial of the Masters' existence was infinitely preferable to his suspecting the truth behind the disguises, as can be seen from an 1886 letter she wrote to Sinnett:

> I know one thing, that if it came to the worst and Master's truthfulness and notions of honour were to be impeached—then I would go to a *desperate expedient*. I would proclaim publicly that I alone was a liar, a forger, all that Hodgson wants me to appear, that I had indeed INVENTED the Masters and thus would by that "myth" of Master K.H. and M. screen the real K.H. and M. from opprobrium. What saved the situation in the Report is that the Masters are *absolutely denied*. Had Hodgson attempted to throw deception and the idea that *They* were helping, or encouraging or even countenancing a deception by *Their* silence—I would have already come forward and proclaimed myself before the world all that was said of me and disappeared *for ever*.[8]

Blavatsky had several reasons to prefer the accusation of having invented the Masters to that of conspiring with them in deception. She had visited India around 1857 and again in 1869, and had devoted herself to spiritual exploration there as she did everywhere. Some of her acquaintances from earlier visits were involved in her decision to relocate to India in 1878–79 and welcomed her help in opposing the efforts of Western missionaries. But there was also a political aspect to her relations with the Masters that, if exposed, could cause trouble for them as well as for her.

The publicly stated objectives of the TS were genuinely valued by HPB and her Masters in India, Egypt, and the West. As usually stated, these were (1) to form a nucleus of universal brotherhood; (2) to study comparative religion, science, and philosophy; and (3) to investigate the hidden laws of nature and the powers innate in humanity. But underlying these unanimous goals were various hidden agendas. The Masonic and Rosicrucian Masters behind the formation of the TS aimed at promoting HPB as a nineteenth-century successor to Cagliostro. Their main interest was in reviving Western occultism and opposing dogmatic Christianity. After arriving in India, HPB served a second hidden agenda defined by the maharajahs and religious leaders with whom she was secretly allied. Broadly defined, their goals were Indian cultural revival and social reform. But this left plenty of room for conflicting interpretations, as became clear almost immediately with Swami Dayananda. By the time of Hodgson's final report, Ranbir Singh was dead and the Singh Sabha was dividing into hostile factions over the privileges of Sikh aristocrats. Not only would full disclosure involve HPB in political controversy, it would deflate Theosophists' faith in the invulnerability of the Masters. Hodgson's denial of their existence left believers unscathed, and in a sense protected HPB.

But HPB was not entirely satisfied with the resultant impasse, which unfairly stigmatized her as a false claimant to esoteric learning.

In fact her search for occult wisdom had been as thorough and far-reaching as any in history, and she was determined to prove it by making her *Secret Doctrine* the classic of esotericism it indeed became. Although to some extent the success of her later writings assuaged the pain of the Hodgson report, HPB felt entrapped by the myth of the Masters, even though it was largely of her own making.

To call the occultist view of the Masters a myth is not to deny its value or validity, but rather to characterize its function for those who accept it. The alleged writings of the Masters are regarded as sacred scripture; they are seen as eternal truths preserved by a secret world-wide fraternity, conveyed to humanity as it becomes ready to receive them. The mythical version of HPB's relations with the Masters portrays them as a monolithic superhuman fraternity that chose her as its messenger to humanity. Her search ended, according to this version, at age twenty, when she first encountered a mysterious Hindu sage in London. Thenceforth she was a mere instrument in the Masters' hands, revealing their teachings progressively under direct orders. Theosophy was an ancient body of doctrine she discovered whole and passed on intact.

In fact, HPB's life provided continual encounters with spiritual teachers of various traditions and nationalities. Her pilgrimage took her from Masonic Masters to Sufi sheikhs, from Kabbalah to Vedanta, from Spiritualism to Buddhism, in no particular order. From early childhood to the end of her life, she was constantly adding to her store of occult learning. Her Theosophy was a brilliant synthesis of elements from dozens of unrelated sources. But she mythologized her search for the Masters in such a way that her real quest remained secret. Her adolescent fascination with the mysterious world of occult Masonry, in which hidden Masters sent unquestioned orders from unknown Oriental locations, led her to present her experiences according to an elaborate hierarchical model. In truth, her Masters constituted not a stable hierarchy but an ever-evolving network.

Whatever wonders HPB had witnessed in her travels were probably exaggerated in her claims to Olcott and others in America. But
compounding her innate tendency to exaggeration was the desperate
hunger of Olcott and her other disciples for the miraculous. Their need
to believe in godlike Mahatmas led HPB to foster a quasi-polytheistic
myth that she would later regret. A letter she wrote to Franz Hartmann clearly acknowledges the extent to which the Masters of Theosophical lore are imaginary:

> Where you speak of the "army" of the deluded—and the "imag-
> inary" Mahatmas of Olcott—you are absolutely and sadly right.
> Have I not seen the thing for nearly eight years? Have I not
> struggled and fought against Olcott's ardent and gushing imagi-
> nation, and tried to stop him every day of my life? Was he not
> told by me . . . that if he did not see the Masters in their true light,
> and did not cease speaking and enflaming [sic] people's imagina-
> tions, that he would be held responsible for all the evil the Society
> might come to? Was he not told that there were no such Mahat-
> mas, who Rishi-like could hold the Mount Meru on the tip of
> their finger and fly to and fro in their bodies (!!) at their will, and
> who were (or were imagined by fools) more gods on earth than a
> God in Heaven could be, etc., etc.? All this I saw, foresaw, de-
> spaired, fought against, and finally, gave up the struggle in utter
> helplessness.[9]

These protests show a rather distorted memory of her relationship
with Olcott, which had begun with an intense effort by HPB to stim-
ulate the very enthusiasm for the Masters that she later came to regret.
Indeed, in the wake of Hodgson's investigation, Olcott was blaming
HPB for the disgrace caused by the phenomena she had performed in
the Masters' name. In August 1885, she complained to Sinnett that Olcott had been "cautiously admitting that I might have substituted bo-

gus for real phenomena; that I am suffering at times from mental aberration." In her view, this implied Olcott's confessing himself to be "the first and chief confederate in the alleged bogus phenomena."[10] By the time HPB wrote to Hartmann in April 1886, the disadvantages of focusing attention on the Masters had become abundantly clear. In fact, the previous month Olcott had threatened to resign as president of the TS unless she promised "total abandonment of sensationalism" which, he said, had "three-fourths ruined the T.S."[11] But HPB protested that the process had begun innocently enough:

> Well, I told him the whole truth. I said to him that I had known Adepts, the "Brothers," not only in India and beyond Ladakh, but in Egypt and Syria,—for there are "Brothers" there to this day. The names of the "Mahatmas" were not even known at the time, since they are called so only in India. That, whether they were called Rosicrucians, Kabalists, or Yogis—Adepts were every-where Adepts—silent, secret, retiring, and who would never divulge themselves entirely.[12]

Idolatry of the Masters began when Olcott met one in person in Bombay, and increased as the Society's membership grew in India:

> Olcott became crazy. He was like Balaam's she-ass when she saw the angel! Then came Damodar, Servai, and several other fanat-ics, who began calling them "Mahatmas"; and, little by little, the Adepts were transformed into Gods on earth. They began to be appealed to, and made puja [worship] to, and were becoming with every day more legendary and miraculous . . . I saw with terror and anger the false track they were all pursuing. The "Masters," as all thought, must be omniscient, omnipresent, om-nipotent. . . . The idea that the Masters were mortal men, limited even in their great powers, never crossed anyone's mind, though they wrote this themselves repeatedly.[13]

There was more than enough blame to go around, although initially HPB refused to admit her own share:

> Is it Olcott's fault? Perhaps, to a degree. Is it mine? I absolutely deny it, and protest against the accusation. It is no one's fault. Human nature alone, and the failure of modern society and religions to furnish people with something higher and nobler than craving after money and honors—is at the bottom of it. Place this failure on one side, and the mischief and havoc produced in people's brains by modern spiritualism, and you have the enigma solved.[14]

But on further reflection, HPB admitted that her own responsibility for false views of the Masters was greater than Olcott's: "If anyone is to be blamed, it is I. I have desecrated the holy Truth by remaining too passive in the face of all this desecration, brought on by too much zeal and false ideas."[15]

Blavatsky's failure to correct distorted views of her Masters was caused in part by the need to keep their identities hidden. After the Hodgson report, she virtually stopped performing paranormal phenomena and rarely referred to the Masters. She insisted that her *Secret Doctrine* be judged not on the basis of any alleged authority, but on its merits alone. Although she attempted to backtrack from the false image of the Mahatmas she had portrayed, she was unwilling to identify her real sponsors or publicly admit the extent to which they had been mythologized. This must have been due in part to the political roles they played; for example, Thakar Singh's final years were devoted to an anti-British conspiracy to restore his cousin, the deposed Sikh Maharajah Dalip Singh, to his throne. But she must also have feared undoing her life's work and undermining the Theosophical movement if she admitted the all-too-human limitations of the Masters.

Her ambivalence about the issue in her later years is illuminated by a strange decision she made as editor of the Theosophical journal *Lucifer.*

Franz Hartmann, to whom HPB confessed her dismay about the cult of the Mahatmas, had been a leading defender of her during her investigation by the Society for Psychical Research. Born in Germany, Hartmann had been in America for several years when he came in contact with Theosophy in the late 1870s. After joining the Society, he journeyed to India, where he spent nine months at the Adyar head-quarters. There he became embroiled in the struggle with Emma and Alexis Coulomb, whose charges of fraud led to the Hodgson report. He published a booklet responding to the Coulombs' charges, and remained a Theosophist through all the struggles that followed. Yet the tone of HPB's 1886 letter to him shows that he had become sadly disillusioned with the cult of the Masters and the leadership of Olcott.

Three years later, Hartmann's anguish about the imaginary Mahatmas produced a fascinating literary work. *The Talking Image of Urur* is as remarkable for the circumstances of its publication as for its contents. Although it is a bitter satire of Theosophy, the Masters, and HPB, she published it in *Lucifer.* In its preface, Hartmann explains that all the events of his tale actually took place, and that the characters are composites of living people. But, he adds, it "has not been written for the purpose of throwing discredit upon any person who may imagine himself caricatured therein" but rather "with the sole object of showing to what absurdities a merely intellectual research after spiritual truths will lead."[16] He respectfully dedicates the book to his "personal friends and teachers" HPB and Olcott, but one cannot imagine that they were completely pleased with their portrayals.

Hartmann's *roman à clef* concerns a young man named Pancho living in San Francisco who is converted to belief in the Mysterious

Brotherhood of Adepts by Mr. Puffer, a traveling lecturer for the Society for the Distribution of Wisdom. Pancho follows him to the Society's headquarters in Urur, South Africa. The Mysterious Brotherhood's best known members are Rataborumatchi and Krashibashi, powerful adepts who live in a secret enclave in the Libyan desert. The Society is led by an American, Captain Bumpkins, but derives its teachings from a curious talking statue that is the mouthpiece of the Mysterious Brotherhood. The Talking Image answers all questions infallibly with the aid of the adepts, and has attracted the attention of many seekers.

Soon after arriving at Urur, Pancho visits the Talking Image but is perplexed by its messages. At times it takes on an unearthly light and utters profound truths, but most often it reflects the prejudices of the inquirers like a mirror and merely confirms their superstitions. Its wisest utterances are least understood by the believers. When an investigator is sent by the Society for the Discovery of Unknown Sciences, he finds the Urur headquarters in an uproar caused by the housekeeper, Mme. Corneille, and her husband, who have joined forces with missionaries to denounce the Talking Image. At the peak of the controversy, the Image vanishes from Urur. Pancho leaves soon thereafter and at the end of the tale he finds it again, now alone in a small Italian town. When the Image tells him that wisdom that comes from the East is the best and must be accepted, he retorts: "There is only one wisdom, because there is only one truth; and it comes neither from the East nor the West, but from the attainment of self-knowledge."[17] This breaks the spell that has bound the soul of the Talking Image in its inanimate form. After an exchange on the nature of divine truth, the final message of the Talking Image concludes the tale:

"No man can teach another the truth if the truth does not manifest itself in and through him. Do not follow those that in a loud voice claim to be able to show you the truth, but seek for the truth itself. . . ."

"What about the Mysterious Brotherhood?" asked Pancho. He received no answer. Before his eyes a great transformation took place. Brighter and brighter shone the light in the interior of the Image, and the statue grew more ethereal and transparent. It was as if the whole substance of its body had become changed into a cloud of living light. . . . At last even the cloud-like appearance was gone; there was nothing of a material character left; the Image had become all soul—a streak of supernatural glory—which slowly faded away.[18]

When HPB was freed from service to hidden Masters, she entered the most productive part of her career. Only after leaving India did she begin to write the books for which she is best remembered. Hartmann's conclusion expresses his perception of the change undergone by HPB when she abandoned sensational claims and phenomena and could focus on conveying the truths gleaned from her years of search.

Although later active in Masonry, Rosicrucianism, and the Ordo Templi Orientis, Hartmann remained a Theosophist. He established an independent Theosophical Society in Germany, fiercely opposed to the cult of the Masters as it flourished in the Adyar TS under the leadership of Annie Besant.

In March 1889, HPB wrote an article for *Lucifer* entitled "On Pseudo-Theosophy," in which she responded to a story in the *Daily News* about Hartmann's novel. The newspaper reported that some Theosophists were distressed by its publication and suggested that "the misgivings that have been awakened will not easily be laid to rest."[19] HPB replies that she is publishing Hartmann's tale precisely in order to awaken misgivings in those who should recognize themselves in it. She adds: "This proceeding of ours—rather unusual, to be sure, for editors—to publish a satire, which seems to the short-sighted to be aimed at their gods and parties only because they are unable to sense the underlying philosophy and moral in them, has created quite a stir."[20]

But although some are offended, HPB wonders, "If 'Mme. Blavatsky'—presumably the 'Talking Image'—does not object to finding herself represented as a kind of mediumistic poll parrot, why should other 'theosophists' object?" She adds: "If the first object of our Society be not to study one's own self, but to find fault with all except that self, then, indeed, the T.S. is doomed to become—and it already has in certain centres—a Society for mutual admiration; a fit subject for the satire of so acute an observer as we know the author of 'The Talking Image of Urur' to be."[21] This was as close to an endorsement of Hartmann's views as she was to come, but her publication of Hartmann's novel is clear confirmation that her adept sponsors were far more human and less godlike than the imaginary Mahatmas he satirized.

In an unpublished article written in the last year of her life, HPB concluded nonetheless that her publicizing of the Masters had done more good than harm:

One of the chief factors in the reawakening of Aryavrta [India] which has been part of the work of the Theosophical Society, was the ideal of the Masters. But owing to want of judgment, discretion, and discrimination, and the liberties taken with their names and Personalities, great misconceptions arose concerning them. I was under the most solemn oath and pledge never to reveal the whole truth to anyone. . . . All that I was permitted to reveal was, that there existed somewhere such great men; that some of Them were Hindus; that they were learned as none others . . . and also that I was a chela of one of them. . . . They were referred to as "Mahatmas." . . . These early misconceptions notwithstanding, the idea of the Masters, and belief in them, has already brought its good fruit in India. Their chief desire was to preserve the true religious and philosophic spirit of ancient India; to defend the ancient wisdom contained in its Darsanas and Upanishads against the systematic assaults of the missionaries, and finally to reawaken the dormant ethical and patriotic spirit in those youths in whom it had almost disappeared.[22]

In a less hopeful mood, HPB lamented the undesirable effects of her life work in her last book, *The Key to Theosophy:*

> Every bogus swindling society, for commercial purposes, now claims to be guided and directed by "Masters," often supposed to be far higher than ours. . . . [H]ad we acted on the wise principle of silence, instead of rushing into notoriety and publishing all we knew and heard, such desecration would never have occurred. . . . But it is useless to grieve over what is done, and we can only suffer in the hope that our indiscretions may have made it a little easier for others to find the way to these Masters.[23]

Although pretended agents of the Masters are now more numerous than ever, access to genuine teachers of authentic esoteric traditions has increased at a comparable rate. Both HPB's hopes and fears about the influence of Theosophy have been fully confirmed in the century since she wrote these words.

Further Reading

My research on the Theosophical Masters is reported in detail in *The Masters Revealed: Madame Blavatsky and the Myth of the Great White Lodge* (1994) and *Initiates of Theosophical Masters* (Albany, NY: 1995), both published by the State University of New York Press. *Tournament of Shadows,* by Karl Meyer and Shareen Blair Brysac (New York: Counterpoint, 1999), gives the fullest account to date of the Great Game between the British and Russian empires in Asia, including some discussion of Blavatsky and her Masters. *Shadows and*

Elephants, by Edward Hower (Wellfleet, MA: Leapfrog Press, 2002), a novel based on years of research on Blavatsky, draws on the thesis that the Masters were fictionalized versions of real persons. *The Maharajah's Box,* by Christy Campbell (New York: Overlook Press, 2002), is a detailed investigation of the conspiracy surrounding Dalip Singh, and provides new evidence of Theosophical involvement.

17

THE APOCALYPTIC STEINER

Rudolf Steiner's teachings predict the growth of humanity's
"spiritual organs" and the spiritualization of matter. Does the
book of Revelation contain the keys to our future destiny?

Anastasy Tousomou

The monumental work of the Western esotericist Rudolf
Steiner is overwhelming in its sheer magnitude. His more
than six thousand lectures, collected into approximately four
hundred volumes, can be quite intimidating to the first-time reader.
The voluminous scope of Steiner's contributions to the fields of art,
medicine, education, organic farming, philosophy, and religion can
lead one on a labyrinthine journey into Western esotericism, and cause
one to lose sight of the center of his work. But diligent and constant
reference to the source and center of Steiner's work reaps its rewards.
Rudolf Steiner's work hinges on his unique Christology and the systematic pursuit of spiritual knowledge grounded in Christ. Every
practical result of Steiner's work can be seen in the light of this
Christology and in his blueprint for human history and its evolutionary
destiny.

Born in 1861 in Austria, Steiner was educated in philosophy and the natural sciences. He is best known for his founding of the Anthropo-sophical Society and its many daughter movements, such as Bio-Dynamic agriculture, Waldorf education, and Eurythmy, and for his contributions to the fields of Goethean science, homeopathic medi-cine, and nutrition. Up to the time of the Anthroposophical Society's formation, Steiner had been the leader of the German section of the Theosophical Society, but he broke with Annie Besant over Krishna-murti's purported reincarnation of Christ. Although Rudolf Steiner's system of Anthroposophy is sometimes confused with its Theosophi-cal parent, it actually differs greatly in its essence and purpose. While Besant considered Christianity to be one of the Lesser Mysteries, the Incarnation of Christ became the historic crux of Rudolf Steiner's pic-ture of cosmic evolution.

In Steiner's time the Theosophical Society was the only public vehi-cle that was open to the kind of Western, esoteric Christianity that he taught from the outset of his leadership in the German section of that organization. The Esoteric Section, or E.S., of the German Theosoph-ical Society practiced a firm-footed Western path with roots in Rosi-crucianism and Johannine Christianity. The recorded German E.S. material contains lectures on cosmology and mantrams, as well as breath and visualization exercises. A large section of this material also deals with Freemasonry, and has recently been published in English under the title *The Temple Legend* (Rudolf Steiner Press). The content of the lectures reflects the E.S. membership's interest in the roots of Western occultism, particularly in the biblical legends of Cain and Abel and of Hiram and Solomon. The theme of two races of human-ity—one race of priests, shepherds, and gardeners, and another of kings, artisans, and builders—is basic to Steiner's anthropology as well as his Christology. Steiner does not see in Jesus Christ a gnostic syzygy of the male and female, but rather the reconciliation of two races of humankind—the Abelite and the Cainite, the Abrahamic and the

Nimrodic. The more receptive, feminine lineage is imprinted with divine revelation; the more active, masculine race is comprised of those who "take heaven by the force" of their own initiative. This characterization of two human types culminates in Steiner's series of lectures entitled Karmic Relationships, in which the leading representative personalities of the two streams are portrayed as "Platonic" and "Aristotelian" souls.

The E.S. can best be studied through the notes of the participants, which are slowly surfacing in German and English manuscripts. A minor but much-talked-about incident in the history of the E.S. is that of the so-called M.D., or Misraim-Dienst (Rite of Misraim), also referred to as the F.M., or Freimaurerei (Freemasons). A small group of E.S. members who had an intense interest in Freemasonry established a lodge with ties to Theodore Reuss and the O.T.O. (Ordo Templi Orientis, a magical lodge later headed by Aleister Crowley). Although this link has been much discussed in print by sensationalists of the occult press, it was, in actuality, a tepid affair. Rudolf Steiner's Memphis and Misraim workings consisted of lecture material and rituals improvised by Steiner in accordance with the number and nature of the participants, both human and angelic. Cursory examination of this M.D. material reveals little in common with orthodox O.T.O. ritual, yet it is much misunderstood and misrepresented.

The work of the Misraim lodge was interrupted by the outbreak of World War I, and when the war was over, Steiner declined to continue it. Disappointed, a number of the members persisted, and the work continues today on a limited basis in northern Germany. One can only imagine that Steiner's extemporaneous form of ritual has been replaced by the authority of manuscripts and the reiteration of old material.

There is presently quite an interest among Anthroposophists in Freemasonry, most notably in Switzerland, near the center of the General Anthroposophical Society in Dornach near Basel. This interest is not surprising. Rudolf Steiner made some very important statements concerning the craft and its mission in the world. According to Steiner, the actual rituals of Freemasonry contain the secrets of the future of human evolution. Much can be said about this future in the light of so-called "mechanical occultism," which works at harnessing the subterranean and elemental forces of the earth. Steiner spoke in intricate detail concerning these mysteries in connection with the Johannine Book of Revelation.

Rudolf Steiner described a cosmos much like that of H. P. Blavatsky, a cosmos ordered into the seven familiar Neoplatonic planetary spheres. These spheres are populated by the nine hierarchic choirs found in Western angelology. Each of these choirs of angels has its own evolution, which interpenetrates the evolution of the other choirs. All the choirs of angels and archangels, however, look to earth, where a cosmic drama of utmost importance unfolds: the grappling of humanity with material substance. This drama of man's involvement with matter parallels the many mythological accounts of the Fall.

The Fall of Man and the resultant acquisition of human self-consciousness and human freedom are major themes in Steiner's works. In his view, the development of agriculture, metallurgy, engineering, and writing were all inspired by this Promethean independence. Evil was also necessary, according to Steiner, providing the opportunity for temptation and resistance in order to further man's spiritual growth. The great religiocultural figures such as Rama, Zarathustra, Hermes, and Moses took measures to realign humanity with the cosmic blueprint. As the very crux of history, the Being of Christ incarnated in order to seed the process of matter's revivification and to give mankind the power to consciously impart spirit to matter. In Steiner's cosmology, man strives upward from the depths of matter in an expansion of his faculties; the spiritual world descends to him to complete the divine-human nexus. The embodiment of this union of ascending and descending processes is the incarnation of the Godman, Jesus

Christ, and the reunification of matter and spirit (originally divided in the Fall).

Steiner's universe is a cosmos confined spatially to the seven planetary spheres and temporally to the world of created time. He speaks little of the cosmos outside of the sphere of Saturn and says nothing of the timeless world of eternity, leaving such descriptions to his esotericist colleagues of the Platonist school. Christ is never regarded by Steiner as the Second Person of the Christian Trinity; instead, he pictures Christ as a hierarchic being at the rank of an Elohim, like the Zoroastrian sun god or the created Christ of Arian Christianity.

ANTHROPOSOPHY'S ESOTERIC PATH AND ITS SCHOOL

The fundamental practice of Anthroposophy consists of basic exercises that school taught for the development of the "spiritual organs," preventing them from becoming one-sided and malformed by self-will. The meditations given by Steiner are mantrams that link both the spiritual world and the world of nature within the being of man. The human being rises through three stages of supersensible ascent: imagination, inspiration, and intuition, marked respectively by spiritual vision, spiritual hearing, and spiritual communion with angelic beings. The present repository of this work is the so-called High School of Spiritual Science, centered at the Goetheanum in Dornach, Switzerland. Originally planned to comprise three grades of esoteric training—the Michael Class, the Sophia Class, and the Christ Class—the school presently consists of one level, referred to as "The First Class." Steiner's premature death in 1925 prevented the establishment of the second and third classes.

RUDOLF STEINER AND THE JOHANNINE REVELATION

Steiner's most well-known contributions are his practical techniques in the fields of education, the arts, medicine, and farming. It is in his work on the book of Revelation, however, that Steiner waxes most profound. His interpretation of this biblical book supplies much of the missing content of the Masonic rituals mentioned earlier, not in their gestures and circumambulations, but rather in secrets of human and earthly evolution, mechanical occultism, and the alchemical transformation of the earth within the pleroma of Christ. For Steiner, the book of Revelation pulls back the veil from the fullness of Jesus Christ, allowing mankind to witness the outpouring of His very Being. Christ is thus revealed as the Ancient of Days, with white hair, feet of brass, and a sword proceeding from his mouth—the future archetype of mankind. In Steiner's interpretation, the Kabbalistic imagery of the book of Revelation describes the way of mechanical occultism, the way of power that is needed for the transformation of matter, and the secrets of the body's resurrection.

The Revelation is a two-edged sword: a critical event that quickens the righteous and smites the wicked. In Steiner's terms, the righteous are those who receive and transform the life-giving etheric forces coming to them from Nature. The wicked are those who reject this path of transformation and exploit Nature in order to perpetuate the status quo of material existence devoid of spirit. It is only the development of the inner faculties, the "spiritual sense organs," that will allow humanity to pass from its present condition to that of the Son of Man. The three aspects of spiritual development are spiritual sight, or imagination (represented by the Sealed Book), spiritual hearing, or inspiration (represented by Angelic Trumpets), and spiritual union, or intuition (represented by the Vials of Wrath).

The Steinerian eschatology would be incomplete without the most important single event designated in the Anthroposophic corpus: the Second Coming of Christ. In keeping with his emphasis on raising the etheric organs to supersensible perception, and his emphasis on the uniqueness of Christ's Incarnation as the crux of history, Rudolf Steiner categorically rejects any notion of a *physical* Second Coming. Steiner's vision of the parousia is instead an *etheric* Return of Christ, which will appear first in the realm of Nature. The return will initially be noticed by Nature mystics and occultists, but the experience will spread gradually to the rest of mankind. According to Steiner, a definite change in Nature will occur (one that he foresaw as starting in the 1930s). Mankind as a whole will be confronted with the events of the Coming of Christ in the etheric realm, as its consciousness gradually evolves and flourishes, or degenerates and withers. Thus Christ comes again, as He left, in the clouds of the etheric world.

What distinguishes Rudolf Steiner's vision of Christ's return is the strictly etheric nature of this event. For many, such as Edgar Cayce, Alice Bailey, and Benjamin Creme, a physical coming is awaited. This presents the possibility of mistaking one spiritual being for another: Anti-Christ for Christ. In Steiner's vision, as well as that of orthodox Christianity, Judaism, and Islam, there will be one who "comes in his own name" and who will do battle with the Prophet Elijah. He will come as a great statesman, a peacemaker, a doer of miracles. His presence will dazzle the crowds and divert their attention from "the Way, the Truth and the Life." His promise of peace, bread, and life is well illustrated in Vladimir Soloviev's *The Antichrist,* an apocalyptic tale that illuminates the central themes of the Steinerian eschatology.

The experience of the Etheric Christ will give new life to those who recognize Him. A process of enlivening the spiritual organs by their permeation with the Christ substance will lead to their eventual resurrection. Humanity will pass to the state of the Son of Man through the etherization of the blood and the transformation of the reproductive organs. Humanity will give birth to a new form whose generative functions will no longer center in the reproductive organs, but instead in a transformed larynx. The solar plexus, the heart, and the larynx will be transformed by the Creative Word and mystical participation in Christ's etheric body. An alchemical *circulatio* (etherization) of the reenlivened blood will raise the human larynx to a state that will empower it to express itself spiritually, that is, to recreate itself in a higher form, "like unto a Son of Man." Not only will this process link one with the Etheric Christ, but also with the realm of Nature and of all created being. Mankind will recognize its own hypostatic union within itself and its union with all Creation. It will no longer be subject to the stars, but will contain them within its breast.

And in the midst of the seven candlesticks one like unto the Son of man, clothed with a garment down to the foot, and girt around the paps with a golden girdle.

His head and his hairs were white like wool, as white as snow; and his eyes were as a flame of fire;

And his feet like unto fine brass, as if they burned in a furnace; and his voice as the sound of many waters.

And he had in his right hand seven stars; and out of his mouth went a sharp two-edged sword; and his countenance was as the sun shineth in his strength.

And when I saw him, I fell at his feet as dead. And he laid his right hand upon me, saying unto me, Fear not; I am the first and the last;

I am he that liveth and was dead; and behold, I am alive forevermore, Amen; and have the keys of hell and of death. (Rev. 1:13–18)

Rudolf Steiner's Christology and eschatology indicate the unfulfilled tasks of Freemasonry and inner alchemy. The obscure symbols of Masonry and the Apocalypse come into focus in the light of Christ's interaction with our spiritual senses and the unveiling and outpouring of His Being. Steiner integrates the evolution of the individual with that of all Creation.

Steiner rejects a Montanist Lordship over the untransformed earth. Instead, he heralds a more subtle, alchemical experience of the Second Coming, a regenerative process for both man and the earth. The Christ dispenses His own Being in order to revivify Creation and to help raise our inner senses to the spirit, so that we may imbue matter with spirit and transform it. Thus, as in the days of Adam, will we regain our stewardship over the earth.

RENÉ SCHWALLER
DE LUBICZ
AND THE INTELLIGENCE
OF THE HEART

One of the twentieth century's great esotericists was certain that

ancient Egypt was based on a way of inner knowing. He dedicated

his life to making that way available to the serious seeker.

Gary Lachman

René Schwaller de Lubicz (1887–1961) is known to English readers primarily for his work in uncovering the spiritual and cosmological insights of ancient Egypt. In books like *Esotericism and Symbol, The Temple in Man, Symbol and the Symbolic, The Egyptian Miracle,* and the monumental *The Temple of Man*—whose long-awaited English translation has finally appeared—Schwaller de Lubicz argued, among other things, that Egyptian civilization is much older than orthodox Egyptologists suggest, a claim receiving renewed interest through the recent work of Graham Hancock and Robert Bauval.

But if this wasn't enough to place him securely beyond the pale, he also argued that the core of ancient Egyptian culture was a fundamental insight into "the laws of creation." Everything about Egyptian civilization, de Lubicz claimed, from the construction of the pyramids to the shape of a beer mug, was motivated by a central, metaphysical vision about the nature of cosmic harmony, and an awareness of mankind's place in the evolution of consciousness.

But as his translator Deborah Lawlor remarks, Schwaller de Lubicz's Egyptian studies are only a part of his overall work as a metaphysician and philosopher.

Born in Alsace-Lorraine, then part of Germany, René Schwaller grew up in a polyglot atmosphere. (He was later given the title "de Lubicz" by the Lithuanian poet and diplomat O.V. de Lubicz Milosz, for his efforts on behalf of Lithuania in the aftermath of World War I.) The territory has oscillated between French and German rule many times since Schwaller's birth, and this Franco-Germanic blend lends a curious characteristic to his work. As Christopher Bamford suggests, Schwaller thought in German but wrote in French.[1] Added to the inherent difficulties of expressing nonlinear, "living" insights in "dead" linear language, this odd combination places many obstacles before a first-time reader. As he wrote apropos the insights into "functional consciousness" presented in his truly "hermetic" work, *Nature Word* (Verbe Nature), "Nature had shown me a great mountain, crowned with a peak of immaculate whiteness, but she was unable to teach me the way leading to it."[2]

Readers wishing to grasp Schwaller's insights may feel that they, too, have found themselves at the foot of a very steep mountain. This challenging prospect would not have fazed Schwaller. He believed knowledge was the right only of those willing to make the effort to achieve it, the elite who would endure suffering in their pursuit of wisdom. This sensibility influenced his political views as well.

EARLY YEARS, BERGSON, AND MATISSE

Schwaller's father was a chemist—apparently wealthy—and the young René grew up in a world of science, nature, and art. Dreamy walks in the Alsatian forests followed hours spent painting and "experimenting." He was also granted two peculiar experiences. In 1894, at the age of seven, Schwaller had a kind of mystical insight into the nature of the divine. This glimpse of metaphysical reality would return seven years later when, at fourteen, he experienced another insight, this one into matter. "What is the origin of matter?" the budding metaphysician asked himself. The question occupied him the rest of his life.

In his late teens, Schwaller left home and went to Paris. He studied painting under Henri Matisse, who at that time was deeply influenced by the work of the most famous philosopher of the age, Henri Bergson. Today Bergson gets little more than a mention in books on the history of philosophy, but in the years before World War I he was world renowned, immensely influential for his philosophy of intuition. Bergson argued against the static, mechanistic perception of the world, in favor of a living vital participation with its essence, the famous *élan vital* or life force. He was also something of a mystic. In one of his last books, *The Two Sources of Morality and Religion* (1932), written after his popularity had declined, Bergson made his famous remark that the universe was a machine for "making gods," a formulation Schwaller would not have found much fault with.

SCIENCE AND THEOSOPHY

Along with Matisse and Bergson, Schwaller came under the influence of the new physics of Albert Einstein and Max Planck. Like many people today, Schwaller believed that the strange world of quantum physics and relativity opened the door to a universe more in line with the cosmologies of the ancients, and less compatible with the Newtonian clockwork world of the nineteenth century. He was especially stimulated by the idea of complementarity, developed by the Danish physicist Niels Bohr, and the uncertainy principle of Werner Heisenberg.

Bohr sought to end the debate over the nature of light—whether it was best described as a wave or as a particle—by opting for a position that would see it as both. Heisenberg's "uncertainty"—which caused Einstein to retort famously that "God does not play dice with the universe"—argued that we cannot know both the position and the speed of an elementary particle: pinpointing one obscures the other.

Schwaller would agree with Einstein about God's attitude toward gambling. But he appreciated that complementarity and uncertainty demand we stretch our minds beyond the "either/or" of syllogistic logic, in order to glean an understanding of how reality works. Complementarity and uncertainty ask us to hold mutually exclusive ideas together—the basic idea behind a Zen koan. The result, Schwaller knew, can be an illogical but illuminating insight.

This "simultaneity of opposite states" plays a great part in Schwaller's understanding of Egyptian hieroglyphics. It characterizes what he calls *symbolique,* a way of holding together the object of sense perception and the content of inner knowing in a kind of creative polarity. When the Egyptians saw the hieroglyph of a bird, he argued, they knew it was a sign for the actual, individual creature, but they also knew it was a symbol of the "cosmic function" that creature exemplified—flight—as well as all the myriad characteristics associated with it. Hieroglyphics did not merely designate; they evoked. As he wrote in *Symbol and the Symbolic,* "The observation of a simultaneity of mutually contradictory states . . . demonstrates the existence of two forms of intelligence"[3]—an idea the early twentieth-century philosopher Alfred North Whitehead would discuss, with many similarities to Schwaller's thought, in his book *Symbolism: Its Meaning and Effect* (1927).

Our rational, scientific intelligence is of the mind and the senses.

The other, whose most total expression Schwaller eventually located in the civilization of ancient Egypt, is of "the heart." This search for the "intelligence of the heart" became Schwaller's life work.

Schwaller believed the appearance of the new physics indicated mankind was moving toward a massive shift in awareness, an idea he shared with his near-contemporary Jean Gebser. He related this to the precession of the equinoxes and the coming Age of Aquarius. But he also believed that science alone couldn't provide the deepest insights into the true character of the world. For this, he argues, a new kind of consciousness is necessary.

He sought signs of this new consciousness among less mainstream thinkers. In 1913–14, Schwaller was active in French Theosophical groups and, one suspects, in occult circles in Paris in general. He read widely in Madame Blavatsky and other occult thinkers, and published a series of fascinating if obscure articles on the philosophy of science in *Le Theosophe*. Soon after, in 1917, at the age of thirty, he published his first book, *A Study of Numbers,* a Pythagorean essay on the metaphysical meaning of mathematics.

The book's central idea is at the heart of Schwaller's thought: the inexplicable splitting—or "scission," as he calls it—of the unmanifest One, the Absolute, into the many—a question that, in a less mystical manner, occupies many leading cosmologists today.

For Schwaller this "irrational" eruption of absolute unity into the world of space and time is the central mystery of existence, the primal secret that will forever elude the simplifying grasp of the purely cerebral mind. Our rational mind is unable to grasp the central mystery, he argues, because our "sensory organization clearly seems to be imperfect." This condition can only be alleviated through a "perfecting of consciousness,"[4] something, he would later argue, the ancient Egyptians knew all about. "I earnestly anticipate the time when an enlightened being will be able to bring the world proof of the mystery of the beginning," he wrote in *Sacred Science.*

ALCHEMY AND FULCANELLI

Dissatisfied with the scientific prejudices of the present, Schwaller sought kindred spirits in the past. The study of alchemy fed his appetite for spiritual knowledge. Unlike many drawn to the occult, Schwaller's interest in science gave him a hard-edged, practical mind, unsatisfied with vague talk of higher worlds. Esotericism, he believed, should include factual knowledge of how the world worked; he rejected Jung's interpretation of alchemy as a purely psychic affair. Alchemy was a spiritual practice involving the consciousness of the alchemist, but it also involved objective insights into the structure of matter. This belief in the reality of objective knowledge fueled Schwaller's later investigations into Egyptian civilization.

He was fascinated with the esoteric secrets of Gothic architecture and became acquainted with the man whose name is most associated with the "mystery of the the cathedrals," Fulcanelli. Sometime between 1918 and 1920 Schwaller met Fulcanelli in Montparnasse. Fulcanelli had gathered a band of disciples around him, called, aptly, "The Brothers of Heliopolis." (Schwaller would later claim that the word "alchemy" meant "out of Egypt.") Alchemy had found a home in the strange world of the Parisian occult underground, and Fulcanelli and the Brothers of Heliopolis studied the works of the great alchemists, like Nicolas Flammel and Basil Valentinus.

Fulcanelli and Schwaller met often and discussed the Great Work, the transmutation of matter, a possibility that the recent advances in atomic theory seemed to bring closer to reality. Then one day, Fulcanelli told Schwaller about a manuscript he had stolen from a Paris bookshop. While cataloguing an ancient book for a bookseller, Fulcanelli discovered a strange piece of writing: a six-page manuscript in fading ink, describing, Fulcanelli claimed, the importance of color in the alchemical process. But, said Schwaller, when it came to alchemy,

Fulcanelli was a materialist, and so he didn't grasp the true nature of color. Schwaller enlightened him. Tired of the distractions of Paris, Schwaller moved to Grasse, in the south of France, where he invited Fulcanelli to join him in an alchemical retreat. There, after much work, they performed a successful opus, involving the secrets of "alchemical stained glass." The peculiarly evocative reds and blues of the rose windows of cathedrals like the unearthly Chartres had eluded artisans since the Middle Ages. In Grasse, Schwaller and Fulcanelli may have cracked the formula.

But there was tension between the two, and the suspicion exists that Fulcanelli stole more than a manuscript from a bookseller. The ideas for his most famous work, *The Mystery of the Cathedrals* (1925), are said to have been taken from Schwaller de Lubicz. Fulcanelli returned to Paris and, against Schwaller's advice, tried to perfom their work again. He wasn't successful. This was, Schwaller claims, because Fulcanelli left out essential ingredients known only to him. Ignoring Schwaller's warnings, Fulcanelli persisted in performing the work in Paris. But his strange death from gangrene, a day before he was to reveal the secret to his students, brought an end to his opus.

ESOTERIC POLITICS

Schwaller found himself moving toward more political methods of embodying esoteric wisdom. He had already met the mystical poet O. V. de Lubicz Milosz, who had bestowed on him a knighthood. Heraldry and chivalric virtue became central items in Schwaller's personal philosophy. As he wrote in *Nature Word*, "The proper path leads you first in search of your 'Totem,' that is to a spiritual Heraldry." This is because "you cannot step into the shoes of another person, for you are yourself a whole, a particular aspect of universal Consciousness."[5] He had also received his mystical name *Aor*, "intellectual light" in Hebrew. In later years, his students would address him in this way.

Esotericism demands one not only deal with esoteric truth intellectually, but as a living practice. Around this time, Schwaller took this maxim to heart, and set out to bring to post–World War I French politics some of the values and ideals of esotericism.

It was not an uncommon idea in the Europe devastated by World War I. Rudolf Steiner had written something of a political bestseller with his book on the restructuring of Europe, *The Threefold Commonwealth* (1919). But Schwaller's political views were very different from Steiner's. Les Veilleurs ("The Watchmen," or "Vigilant Ones"), the political society Schwaller and Milosz began, espoused a decidedly conservative and elitist philosophy. Aside from a few exceptions, this seems common to many occult thinkers at that time, from W. B. Yeats to the more dubious individuals making up the notorious Thule Society. (Oddly enough, Rudolf Hess, a member of the Thule Society, was also one of "The Vigilant Ones.") Isha Schwaller de Lubicz, Schwaller's wife (herself the author of a strange work of Egyptian esoterica, *Her Bak*) wrote that the aims of Les Veilleurs included "the common defense of the principles of human rights . . . the supreme safeguards of . . . independence."[6]

Yet according to André VandenBroeck, author of *Al-Kemi: Hermetic, Occult, Political, and Private Aspects of R. A. Schwaller de Lubicz* (1987), these sentiments were mixed with less democratic views—as well as a taste for dark shirts, riding pants, and boots, a questionable fashion statement in the years leading up to Hitler. A distaste for modern society and civilization runs throughout Schwaller's writings, a dissatisfaction with "mass man," a Nietzschean disdain of "the herd" he shares with other esoteric thinkers like Julius Evola and René Guénon. It's clear that individuals like Schwaller would find our increasingly lowest-common-denominator society revolting, and we must see his interest in the pharaonic theocracy of ancient Egypt in light of his belief in the absolute value of the individual consciousness in a time of increasing spiritual and cultural mediocrity. But

Schwaller's belief that contemporary human beings are by and large degenerate and his faith in an esoteric elite preparing for a spiritual renaissance often smack unappetizingly of less philosophically informed attempts to reestablish "traditional values" in the modern world.

Schwaller soon realized that politics are an unwieldy vehicle for truth, and accepted that a literal theocracy wasn't feasible in his time. From the chivalric Les Veilleurs, he moved to a more withdrawn, communal approach. In the 1920s, René and Isha moved to Switzerland and established Station Scientific Suhalia, a center for research in a variety of scientific and alchemical studies. Physics, chemistry, microphotography, homeopathy, astronomy, wookworking, printing, weaving, glassmaking, and theatre all found a place in Suhalia. There Schwaller developed a motor that ran on vegetable oil, which he hoped would help France use less petrol, an ecological vision ahead of its time. A ship designed according to the "principle of number and proportion" showed considerable capacities for speed and balance. At the same time he studied botany, and perfected his method of producing "alchemical glass."

Also at Suhalia, Schwaller's views on the evolution of consciousness began to coalesce. In a book distributed to his students called *L'Appel du Feu* (1926), he recorded a series of inspirations via a higher intelligence he called "Aor." These revealed to him the true significance of time, space, measure, and harmony. The basic insight was to think simply, to abstract oneself from time and space, and to "consider only the aspect common to everything and every living impulse." As he would later write, "to cultivate oneself to be simple and to see simply is the first task of anyone wishing to approach the sacred symbolism of Ancient Egypt."[7] This is necessary because "the obvious blinds us," the obvious being our perception of the world via cerebral consciousness alone, which divides, analyzes, and "granulates" experience—Bergson's "static perception." Schwaller would later discover that the Egyptians associated this type of consciousness with the "evil" god Set; its opposite, the "intelligence of the heart," they associated with Horus.

Schwaller claimed that the knowledge he received at Suhalia was from a past life. Like Plato, Schwaller believed that all real knowledge is a kind of re-membering—a bringing back together what had been separated, a reparation of the "primordial scission."

Suhalia continued until 1929, when finances caused Schwaller to shut down. The next eight years were spent at Grasse, and aboard his yacht. Two years of comparative solitude in Palma de Mallorca ended with the outbreak of the Spanish Civil War. The moment seemed right to follow up an idea Isha and René had toyed with for some time—a journey to Egypt.

LUXOR AND CONSCIOUS MAN

Ironically, it was Isha, not René, who first felt the pull of Egypt. Concerned with alchemy, matter, and the evolution of consciousness, Schwaller hadn't thought much of it. But Isha knew they had to go. In 1936, on a visit to the tomb of Rameses IX in Alexandria, Schwaller had a kind of revelation. A picture of the pharoah showed him represented as the hypotenuse of a right-angled triangle with the proportions 3:4:5; his upraised arm added another unit. Schwaller thought: the Pythagorean theorem, centuries before Pythagoras was born. From the picture it was clear the knowledge of the Gothic masons had its roots in ancient Egypt. For the next fifteen years, until 1951, Schwaller de Lubicz remained in Egypt, investigating the evidence for what he believed was an ancient system of psychological, cosmological, and spiritual knowledge.

Most of Schwaller's work was done at the temple at Luxor, his study of its remarkable architecture and design a natural outcome of his early fascination with the mystery of numbers. On his first visit in 1937, Schwaller was hit with a tremendous insight. The temple, with its strange, "crooked" alignments, was, he was certain, a conscious exercise in the laws of harmony and proportion. He called it "The Parthenon of Egypt"—somewhat anachronistically, since he believed Luxor was concrete proof that the Egyptians understood the laws of harmony and proportion before the Greeks.

Schwaller searched for evidence of the golden section, phi.[8] If the golden section had been used, this would prove the Egyptians had knowledge of it much earlier than the Greeks, a revelation that alone would cause an uproar in orthodox Egyptology. But as John Anthony West points out in *The Serpent and the Sky* (1978), a study of Schwaller de Lubicz, phi is more than a central item in classical architecture. It's the mathematical archetype of the manifest universe, the means by which we have an "asymmetrical," "lumpy" world of galaxies and planets, and not a bland, homogenous sameness, a question that contemporary cosmologists are concerned with. Schwaller linked phi to the orbits of the planets, the proportions of Gothic cathedrals, and the forms of plants and animals. It was a "form constant," a blueprint for reality, a law of creation. And the Egyptians knew it.

The Egyptians knew much else: the precession of the equinoxes, the circumference of the globe, the secrets of pi: the knowledge of the Egyptians indeed made the Greeks seem like children. Their forgotten mathematical wisdom led Schwaller increasingly to realize that Egyptian civilization must be far older than we suspect—the clear evidence of water erosion on the Sphinx also suggests that. He concluded that their knowledge may have been inherited from vanished Atlantis. But more important than any of those conclusions was his growing conviction that the Egyptians had a radically different consciousness from ours. They viewed the world symbolically, seeing in nature a "writing" conveying truths about the metaphysical forces behind creation—"the Neters," as Egyptian gods are called. It was a vision Schwaller believed we desperately need to regain.

At the center of this vision was Conscious Man, the King. For the ancient Egyptians, Conscious Man was the crown and aim of the universe, a perception many nature-centered mystics would dispute. But Conscious Man was not "man as we know him." He was the individual in whom the "intelligence of the heart" has awakened, one who has had the experience of "functional consciousness."

FUNCTIONAL CONSCIOUSNESS

Schwaller believed Luxor was a kind of living organism, a colossal compendium of esoteric truth, whose every detail, from its total design down to its very materials, voiced one central revelation: that Conscious Man was the goal of cosmic evolution. "Each individual type in Nature is a stage in the cosmic embryology which culminates in man,"[9] he wrote. Different species, Schwaller believed, developed various "functions"—what the Egyptians called "Neters," and we translate as "gods"—which have their apotheosis and integration in Conscious Man.

The essence of Schwaller's evolutionism has to do with what he calls "functional consciousness," an idea we can benefit from understanding, regardless of our opinions of elites or theocracies. And although Schwaller developed his ideas about functional consciousness in an Egyptian context, that context is ultimately not necessary. The essence of those ideas goes back to Bergson and "intuition." Needless to say, Schwaller took this basic insight and, with his Egyptian revelations, developed an original, powerful, and imaginatively thrilling symbolic system.

"Functional consciousness" is a way of knowing reality from the inside. Schwaller believed ancient Egypt was based on this inner knowing, very unlike our own outer-oriented one. The ancient Egyptians, he argued, were aware of the limitations of purely cerebral consciousness, the Sethian mind that "granulates" experience into fragments of time and space, and that is behind our increasing abuse of nature and each other. Granulated experience produces our familiar world of

disconnected things, each a kind of "island reality." From this perspective, when I look at the world, I see a foreign, alien landscape,
which I can know only by taking apart and analyzing it. As the poet
Wordsworth wrote, "We murder to dissect."

But as Schwaller wrote in *Nature Word,* "The Universe is wholly activity." There is another way of knowing, one very similar to Taoist
forms of perception, that can heal the ruptures of cerebral consciousness, without recourse to dubious ideas of elites or theocracies. In a section called "The Way," Schwaller advises us to "leave all dialectic
behind and follow the path of the Powers." Poetically, he continues by
calling on us to

> *Tumble with the rock which falls from*
>   *the mountain.*
> *Seek light and rejoice with the rosebud*
>   *about to open:*
>
>   . . .
>
> *labour with the parsimonious ant;*
>   *gather honey with the bee;*
>   *expand in space with the ripening fruit;*[10]

All of those injunctions are classic examples of the kind of "knowing from the inside" that Bergson had in mind in his talk on intuition.
In this way, we participate with the world, rather than hold it at arm's
length, objectifying it, as modern science is prone to do. With recent
developments in genetics, this "objectification" is now dangerously focused on ourselves.

My aim is not to reduce Schwaller's remarkable achievement to
a simple variation on Bergson. Understanding what "functional consciousness" is and developing methods of achieving it are two different
things. Schwaller's immense work on an entire civilization devoted to

"inner knowing" entails ways of reaching this deeper perception, and we would be wrong to ignore it. But I think it's important to bring the essence of Schwaller's thought to an audience possibly put off by his talk of elites. The "intelligence of the heart" may be difficult to acquire, but it's something we and the world —not only a select group of enlightened theocrats—can benefit from by experiencing. In the long run, Schwaller himself understood this. "To be of the Elite," he wrote, "is to want to give and to be able to give . . . to draw on the inexhaustible source and give this food to those who are hungry and thirsty."[11] With his study of ancient Egypt, this is a truth Schwaller de Lubicz took to heart.

G. I. GURDJIEFF

MEETINGS WITH A REMARKABLE PARADOX

What kind of sense can we make of the enigmatic

life of this influential teacher?

Richard Smoley

He was by any account one of the most remarkable men the human race has produced.

His name was George Ivanovich Gurdjieff (pronounced "gur-*jeef*" or "*gur*-jeff"), and he proved to be one of the most challenging, paradoxical, and enigmatic spiritual teachers of our time. His principal biographer called him "a fraud, a liar, a cheat, a scoundrel"— and then went on to note his "sympathy, compassion, charity," and his "eccentric code of honor."[1] He is chiefly remembered for imparting, through the most extraordinary and difficult methods, the fundamentals of an esoteric system known as the Fourth Way—also called, austerely, "the Work."

WHAT IS THIS Fourth Way? Gurdjieff said there were three comparatively common ways to spiritual attainment: the way of the fakir, that is, the man who masters his physical organism to the point where he can, say, stand "motionless in the same position for hours, days, months, or years."[2] The second is the way of the monk, the man who masters his emotions through prayer and devotional practices. The third way is the way of the yogi, the man who gains control of his mind.

Yet, Gurdjieff believed, none of these ways is complete in itself. A man, for example, may master his mind—he may genuinely know something—but may be incapable of putting it into action. Or his emotions may be developed, but his intellect may remain at its primitive state. To compound these difficulties, each of these first three ways requires withdrawal from the world, from day-to-day life.

Then there is the Fourth Way—"the way of the sly man." It does not require withdrawal from the world, but can be pursued in the midst of ordinary life. And instead of working with just the mind, the emotions, or the body, it works with all three. It is, Gurdjieff claimed, faster and more efficient than the other ways. "The 'sly man' knows the secret," said Gurdjieff, "and with its help outstrips the fakir, the monk and the yogi."[3]

So who was this Gurdjieff man? What secret did he possess, and was he able to pass it on?

About his early life little is known. Even his surname is questionable; perhaps it was originally "Gurdjian" or even "Georgiades," the racial salad of the Caucasus—where Gurdjieff was born—occasionally imposing the convenience or necessity of name changes upon its inhabitants. His birth date? His passport said 1877, but some believe he was born as early as 1873 or as late as 1886. His birthplace can be fairly well established as Alexandropol (now Leninakan), a small town on the Russo-Turkish border. His father was Greek, his mother Armenian.[4]

So much can be said. But of the rest of the first thirty-seven years (more or less) of Gurdjieff's life, we have no other authority than his own written works, particularly the autobiography *Meetings with Re-*

markable Men. Entertaining and profound as it is, much of this book is clearly not literal truth. Curious seekers and even serious scholars have invoked speculation, rumor, and sheer fiction to fill the gap.

The most intriguing part of Gurdjieff's legend is one he fostered himself: that he began, at an early age, on a search for some deeper truth about man and the universe. Along with a small band of fellow seekers, he eventually made his way to a school in Central Asia called the Sarmoun Brotherhood and there learned the secrets he would later impart to his students.

Where this brotherhood was, or even if it really existed, has never been conclusively proven. Nor do we have any clear picture (other than Gurdjieff's own) of his companions in this search. Gurdjieff did his best to cover his tracks; to a large extent he succeeded. The first conclusive evidence we have of his whereabouts is in Moscow around 1914, where he began to teach the System (like the Work, it is usually capitalized) for which he would become renowned.[5]

In 1915 Gurdjieff met his most famous student, the man who, much more than Gurdjieff himself, would become the most widely read exponent of the Fourth Way: Pyotr Demianovich Ouspensky (1878–1947). Ouspensky, a bespectacled mathematician preoccupied with the nature of the universe, had just come back from a journey from India to find hidden wisdom (which he had failed to do). He suspected Gurdjieff had the secrets he had been searching for. Ouspensky gives a vivid account of their first meeting:

> We arrived at a small café in a noisy though not central street. I saw a man of an oriental type, no longer young, with a black mustache and piercing eyes, who astonished me first of all because he seemed to be disguised and completely out of keeping with the place and its atmosphere. . . . This man with the face of an Indian raja or an Arab sheik whom I at once seemed to see in a white burnoose or a gilded turban, seated here in this little

café . . . in a black overcoat with a velvet collar and a black bowler
hat, produced the strange, unexpected, and almost alarming im-
pression of a man poorly disguised, the sight of whom embar-
rasses you because you see he is not what he pretends to be and
yet you have to speak and behave as though you did not see it.[6]

Ouspensky's account of his experiences is contained in what is perhaps the best and most famous book about the Gurdjieff Work: *In
Search of the Miraculous.* In it Ouspensky presents an elaborate and
fantastic esoteric system, emphasizing the mechanicalness of human
behavior and how man, in his ordinary situation, cannot do anything;
things happen to him. Man, in fact, is not even one consistent being: he
is a stage on which a constant succession of different identities perform, each of them wanting and doing one thing one minute and another the next. By this view we are scarcely different from those cases
of multiple identities recorded in psychiatric journals. Yet Gurdjieff
also taught that man, by dint of intense work upon himself, can *become* a unified being, possessing will and consciousness and able to *do*
in the real sense of the word.

In Moscow and later in Petrograd, Gurdjieff managed to collect a
small band of students dedicated to working on these premises. From
one point of view, their circumstances were far from auspicious, those
being the grim days of World War I, when the fabric of imperial Russia was beginning to rend. From another point of view, however, the
circumstances were ideal, since, as Gurdjieff himself said, "sometimes,
revolutions and all consequent difficulties can help real Work."[7] The
turmoil of the Russian Revolution and subsequent civil war would
supply ample conditions for the "superefforts" that Gurdjieff required
of his students.

When the revolution finally came in 1917, Gurdjieff led his followers down to the Caucasus, which was still free from the Bolsheviks and
provided some refuge for Gurdjieff and his White Russian followers.

There he put his pupils through a remarkable odyssey that led them to make the most extraordinary demands upon themselves.

At one point, for example, Gurdjieff formed something called the "International Idealistic Society" and required his students not only to join it, but to give up all their possessions to it. The move at first glance smacks of opportunism and chicanery, but it turned out to have a useful purpose; according to Thomas and Olga de Hartmann, the aristocratic composer and his wife who accompanied Gurdjieff on this journey, "the papers we had written stating we were giving up all our personal belongings were used later to convince the Bolshevik authorities that we were not unsympathetic toward the idea of common ownership of property," thus winning them a certain measure of freedom.[8] On another occasion, Gurdjieff persuaded the Bolsheviks that he knew where gold could be found in the Caucasus and organized a "scientific expedition" to find it. He and his followers used the pretext to organize their escape from Soviet Russia in a harrowing mountain trek.

Neither Gurdjieff nor his followers would ever return to their native country. Instead, after sojourns in Constantinople and Berlin, they arrived in France in 1922. Here Gurdjieff was finally able to establish his school, the "Institute for the Harmonious Development of Man," in an old chateau known as the Prieuré, near Fontainebleau, forty miles from Paris. For the rest of his life Gurdjieff would live here and in the capital, drawing a collection of students, famous and obscure, from around the world.

One of Gurdjieff's most renowned pupils was A. R. Orage (pronounced "or-*azh*"), who was editor of the respected British journal *The New Age* and was hailed by T. S. Eliot as "the best literary critic of that time in London."[9] Orage, who had first come to the Work in London through Ouspensky (who had gone there after leaving Russia), eventually went to the Prieuré. There Gurdjieff turned him to manual labor; one visitor recalled Orage being set to digging ditches in the

Prieuré garden—only to be told to fill them in again as soon as he was done.[10]

Orage joined Gurdjieff and his group for their first trip to America in 1924. In New York and Chicago Gurdjieff and his troupe gave demonstrations of the movements and sacred dances on which he particularly prided himself. Though the dances created a certain *éclat* in the novelty-hungry America of the twenties, they did not furnish Gurdjieff with the recognition (or the money) he sought. It was Orage— urbane, intelligent, "the most persuasive man I have ever known," according to one observer—who laid the foundations for the Gurdjieff Work in New York.[11] When Gurdjieff and his troupe returned to France, Orage stayed behind to develop Work groups. It was his interpretation of Gurdjieff's teachings that would dominate the Work in America for the rest of the decade.

GURDJIEFF TAUGHT THAT man in his undeveloped state was subject to the law of accident. Unless we are able to take our lives in hand with consciousness and will, we cannot effectively do anything; we are bounced around by circumstance like coins in a pocket. And it was precisely to exempt oneself from this law of accident that one undertook the Work.

Given this context, one can imagine the shock created when the master had an accident himself—and a severe one. Driving to Fontainebleau from Paris on July 5, 1924, he crashed into a tree. Gurdjieff went into a coma that lasted for several months.

The incident was a severe test for everyone associated with him. In part this was a sheer matter of practicality, since the master had directed the day-to-day activities of the Institute. But for some—including Ouspensky—the crisis went deeper.

Ouspensky had had misgivings about Gurdjieff for some time, centered on Gurdjieff's eccentric behavior and his disregard for conventional morality. He told his pupils his association with Gurdjieff had ended around the time of the latter's first trip to America. Nonetheless Ouspensky went to France soon after Gurdjieff's accident. During his stay he met with his friend Boris Mouravieff. Mouravieff knew (and liked) Ouspensky and knew (but did not like) Gurdjieff; moreover, since he was himself an esotericist of no mean caliber, his testimony is of interest:

> Several days [after Gurdjieff's car wreck], Ouspensky came to Paris from London; and we both went together to the site of the accident.
>
> Despondent, crushed, after a long silence, he told me:
>
> "I'm afraid . . . It's terrible . . . George Ivanovich's Institute was created to escape the influence of the *law of accident* under which we live. And here he is himself fallen under the realm of the same law . . .
>
> "I wonder if it's really just an accident? Gurdjieff always made light of honesty, just as he did of human personality in general. Hasn't he gone too far? I tell you, I'm terribly afraid!"[12]

Although Ouspensky continued to teach his own version of the System, and although he and Gurdjieff remained in occasional contact for the rest of their lives, they never mended the breach between them. Possibly its cause was dispositional: Ouspensky was a man of extraordinary decency and refinement; Gurdjieff's antics, often coarse and not infrequently brutal, must have gone strongly against his grain.

The effects of the accident were felt in other ways too. As soon as Gurdjieff regained consciousness several months later, he sent away most of the students from the Prieuré, allowing only Americans to stay (in recompense for the generosity of American students who, mostly thanks to Orage, gave Gurdjieff a lot of money).[13] Withdrawing into himself, Gurdjieff began the enormous project of setting down his teachings in written form.

He originally intended to write books in three series: the first would provide "an objectively impartial criticism of the life of man," and would "destroy mercilessly . . . the beliefs and views . . . of everything existing in the world." The second would "acquaint the reader with the material required for a new creation," while the third would "assist in the arising of a veritable, non-fantastic representation . . . of the world existing in reality."[14] Of this series, only the first, later published as *Beelzebub's Tales to His Grandson,* would ever be finished more or less as Gurdjieff had first envisioned it. The second, *Meetings with Remarkable Men,* was eventually finished in a shorter form, and is the most readable of Gurdjieff's writings; the third series, published under the title *Life Is Real Only Then, When "I Am,"* is fragmentary.

Working at an intense pace, mostly at the Cafe de la Paix in Paris, Gurdjieff "wrote and rewrote 10,000 kilos of paper" by his own estimation.[15] Like Gurdjieff's other works in this series, *Beelzebub* was not published until after his death. It is an enormous book, over twelve hundred pages long, and contains, under the guise of narrations by the aforementioned Beelzebub, its author's views of man and the cosmos.

Gurdjieff sent pages of this work to Orage in New York, who returned at least one section as completely unintelligible: later versions, though no doubt improved, were to prove difficult enough. Partly this was deliberate: Gurdjieff believed nothing comes without effort and wanted to make *Beelzebub*'s wisdom difficult to extract. On the other hand, he himself lamented that the book was only comprehensible to those who "in one way or another, were already acquainted with the Peculiar form of my mentation."[16]

He had good reason to think so. Written in an extraordinarily convoluted style and laced with words of Gurdjieff's own coinage like "Rastropoonilo" and "Ikriltazkakra," *Beelzebub* is the *Finnegans Wake* of esotericism: worth reading, no doubt, but almost unreadable, and studied exclusively by the few who have decided to surmount its obscurities—usually with the help of a group.

Despite the Support Orage and his American groups gave for *Beelzebub,* Gurdjieff, upon his visit to New York in 1930, decided Orage had not done a good job teaching the System, and asserted that Orage had only wanted to stay in New York because he had "started a romance . . . with [a] saleswoman in [a] bookshop."[17] He made his students sign a piece of paper saying they would have nothing more to do with Orage. (To Gurdjieff's discomfiture, Orage signed the paper himself.)

The pattern is a familiar one, for Gurdjieff was to experience breaks with many of his students at some point or another. Ouspensky's reaction we have already seen. Even Thomas and Olga de Hartmann, who accompanied Gurdjieff out of Russia and whose account of their years with him provides one of the warmest and most sympathetic treatments of Gurdjieff and his Work, were forced to break with him in 1929—according to Olga de Hartmann, because Gurdjieff demanded that they accompany him to New York when her husband was extremely ill.[18]

Though these breaks are difficult to explain—except perhaps by saying Gurdjieff did not wish to foster dependency in his students—in some cases they proved damaging to him. Olga de Hartmann had been his secretary for many years and had taken down much of the dictation for *Beelzebub.* The break with Orage was even more costly, losing Gurdjieff not only a great deal of his financial support but also many of his students. By the early 1930s, Gurdjieff was a bit down-at-heel, having alienated many of even his most loyal followers; in 1933 he sold the Prieuré.

The last fifteen years of Gurdjieff's life seem to a certain extent anticlimactic. He remained in Paris throughout World War II (and indeed seemed surprisingly—and to some suspiciously—exempt from the want imposed by the Nazi occupation); two or three years after it was over his reputation rose again, and his flat was filled with disciples, his own as well as old students of Orage and Ouspensky. Plans were even made to publish *Beelzebub*; those who had found it useful were invited to support its publication by paying a subscription fee of one hundred pounds.[19]

Nonetheless, even at this late stage of his life, Gurdjieff did not seem to elude the law of accident. Rammed by a drunken driver in 1948, he suffered severe internal injuries. Though he recovered, he was never quite the same, and he died on October 29, 1949, at the age of (perhaps) seventy-two. His last words are rumored to have been addressed to his disciples: "Vous voilà dans des beaux draps!" ("Here you are in a fine mess!")

James Webb, the most dispassionate of Gurdjieff's biographers, asked someone who had been present if Gurdjieff really had said that. "He did *not*," the man replied, "but it was true!"[20]

As for Ouspensky, he had died two years earlier, in 1947, shortly after repudiating Gurdjieff's System as he had known and taught it.[21] Gurdjieff had told some American pupils that Ouspensky had "perished like a dog."

What is one to make of the strange case of G. I. Gurdjieff? Was he a "good man"? What was his aim? And can the seeker do anything with his System?

To the question of whether Gurdjieff was a "good man" or not, one can only shrug. As Ouspensky pointed out, Gurdjieff made light of conventional morality and honesty; in *Meetings with Remarkable Men* he tells of a time when, hard up for cash, he gets hold of some sparrows, paints them with aniline dyes, and sells them as "American canaries." Nor was he known for sexual restraint; several of his female disciples ended up carrying his children.

On the other hand, Gurdjieff does not seem to have been concerned with the empire-building so beloved of contemporary gurus in the United States; he drove away as many students as he attracted; and many of the people who stayed at the Prieuré were Russian refugees whom he had to support. True to his Caucasian heritage, he dispensed hospitality in abundant quantities. To Aleister Crowley, for example, who came to the Prieuré for help with his drug addiction, Gurdjieff showed all due consideration—until Crowley was about to leave.

> "Mister, you go?" Gurdjieff inquired. Crowley assented. "You have been guest?"—a fact which the visitor could hardly deny. "Now you go, you are no longer guest?" Crowley—no doubt wondering whether his host had lost his grip on reality and was wandering in a semantic wilderness—humored his mood by indicating that he was on his way back to Paris. But Gurdjieff, having made the point that he was not violating the canons of hospitality, changed on the instant into the embodiment of righteous anger. "You filthy," he stormed, "you dirty inside! Never again you set foot in my house.". . . Whitefaced and shaking, the Great Beast crept back to Paris with his tail between his legs.[22]

Amusing as it is, this incident also displays some of the problems one faces when trying to make sense of Gurdjieff. More so, perhaps, than any other mage of our time, he seems to have been operating under premises that were obscure or difficult for the ordinary person to sort out—in this comparatively simple case, the obligations of hospitality versus his dislike and distrust for Crowley. As for his larger aims, which could tell us something about the direction of his Work and what he hoped to accomplish with it, we have little if any idea. (He himself told Ouspensky, "My aim cannot have any meaning for you.")[23]

But if we cannot know Gurdjieff's aim, let us permit ourselves to guess. And that brings us to the question of the source of Gurdjieff's teaching—a difficult, and to some insoluble, problem. Most would agree at least up to a point with Boris Mouravieff's evaluation: some of Gurdjieff's teachings came from the esoteric tradition of Orthodox Christianity; some came from Muslim traditions; and some were Gurdjieff's own ideas and creations.[24] (To this one could add the teachings he might have taken from Buddhist or shamanistic traditions in Central Asia and elsewhere.) What people don't agree on is the degree of the admixture. Claudio Naranjo, the Chilean physician and esotericist, believes Gurdjieff's teaching reflects a northern strain of Sufism indigenous to Central Asia and less connected to orthodox Islam than more southerly versions. And Robin Amis makes an intriguing case for finding the sources of Gurdjieff's teaching in Eastern Orthodoxy; after all, Gurdjieff himself said his System was "esoteric Christianity."[25] Each year to this day Gurdjieff's death is commemorated in Paris by Russian Orthodox services.[26]

BUT PERHAPS ANOTHER answer lies in the notion of the Fourth Way, the way beyond that of the fakir, the monk, and the yogi—meaning the Muslim, Christian, and Hindu. Robert Amadou, in an article on Gurdjieff's relation to Sufism, points out:

These three mystic ways [are] always open to the Muslim, the Christian, or Hindu who wishes to perfect his religion. . . . Then—a Fourth Way, which Gurdjieff traced . . . and on which he leads those unfortunates, the monsters without religion. . . . The primordial trick of Gurdjieff is to have, in his teaching and practice, hidden the latent religious side and manifested the psychological.[27]

So possibly Gurdjieff took on the project of bringing certain ancient esoteric doctrines to overintellectualized Western man, for whom God is a nullity or an abstraction, and who can only appreciate such teachings if presented in a psychological or "scientific" cloak. If this was in fact his task, he was to devote his entire life to it.

Did he succeed? The difficulty of the Work, its inaccessibility to all but a tiny fraction of humankind, is admitted and even celebrated by its adherents. Yet, we find the teachings of Gurdjieff cropping up in the most unlikely places—in books on pop psychology, in corporate management classes, even on sneakers and key chains.

Gurdjieff himself, most likely, would have laughed at such attempts and branded them as counterfeits—as they may well be. And they point to a goal Gurdjieff would have found ridiculous: the collective awakening of mankind. Gurdjieff, who believed human beings were on a low rung of an enormous cosmic food chain, did not think awakening was possible for any more than a few isolated individuals working together, who, like prisoners digging a tunnel, may be able to find a way out.

I can't quite bring myself to disagree with Gurdjieff about this point, but I can't bring myself to agree with it either. True, awakening is extraordinarily difficult, even when pursued along definite lines and with the help of a group dedicated to this purpose. On the other hand, we have reached the point in human history when we have no choice: individual awakenings are not enough. Boris Mouravieff believed that we are on the threshold of the Era of the Holy Spirit, which will open up enormous possibilities for human evolution, but if we do not successfully pass over into this epoch, we will be subject to the deluge of fire mentioned by the Apostle Peter.[28]

An extravagant statement; but to view it another way, Mouravieff is simply stating what we all know: if we don't come to our senses, we will blow ourselves up.

What role do the Gurdjieff teachings have to play in this drama? This is not clear to me. Perhaps it lies in the notion that man is asleep and needs to wake up. But Gurdjieff taught that awakening requires a school, and few have bothered to involve themselves with the Gurdjieff Work as he envisaged it. (Nor, I suspect, is it an ideal path for many.) Moreover, many students—apparently including Ouspensky—did not reach the goals Gurdjieff set out. If the "sly man" had a secret, it is far from an infallible one.

And yet Gurdjieff retains an incontestable allure despite his paradoxes and inconsistencies. Or perhaps because of them. For it seems quite clear that Gurdjieff as a man makes little sense in any kind of rational or logical way—nor did he intend to. Was this hypocrisy or schizophrenia on his part, Gurdjieff exemplifying his own teaching that we have no one consistent "I"? Possibly. But beyond a certain point it may be more useful to set aside our judgments of Gurdjieff and ask instead what we can learn from him.

Gurdjieff's abundant sense of humor, his relentless will, the depth of his teachings, the richness and drama of his life all retain the capacity to fascinate and inspire even now, forty years after his death. As for his darkness—for there was darkness, despite his followers' best efforts to excuse it or cover it up—that too has its place: if we are to be sly men and women, we must make use of darkness as well as light. For myself, as I try to distill some wisdom from my reflections on Gurdjieff's strange and mysterious career, I keep coming back to a piece of advice given to him by his father: "to be outwardly courteous to all without distinction . . . but inwardly to remain free and never to put much trust in anyone or anything."[29]

And of course that would include Gurdjieff himself.

20

FACING THE
TRADITIONALISTS
AN APPROACH TO RENÉ GUÉNON
AND HIS SUCCESSORS

This uncompromising camp of esoteric thinkers has much

to offer in their critique of the modern world,

despite certain dispeptic quirks.

Joscelyn Godwin

One's first encounter with the mind of René Guénon (1886–1951) can be a traumatic experience. Anyone who feels at ease with the intellectual attitudes and the scientific theories of our time should think twice before opening *The Crisis of the Modern World* or *The Reign of Quantity and the Signs of the Times,* for they may find, with this author, that their worldview suffers a blow from which it will never recover. Guénon aims, with deadly effect, at the very vitals of the modern age: not just at the easy target of its materialism, but at most of its spiritual aspirations as well.

Guénon and those who more or less share his principles, grouped together for convenience as "Traditionalists," have long been a recognized intellectual, even a political, force in his native France. In Britain, more resistant to esoteric ideas, a small but faithful group published *Studies in Comparative Religion* for many years, a journal whose title belied its far from academic concerns. In the United States, Traditionalism has been represented by two immigrants, the brilliant Iranian scholar Seyyed Hossein Nasr and the profound and prolific Frithjof Schuon, while professors Jacob Needleman and Huston Smith have also helped to publicize it. There is every reason to welcome their efforts.

First, the Traditionalists cut across the barriers that separate East from West and one religion from another, to find the esoteric truth that reconciles them. Once this is in view, their differences can be seen for what they are: exoteric, hence contigent on the time, place, and style of each religious revelation. Esoteric doctrines, on the other hand, and the initiatic experiences that accompany them, can only be the same, always and everywhere. Thus a man like Frithjof Schuon can write with equal authority on Islam, Buddhism, Hinduism, or Christianity, "believing" in all of them because he is able to appreciate their transcendent unity.

This unity is first approached theoretically, through the study of metaphysics. The Traditionalists use this term specifically to refer to the ultimate realities, beyond cosmology and beyond theology. Theologies differ (are there many gods, as in Hinduism, or only one, as in the Abrahamic religions?), but metaphysical principles do not: instead, they provide the means for reconciling apparent contradictions, and of seeing each belief system on its own terms and at its own level. Eventually these principles are known experientially. But the quest begins with intellectual knowledge, as one might set out on a pilgrimage prepared with a map of the territory. Without this knowledge one is no better off than the narrow sectarians, even the mystics among them, for whom their own religious path is the only true one. Mystical experience and religious devotion are certainly intrinsic elements of the spiritual path, but as Guénon never tired of emphasizing, the ultimate realization of a human being is through Knowledge.

Some may find this whole approach too intellectual, but they cannot deny that the Traditionalists' discipline of metaphysics cuts like a razor through the sloppy thinking and sentimentality prevalent among "New Age" types. It sets standards of integrity, against which other spiritual teachings either stand or fall. It assumes from the outset that absolute truth has always been there for the finding, so it has no time for the fumblings of Western philosophy, so-called, or for a science whose basic dogma is that man is still searching for the truth. And it incidentally forces a revaluation of all the modern ideals that most North Americans take for granted, such as individualism, equality, evolution, and progress. One looks at the world with new eyes once one has passed through a Traditionalist reeducation.

One might stop here, simply recommending the study of Guénon and his successors to whoever feels the urge to embark on it. But it seems advisable, while doing so, to explain some of the obstacles that these thinkers have placed in the way of their audience. For one soon discovers that this movement, in one sense the broadest of all since it is based on the reconciliation of all religions, tends in other respects toward the narrowness of a cult. The natural revulsion that many people feel at this point may turn them against the Traditionalists forever, and that would be a pity. Better to face their challenge with equanimity and discrimination, accepting what is of value and discarding what is prompted by animus and prejudice. This article begins, in a very modest way, to sift the two apart.

One of the first shocks for those who already sense a spiritual dimension to life, beyond what an agnostic or exoteric upbringing may have offered them, is the Traditionalists' insistence that spiritual development is virtually impossible outside the great religions. There is, they say, no other salvation, whether for those who need only the reassurance and regularity of faith and worship, or for the aspirants to mystical, initiatic, or philosophic paths. While admitting that in the past there have been a few "independents," any modern leanings in that direction are firmly put down as spiritual pride. The Traditionalists' view is that an orthodox exoteric practice is essential to discipline the body and soul, and to provide a firm foundation for the higher flights of esotericism for which only a few are qualified. And in the present age, they add, one surely needs all the help one can get.

One cannot doubt the sincerity of those who have followed this precept and found their home in one of the living religions. Few of the Traditionalists, however, have stayed with the one in which they were born or brought up, for reasons that will soon be apparent. Several of the most prominent have followed Guénon's own example in entering Islam and making connections with esoteric Sufi orders. Those who have stayed within Christianity have usually gravitated toward the Orthodox churches, for modern Catholicism is considered very dubious, while all Protestants are by definition antitraditional. Orthodox Judaism is the obvious choice for Jews, but difficult to enter from outside, since gentile converts are not exactly welcomed by Hasidic and suchlike communities. "Reformed" Judaism, on the other hand, is no better than Protestantism, having made fatal compromises with the modern world. A fourth and last possibility is Buddhism, though Guénon accepted it only grudgingly and late in life. Hinduism is excluded for Westerners because one cannot be a genuine Hindu unless one was born into one of the castes. The traditions of the American Indians, of Black Africa, and the Far East (Taoism, Shinto) are barely feasible nowadays, especially in view of the difficulty of finding any living esoteric masters. Moreover, in all these cases it is only the most ancient and integral streams that are acceptable: most of the so-called Sufi, Vedantic, and Buddhist groups in the West are suspect, having become polluted with modern ideas. So the choice of an exoteric religious allegiance is extremely limited, if not geographically inaccessible, for many people.

The reader can perhaps sense already, behind this quest for perfect doctrinal purity, that the Traditionalists have a kind of blacklist of what they consider pseudo- or antitraditions. There are of course degrees of leniency among them, as in any broad and disparate group. But to the strictly orthodox, the vast majority of the world's Christians (to take the example closest to home) are schismatics and heretics, cut off—maybe through no fault of their own—from the authentic transmission from Jesus Christ through his Church. The fiercest Traditionalists accuse the Roman Church of having disqualified itself through the doctrinal and liturgical innovations of the past century, so that the only Catholics left are those who defy the pope—or rather the current antipope—by maintaining the Latin Mass and other traditional rites. With a literalism that is truly medieval, they say that the bishops and priests consecrated and ordained under the new liturgy are technically incapable of performing transubstantiation and of making the sacraments effectual for their people.

This kind of extremism betokens a strange mentality and a stranger conception of God. For while willing to accept that he reveals himself through different religions, they seem to imagine him only willing to funnel his grace through a very narrow channel in each case. There is little difference between this attitude and that of the fanatical Christian to whom all non-Christians are damned: it is the same desire to limit God's grace to oneself and one's community, and its roots cannot be anything but psychological. To Guénon, any considerations of a psychological nature were beneath contempt, and any mention of such motives strikes Traditionalists as very insulting. But like it or not, the compulsion to divide one's fellow humans into sheep and goats is of a psychological order; metaphysically it is meaningless, as they should know who acknowledge the inherent divinity of every person.

When we turn from this to the particular case of René Guénon, we find at his best a vast and liberating vision for which every serious reader (and that does not include those who stop with *The Reign of Quantity,* or, worse, *The Lord of the World*) will be grateful. He shares with Plotinus, Meister Eckhart, and Jakob Boehme the privilege of access to the very summits of conceptual thought. For he does not conclude his philosophical ascent with Being, nor does his theology begin with God the Creator. Beyond both, and beyond any distinction of philosophy from religion, lies the ultimate mystery to which those few Western masters have alluded. Guénon calls it Non-Being, surpassing the limits of manifestation and thought, yet paradoxically supporting them both. This is the Nirvana of the Buddhists, eternally copresent with Samsara, the nonmanifest with the manifest. Those who wish to follow him into these realms will read *Man and His Becoming According to the Vedanta, The Symbolism of the Cross,* and *The Multiple States of Being,* and perhaps they will do best to ignore the rest of the Traditionalist literature.

Guénon himself, however, could not resist descending from these philosophical peaks to wander through the forest of symbolic images and to do battle down on the plains where Opinion holds sway. In private life he was a gentle soul, an introverted family man with no financial or social ambitions. There is no record of his ever doing a mean act or of saying anything to hurt an individual, while the last thing he wanted was to head a "Guénonian" cult. In his writings, however, there is no denying that he is intellectually arrogant, polemical, and opinionated, never considering himself as less than an absolute authority—on everything.

Two of Guénon's earliest books cleared the way for his doctrinal work by disposing of his rivals in the esoteric field. Translated, but still unpublished in English, they are *Le Théosophisme, Histoire d'une Pseudo-religion* ("Theosophy, the History of a Pseudo-religion," 1921) and *L'Erreur Spirite* ("The Spiritualist Error," 1923). The work on modern theosophical movements, which is a feast of esoteric gossip, is aimed at Madame Blavatsky, the Rosicrucian revival, Annie Besant, C. W. Leadbeater, the young Krishnamurti, and Rudolf Steiner, to name only the most eminent targets. The one on Spiritualism, in turn, exposes the origins and absurdities of that movement, showing that whatever is contacted in séances, it is not the spirits of the dead. But what emerges from the two books, besides many entirely valid criticisms, is Guénon's refusal to make moral judgments except in absolute terms. Either someone is an authentic representative of Tradition, or else they are antitraditional and hence subversive of all that is truly sacred. Later he would coin for the latter the term "Counter-initiation."

From the 1920s onward Guénon contributed hundreds of book reviews and articles to the journal *Le Voile d'Isis,* later renamed *Études Traditionnelles.* Here he had free rein as arbiter of the whole esoteric and pseudoesoteric world, never in any doubt as to who belonged where, often amusing in a sardonic way. Following more ponderously in his footsteps, his disciples continue the heresy-hunting, picking on figures as various as Vivekananda, Aurobindo, the later Krishnamurti, Gurdjieff, Teilhard de Chardin, Hans Küng, Mircea Eliade, Chögyam Trungpa, and last but not least, C. G. Jung. But one does not have to be much of a Jungian to notice in these polemics a certain projection of their own shadows.

This brings us to the matter of Guénon's shadow, which was projected not so much on personalities as on the whole modern world. In his view of history, based on the Hindu system of cycles, mankind deteriorates in the course of each cycle of four ages, becoming ever more materialist—more materialized, even—and ignorant of spiritual realities. At the start of each cycle a "primordial tradition" is revealed that is progressively obscured and distorted, yet never entirely lost. It is preserved in the symbolism of the revealed religions, each one a certain specialization and limitation of it, and its esoteric purposes are fulfilled in their initiations. Contrarily to the traditional Hindu dating, which gives the current dark age (Kali Yuga) many thousands of years still to run, Guénon believed it to be now nearing its close, and consequently that the modern age represents the *ne plus ultra* of spiritual decline. He used the memorable phrase "the Reign of Quantity" to describe a civilization for which qualitative considerations no longer counted. In deliberate distinction from the imagination of mankind striding ever upward, evolving from ape to technocrat, focusing its energies and its aspirations to progress on the material world alone, Guénon saw the rot setting in as far back as ancient Greece, with its rationalism and religious skepticism. Having little regard for Classical civilization and none at all for the Renaissance, he deplored the end of the Middle Ages and of any possibility of a Christian theocracy in Europe. Since that time, he saw the sacred giving way to the secular on every front: in religion, with the fragmentation of the Christian tradition and the driving of esoteric knowledge underground; in philosophy, with its denial of true metaphysics and its futile attempt to dispense with any sacred foundations; in society, with the lower elements usurping the controlling functions of the priestly and noble castes; and in the arts, always the surest barometer of a civilization's soul. Yet what else could one expect at the end of a dark age? Perhaps the most realistic response is that of Jean Robin, author of two books on Guénon, who actually welcomes that bogeyman, the "Counter-initiation," for hastening the end of this wretched time and the advent of a new postapocalyptic golden age.

In *The Reign of Quantity and the Signs of the Times,* Guénon created an imagination all his own, a living myth complete with picturesque details through which to view the end of an age. Yet the spread of his own ideas since 1945 and the very existence of the Traditionalists shows that things are not so simple, and that the ascendancy of the West is not synonymous with mankind's degradation. In those Middle Ages of which they seem so fond, they would all have been burnt for heresy and apostasy—if they could ever have learnt what they now know. The secular humanism they abhor is a far more favorable climate for their work than the fundamentalism that would at least burn all their books if it came to power again. One would think that past and present held enough lessons on the evils to which exoteric religion is prone for them at least to hesitate in their support of it. But unlike Guénon, who lived in Cairo from 1930 onward, most of them support it from a safe distance, enjoying the advantages of life in Switzerland, Britain, the United States, and other strongholds of the Reign of Quantity, while cherishing some fantasy of traditional civilization that probably never existed on earth. Certainly there is a need for a polemic against the modern frame of mind, as there is for a critique of phony religions. But the Traditionalist approach lacks subtlety. It lacks it, first, in its determination to make orthodoxy a moral issue, choosing not to admit that the construction of orthodoxies themselves is at best a dubious historical process. Second, it makes a far too simplistic condemnation of this extraordinary and unprecedented age, as if time had no lessons for mankind, or as if the Kali Yuga were a mistake on Ishvara's part.

Although Guénon's eschatology does indeed foresee the return of the blissful Satya Yuga at the start of a fresh cycle, he evidently did not expect any of us to be around to enjoy it, not even in some future incarnation. He felt very strongly on this point, and always waxed emotional when he mentioned it in print. While the question of reincarnation is a secondary one, the main point being to get liberated here and now, it is a commonplace in many esoteric doctrines, and Guénon made some quite erroneous statements in his attempt to gloss over this fact. In *Le Thésophisme,* chapter 11 and *L'Erreur Spirite,* chapter 6, he points out that homo sapiens is only one among many other states that a being can occupy, but draws the unwarranted conclusion that the repetition of any state is "metaphysically impossible," so that no soul can ever return to earth again. A. K. Coomaraswamy, sharing Guénon's aversion, would also try to prove it in an article on "The One and Only Transmigrant," but his argument on the level of the Supreme Self, by all means the only ultimate reality in man, cannot honestly be transposed to the secondary reality of the reembodying soul.

The debate *pro* and *contra* reincarnation had long been in the forefront of spiritualist literature, each side amply supported by the revelations of its spirits. The rejection of reincarnation had become a cornerstone of the anti-Theosophical camp in French occultism, with which Guénon was aligned from his early spiritualistic experiments. Subsequently, when Guénon's hopes centered for a while on the restoration of a Catholic traditionalism, he had no reason to change his position: anything else would have wrecked his chances, as it would later have made him a suspiciously unorthodox Muslim. However, it would be a very odd Buddhist or Hindu who denied the possibility of ever returning to earth as a human being, however little they wanted to dwell on the question. I have dwelt on it here only to show how one man's psychological or political needs can become entrenched as dogma and defended as "metaphysical necessity." No doubt the history of religions could furnish other examples.

One must finally admit that the whole Traditionalist movement has been colored, so far, by Guénon's own decision to enter the Islamic tradition. However irrelevant it may be on the mountaintop of metaphysics, the choice of religion based on an unquestionable book and on the exhortation to holy war betokens a certain "spiritual style." How different Guénon's dogmas, and the attitudes of his followers, might have been if his first initiation had been into Buddhism, for instance, or if he had managed to find a *modus vivendi* with Christianity. Nevertheless, he is to be thanked for inspiring a group of writers and teachers who are among the guiding lights of our time. Besides those whose names have already been mentioned, the works of Marco Pallis, Titus Burckhardt, Martin Lings, and Philip Sherrard stand out like gems from the occult and pseudoesoteric trash that delays the seeker after wisdom.

Like all the best spiritual literature—like "revealed" scripture itself—the work of the Traditionalists is not easily faced. It threatens the very ground on which one stands. But that is no reason to let it sweep one off one's feet. My own heresy, and one I would hope other students of the Traditionalists might share, is that the holy trinity of reason, compassion, and intuition, taken together, are better guides than any authority whatsoever. There is no tradition on earth that is not tarnished with age, no revelation that can, or need, be reconstituted in its pristine purity hundreds or thousands of years later and on another continent. The Spirit still descends as it will, indifferent as a bird to anyone's notions of where it should or shouldn't land. It descends on Quakers and Theosophists as well as on Traditionalists, and even on those who wear no label at all.

BIBLIOGRAPHICAL NOTES

All of Guénon's books are available in French. Sophia Perennis Books of Ghent, New York, has published many of Guénon's works in English translation, including: *East and West, The Crisis of the Modern World, The Symbolism of the Cross, The Reign of Quantity and The Sign of the Times, Perspectives on Initiation, Spiritual Authority and Temporal Power, Insights into Christian Esoterism,* and *Initiation and Spiritual Realization.*

   Also translated are:

Initiation and the Crafts (Ipswich, Suffolk, UK: Golgonooza Press, 1973); *The Lord of the World* (Ellingstring, No. Yorkshire, UK: Coombe Springs Press, 1983); *The Multiple States of Being* (Burdett, NY: Larson, 1984); and *Studies in Hinduism* (Columbia, MO: South Asia Books, 1986).

   Some representative works by the other authors mentioned are:

Titus Burckhardt, *Alchemy: Science of the Cosmos, Science of the Soul* (Baltimore: Penguin Books, 1972), and *Sacred Art in East and West* (Bedfont, Perennial Books, 1967).

A. K. Coomaraswamy, *Christian and Oriental Philosophy of Art* (New York: Dover, 1957), and *Selected Papers, vol. 2, Metaphysics* (Princeton: Princeton University Press, 1977).

Martin Lings, *Muhammad: His Life Based on the Earliest Sources* (London: Allen and Unwin, 1984).

Seyyed Hossein Nasr, *Knowledge and the Sacred,* the Gifford Lectures (New York: Crossroad, 1981), and *The Heart of Islam: Enduring Values for Humanity* (San Francisco: HarperSanFrancisco, 2002).

Jacob Needleman, ed., *The Sword of Gnosis: Metaphysics, Cosmology, Tradition, Symbolism* (essays from *Studies in Comparative Religion*) (New York: Methuen, 1986).

Marco Pallis, *Peaks and Lamas* (1939; reprint, Totowa, NJ: Biblio Distribution Center, 1974), and *A Buddhist Spectrum* (London: Allen and Unwin, 1980).

Jean Robin, *Les Sociétés Secrètes au rendez-vous de l'Apocalypse* (Paris: Guy Trédaniel, 1985).

Frithjof Schuon, *Esoterism as Principle and as Way* (Bedfont, Middlesex, UK: Perennial Books, 1981).

Philip Sherrard, *The Eclipse of Man and Nature* (Rochester, VT: Inner Traditions, 1986).

Huston Smith, *Forgotten Truth: The Primordial Tradition* (San Francisco: Harper and Row, 1977).

Other works of interest are:

Whitall N. Perry, ed., *A Treasury of Traditional Wisdom* (London: Allen and Unwin, 1971), and *Gurdjieff in the Light of Tradition* (Bedfont, Middlesex, UK: Perennial Books, 1978).

Rama P. Coomaraswamy, *The Destruction of the Christian Tradition* (Bedfont, Middlesex, UK: Perennial Books, 1981).

Robin Waterfield, *René Guénon and The Future of the West: The Life and Writings of a Twentieth-Century Metaphysician* (Rochester, VT: Inner Traditions, 1987).

CONTRIBUTORS

CHAS S. CLIFTON teaches writing at Colorado State University–Pueblo and edits *The Pomegranate: The Journal of Pagan Studies*. Thirty years after receiving his first Tarot deck, he still thinks that "the cards never lie."

PRISCILLA COSTELLO is a long-time counseling astrologer, teacher, and writer. She serves as chapter affairs coordinator for the National Council for Geocosmic Research and is founder of The New Alexandria, a center for religious, spiritual, and esoteric studies in Toronto.

PINCHAS GILLER is professor of Jewish thought at the University of Judaism in Bel Air, California. He is the author of *The Enlightened Will Shine* (1993) and *Reading the Zohar, The Sacred Text of the Kabbalah* (2001).

JOSCELYN GODWIN is professor of music at Colgate University

and the author of over fifteen highly regarded books on music, harmony, and the Western esoteric traditions. Among them are *Robert Fludd: Hermetic Philosopher and Surveyor of Two Worlds, Mystery Religions of the Ancient World, The Theosophical Enlightenment,* and most recently *The Pagan Dream of the Renaissance* (2002).

JUDY HARROW has been high priestess of Proteus Coven since 1980. She holds a master's degree in counseling, is president-elect of the New Jersey Association for Spiritual, Ethical and Religious Values in Counseling (a division of the New Jersey Counseling Association) and chair of the Pastoral Counseling Program of Cherry Hill Seminary. Judy has written two books: *Wicca Covens* (1999) and *Spiritual Mentoring* (2002). She also edited and contributed to the anthology *Devoted to You* (2003).

KABIR HELMINSKI is a shaikh of the Mevlevi Order, which traces back to Rumi. He is the codirector of the Threshold Society (sufism.org) and the author and translator of various books, including *Living Presence* and *The Knowing Heart.*

STEPHAN A. HOELLER is the author of *The Gnostic Jung and the Seven Sermons to the Dead* (1982), *Jung and the Lost Gospels* (1989), and *Gnosticism: New Light on the Ancient Tradition of Inner Knowing* (2002). He is the director of the Gnostic Society of Los Angeles and is a leading figure in contemporary Gnostic activities.

K. PAUL JOHNSON is author of *The Masters Revealed: Madame Blavatsky and the Myth of the Great White Lodge* (1994), *Initiates of Theosophical Masters* (1995), and *Edgar Cayce in Context* (1998).

GARY LACHMAN is author of *Turn Off Your Mind: The Mystic Sixties and the Dark Side of the Age of Aquarius* (2002) and *A Secret History of Consciousness* (2003). As Gary Valentine, he was a performer and composer with the rock group Blondie.

CAITLÍN MATTHEWS is the author of forty books on Western spirituality and on Celtic and ancestral wisdom, including *Sophia: Goddess of Wisdom, Bride of God* (Wheaton, IL: Quest Books, 2001).

With John Matthews, she is co-founder of the Foundation for Inspirational and Oracular Studies, dedicated to the sacred arts. They teach worldwide. For details of their courses, see www.hallowquest.org.uk.

CHRISTOPHER MCINTOSH is author of several books on the history of Western esotericism, including *The Rosicrucians* (1980) and *The Rose Cross and the Age of Reason* (1992). He presently works for an institute of UNESCO in Hamburg, Germany.

THEODORE J. NOTTINGHAM is an author and translator whose work has included historical and metaphysical fiction, screenplays, children's books, and nonfiction works on spirituality. He is also a television and video producer. He has been involved in the study of spiritual development for over twenty years.

ROBERT RICHARDSON is a longtime student of the Western esoteric traditions. His writings have appeared in *Gnosis* magazine and *New Dawn* magazine.

RICHARD SMOLEY was editor of *Gnosis* magazine from 1990 to 1999. He is the author of *Inner Christianity: A Guide to the Esoteric Tradition* (2002) and coauthor (with Jay Kinney) of *Hidden Wisdom: A Guide to the Western Inner Traditions* (1999).

KENNETH STEIN is a student of esoteric, occult, and theosophical thought, particularly Neoplatonism, Kabbalah, and William Blake.

ANASTASY TOUSOMOU is the pen name of a Christian theologian with an interest in esotericism and matters alchemical.

THOMAS D. WORREL, a past master of Mill Valley Masonic Lodge, is the author of several articles in Masonic research periodicals and publications. He has also held several positions in various Masonic organizations. He holds graduate degrees in both business and religious studies and has been an avid student of esoteric studies for over thirty-four years. He resides in Mill Valley, California.

NOTES

INTRODUCTION
by Jay Kinney

1. John L. Brooke, *The Refiner's Fire: The making of Mormon Cosmology, 1644–1844* (New York: Cambridge University Press, 1994), p. 71.
2. Ibid., p. 31.
3. Francis King, *The Rites of Modern Occult Magic* (New York: Macmillan, 1971), p. 127.
4. Noel L. Brann, *Trithemius and Magical Theology* (Albany, NY: SUNY Press, 1999), p. 154.

CHAPTER I. HERMES AND ALCHEMY
by Richard Smoley

1. Brian P. Copenhaver, introduction to *Hermetica: The Greek Corpus Hermeticum and the Latin Asclepius in a New English Translation with Notes and Introduction* (Cambridge, UK: Cambridge University Press, 1992), pp. xiii–xiv.

2. Quoted in ibid., p. xlviii.

3. Ibid.

4. Antoine Faivre, *The Eternal Hermes: From Greek God to Alchemical Magus* (Grand Rapids, MI: Phanes Press, 1995), pp. 104–5.

5. Faivre says that the term "Hermetism" should be used to refer to the *Corpus Hermeticum* and the literature directly inspired by it, while "Hermeticism" should be used in a wider sense to refer to "many aspects of Western esotericism, such as astrology, alchemical speculations, and the like" (introduction to *Modern Esoteric Spirituality,* coedited with Jacob Needleman [New York: Crossroad, 1992], p. 3). But this distinction strikes me as more likely to confuse than enlighten the general reader, so I have chosen simply to use the term "Hermeticism" in all instances.

6. Peter French, *John Dee* (London: Ark Paperbacks, 1987), p. 146.

7. Fulcanelli, *Le mystère des cathédrales,* trans. Mary Sworder (Albuquerque, NM: Brotherhood of Life, 1984). Reviewed in *Gnosis* 10 (Winter 1989).

8. Julius Evola, *The Hermetic Tradition: Symbols and Teachings of the Royal Art,* translated by E. E. Rehmus (Rochester, VT: Inner Traditions International, 1995), p. 23. For an overview of Evola's writings available in English, see *Gnosis* 40 (Summer 1996): 64.

9. Evola, *Hermetic Tradition,* p. 25. Emphasis, here and in other quotations, in the original.

10. Ibid., pp. 36–7.

11. Annie Besant, *Thought Power* (Wheaton, IL: Theosophical Publishing House, 1966), p. 13. Besant does not, however, explicitly equate the Knower with alchemical *sol.*

12. Fulcanelli, *Cathèdrales,* p. 46.

13. Evola, *Hermetic Tradition,* p. 140.

14. Ibid., p. 147.

15. Quoted in Fulcanelli, *Cathèdrales,* p. 53.

16. Evola, *Hermetic Tradition,* p. 164.

17. Isha Schwaller de Lubicz, *The Opening of the Way: A Practical Guide to the Wisdom Teachings of Ancient Egypt* (Rochester, VT: Inner Traditions International, 1981), pp. 39–40.

18. See Robert Masters, *The Goddess Sekhmet: The Way of the Five Bodies* (Amity, NY: Amity House, 1988), and *Neurospeak* (Wheaton, IL: Quest Books, 1994); also Jean Houston, *The Passion of Isis and Osiris* (New York: Ballantine, 1995).

19. See, for example, C. G. Jung, "The Psychology of the Transference," quoted in

Jung on Alchemy, edited by Nathan Schwartz-Salant (Princeton: Princeton University Press, 1995), p. 69.

CHAPTER 2. THE STAR-GODS OF NEOPLATONISM
by Kenneth Stein

1. Plotinus, *The Enneads,* translated by Stephen MacKenna (Burdett, NY: Larson, 1992), II.1.4.

2. Ibid., V.1.2; see also II.1., II.2.

3. Ibid., II.3.5.

4. Ibid., IV.8.7. ("Intellectual," as used here, refers to the higher realm of Divine Intellect, not to human thought.—Ed.)

5. Ibid., VI.9.1.

6. Proclus, *Elements of Theology,* edited by E. R. Dodds (Oxford: Oxford University Press, 1963), pp. 271, 292.

7. Ibid., prop. 7.

8. Proclus, *Commentaries of Proclus on the Timaeus of Plato,* translated by Thomas Taylor (1823; reprint, Hastings, UK: Chthonios Books, 1988), vol. 1, p. 426.

9. Porphyry, "Auxiliaries to the Perception of Intelligible Natures," translated by Thomas Taylor, in *Select Works of Porphyry* (1823; reprint, Lawrence, KS: Selene Books, 1988), p. 230.

10. Proclus, *Commentaries,* vol. 2, pp. 227–31.

11. Ibid., p. 387. See also *Elements,* p. 304.

12. Porphyry, "On the Cave of the Nymphs," in *Select Works,* pp. 178–80.

13. Proclus, *Elements,* p. 307.

14. Proclus, *A Commentary on the First Book of Euclid's Elements,* translated by G. R. Morrow (Princeton: Princeton University Press, 1970), p. 17.

15. E. R. Dodds, ed., *Select Passages Illustrating Neoplatonism* (1923; reprint, Chicago: Ares, 1979), p. 14.

16. Kathleen Raine and G. M. Harper, eds., *Thomas Taylor the Platonist* (Princeton: Princeton University Press, 1969), p. 193.

17. Plotinus, *Enneads,* II.3.18, III.8.4.

18. Ibid., IV.4.40–44.

19. Proclus, *Platonic Theology,* translated by Thomas Taylor (1816; reprint, Kew Gardens, NY: Selene Books, 1985), vol. 1, p. 181.

20. E. R. Dodds, *The Greeks and the Irrational* (Berkeley: University of California

Press, 1971), pp. 283–311, explains the séance connection. For a discussion of meditation in theurgy, see Ruth Majercik, *The Chaldean Oracles* (Leiden: Brill, 1989), pp. 1–46.

21. Proclus, "Excerpts from the Commentary of Proclus on the Chaldean Oracles," translated by T. M. Johnson, in *Iamblichus: The Exhortation to Philosophy* (Grand Rapids, MI: Phanes Press, 1988), pp. 123–8.

CHAPTER 3. THE QUEST FOR SPIRITUAL FREEDOM
by Stephan A. Hoeller

1. Giovanni Filoramo, *A History of Gnosticism* (Oxford, UK: Basil Blackwell, 1990), p. xiv.

CHAPTER 4. KABBALAH AND JEWISH MYSTICISM
by Pinchas Giller

1. Nahmanides' Commentary to the Torah 17:11, *Mikraot Gedolot Meorot* (Jerusalem: Meorot, 1999), p. 149.

CHAPTER 5. THE MYSTICISM OF CHRISTIAN TEACHING
by Theodore J. Nottingham

1. Evelyn Underhill, *The Essentials of Mysticism* (New York: Dutton, 1920), p. 12.
2. Ibid., p. 15.
3. Evelyn Underhill, *Practical Mysticism* (New York: Dutton, 1943), p. xi.
4. Ibid., p. 3.
5. Ibid.
6. G. I. Gurdjieff, *Views from the Real World* (New York: Dutton, 1975), p. 153.
7. Jacob Needleman, *Lost Christianity* (New York: Bantam Books, 1982), p. 131.
8. Maurice Nicoll, *The New Man* (New York: Penguin Books, 1979), p. 143.
9. Thomas Merton, *New Seeds of Contemplation* (Toronto: New Directions, 1961), p. 126.
10. Ibid., p. 127.
11. Ibid., p. 131.

CHAPTER 6. SUFISM
by Kabir Helminski

Unless otherwise indicated, the quoted translations are the author's.

1. Muhammad Asad, *The Message of the Qur'an* (Putney, VT: Threshold Books, 1993), 50:37 and 4:82.

2. Khwaja 'Abdullaah Ansaari, *Rasaa'el-e Ansaari,* in Javad Nurbakhsh, *Sufism: Meaning, Wisdom, Unity* (New York: Khaniqa-Nimatullahi, 1981), p. 23.

3. Abu Sa'id, *Asraar al-Tawhid,* quoted in Nurbakhsh, *Sufism,* p. 21.

4. Jelaluddin Rumi, *Mathnawi,* II, 1834–37.

5. From traditional sources.

6. Yunus Emre, *The Drop That Became the Sea,* translated by Kabir Helminski and Refik Algan (Putney, VT: Threshold Books, 1989), p. 34.

7. Hakim Sanai, *The Walled Garden of Truth,* translated by David Pendlebury (New York: Dutton, 1972).

CHAPTER 7. THE QUEST OF THE MAGUS
by Thomas D. Worrel

1. Antoine Faivre, *Access to Western Esotericism* (Albany: SUNY Press, 1994), pp. 10–5.

2. Antoine Faivre and Jacob Needleman, eds., *Modern Esoteric Spirituality* (New York: Crossroad, 1992) p. 4.

3. Charles H. Kahn, *The Encyclopedia of Philosophy* (New York: Macmillan, 1972), p. 497.

4. Jim Tester, *A History of Western Astrology* (New York: Ballantine, 1987), p. 19.

5. Ibid., p. 14.

6. Gregory Shaw, *Theurgy and the Soul: The Neoplatonism of Iamblichus* (University Park: Pennsylvania State University Press, 1995), p. 30.

7. Ibid., p. 67.

8. Ibid., p. 185.

9. Ibid., p. 91.

10. From the introduction to *The Letters of Marsilio Ficino,* vol. 1 (Bury St. Edmunds, Suffolk, UK: St. Edmundsbury Press, 1975), p. 23.

11. D. P. Walker, *Spiritual and Demonic Magic* (University Park: Pennsylvania State University Press, 2000), pp. 36–7.

12. Thomas Moore, *The Planets Within* (Hudson, NY: Lindisfarne Press, 1990), p. iii.

13.   Joscelyn Godwin, *Music and the Occult* (Rochester, NY: University of Rochester Press, 1995), pp. 23–4.

14.   Frances A. Yates, *Giordano Bruno and the Hermetic Tradition* (Chicago: University of Chicago Press, 1964), p. 199.

15.   V. Perrone Compagni, ed., *Cornelius Agrippa, De occulta philosophia, Libri tres* (Leiden: Brill, 1992), p. 2.

CHAPTER 8. THE UNEXAMINED TAROT

by Chas S. Clifton

Bibliography

Agrippa, Henry Cornelius. *The Philosophy of Natural Magic*. (Secaucus, NJ: University Books, 1974). (First published in 1531.)

Anonymous. *Meditations on the Tarot: A Journey into Christian Hermeticism*. (Warwick, NY: Amity House, 1985). (First published in France in 1967.)

Buckland, Raymond. "Gypsies and the Tarot." *Fate* (July 1990): 58–65.

Butler, Bill. *Dictionary of the Tarot*. (New York: Schocken Books, 1975).

Cavendish, Richard. *The Tarot*. (New York: Harper and Row, 1975).

Doane, Doris Chase, and King Keyes. *How to Read Tarot Cards*. (New York: Funk and Wagnalls, 1967).

Eliade, Mircea. *A History of Religious Ideas*. Vol. 1. (Chicago: University of Chicago Press, 1978).

Franklin, Stephen E. *Origins of the Tarot Deck*. (Jefferson, NC: McFarland, 1988).

Gray, Eden. *The Tarot Revealed*. (New York: New American Library, 1969).

Hoffman, Detlef. *The Playing Card: An Illustrated History*. (New York: New York Graphic Society, 1973).

Kaplan, Stuart R. *Encyclopedia of Tarot*. 3 vols. (New York: U.S. Games Systems, 1978).

O'Neill, Tim. "Dancing with Doctor Dee." *Gnosis* 17 (Fall 1990): 56–7.

Petrarch, Francesco. *The Sonnets, Triumphs and Other Poems*. (London: George Bell, 1897).

Spence, Lewis. *An Encyclopaedia of Occultism*. (New Hyde Park, NY: University Books, 1960). (First published in 1920.)

Tuchman, Barbara W. *A Distant Mirror: The Calamitous Fourteenth Century*. (New York: Knopf, 1978).

Weigle, Marta. *Brothers of Light, Brothers of Blood*. (Albuquerque: University of New Mexico Press, 1976).

CHAPTER 9. LADDER TO LABYRINTH
by Priscilla Costello

1. Alexander Marshack, *The Roots of Civilization: The Cognitive Beginnings of Man's First Art, Symbol, and Notation* (New York: McGraw-Hill, 1972).

2. I am indebted to Robert Hand for an overview of this early period. His sources include B. L. van der Waerden, *Science Awakening,* vol. 2 (New York: Oxford University Press, 1970); Otto Neugebauer, *The Exact Sciences in Antiquity* (New York: Dover, 1989); Otto Neugebauer and H. B. van Hoesen, *Greek Horoscopes* (Philadelphia:American Philosophical Society, 1969); and the works of Cyril Fagan.

3. A. Sachs, "Babylonian Horoscopes," *Journal of Cuneiform Studies* 6 (1952): 49–75.

4. *The Three Steles of Seth,* in *The Nag Hammadi Library in English,* edited by James M. Robinson, 3rd ed. (San Francisco: Harper and Row, 1988), p. 401.

5. Quoted in Origen, *Contra Celsum,* in *The Ancient Mysteries, A Sourcebook: Sacred Texts of the Mystery Religions of the Ancient Mediterranean World,* edited by Marvin W. Meyer (San Francisco: Harper and Row, 1987), p. 209.

6. The *Poimandres* of Hermes Trismegistus, in *Hermetica: The Ancient Greek and Latin Writings which Contain Religious or Philosophic Teachings Ascribed to Hermes Trismegistus,* edited and translated by Walter Scott (1924; reprint, Boston: Shambhala, 1985), pp. 121–3.

7. Ibid, p. 119.

8. Ibid., p. 127.

9. Ibid., p. 119.

10. A full correlation of astrology and Jungian psychology is beyond the scope of this article. Readers may wish to peruse Liz Greene's books, which provide the most consistent and thorough exploration of astrology in Jungian terms.

11. C. G. Jung, interview with André Barbault, *Astrologie Moderne,* May 26, 1954, cited in Stephen Arroyo, *Astrology, Psychology, and the Four Elements* (Sebastopol, CA: CRCS, 1975), pp. 33–4, 189.

12. Robert Lawlor, *Sacred Geometry: Philosophy and Practice* (London: Thames and Hudson, 1982), p. 74.

13. C. G. Jung, *The Archetypes and the Collective Unconscious,* in *Collected Works,* vol. 9i, translated by R. F. C. Hull (Princeton: Princeton University Press, 1969), p. 310.

CHAPTER 10. SOPHIA

by Caitlín Matthews

1. C. S. Lewis, *Til We Have Faces* (London: Collins, 1956), p. 283.
2. "The Thunder-Perfect Intellect" 16:9–17, in *The Gnostic Scriptures: A New Translation with Annotations and Introduction by Bentley Layton* (London: S.C.M. Press, 1987), p. 82.
3. "The Gnostics According to St. Epiphanius" 26:3.1, in *The Gnostic Scriptures,* p. 205.
4. C. G. Jung, *Answer to Job* (London: Routledge and Kegan Paul, 1954), p. 159.
5. Quoted in Barbara Newman, *Sister of Wisdom: St. Hildegard's Theology of the Feminine* (Aldershot, UK: Scolar Press, 1987), p. 261.
6. Quoted in Samuel D. Cioran, *Vladimir Solov'ev and the Knighthood of the Divine Sophia* (Waterloo, Ontario: Wilfred Laurier University Press, 1977), p. 150.
7. *Aurora Consurgens,* edited with commentary by Marie-Louise von Franz (New York: Bollingen Foundation, 1966), p. 43.
8. *The Book of Enoch* 42:1, translated by R. H. Charles (London: S.P.C.K., 1982), p. 61.
9. "The First Thought in Three Forms" 42:17–20, in *The Gnostic Scriptures,* p. 95.
10. Wisdom of Solomon 8:17.
11. Rudolf Steiner, *The Search for the New Isis, Divine Sophia* (Spring Valley, NY: Mercury Press, 1983), p. 21.
12. Proverbs 8:17.

CHAPTER 11. EXPLAINING WICCA

by Judy Harrow

1. Leonard Swidler, "The Intimate Intertwining of Business, Religion and Dialogue," a paper presented at the First World Congress of the International Society of Business, Economics, and Ethics, July 25–28, 1996, Tokyo, Japan. http://www. usao. edu/~facshaferi/DIALOG03.HTML.

CHAPTER 12. THE HIDDEN SAGES AND THE KNIGHTS TEMPLAR

by Robert Richardson

1. Paraphrased from Michael Baigent, Richard Leigh, and Henry Lincoln, *Holy Blood, Holy Grail* (New York: Delacorte Press, 1982).

2. For more esoteric studies of Egypt, see the works of R. A. Schwaller de Lubicz. (Also, see chapter 18.–Ed.)

3. Gaetan DelaForge, *The Templar Tradition in the Age of Aquarius* (Putney, VT: Threshold Books, 1987), p. 63.

4. Vaclar Havel, letter to Alexander Dubcek, August 1969. Quoted in Vaclav Havel, *Disturbing the Peace* (New York: Knopf, 1990), chapter 3.

5. Peter Dawkins, *Dedication to the Light: The Francis Bacon Research Trust Journal, Series I, Vol. 3* (Alderminster, Warwickshire, UK: Francis Bacon Research Trust, 1984) pp. 65–7.

6. For a more detailed study of this period, see the works of the Francis Bacon Research Trust.

7. For more information on this period and the seeds it sowed, see Francis A. Yates, *The Rosicrucian Enlightenment* (London: Ark, 1986). (Also, see chapter 13.–Ed.)

CHAPTER 13. THE ROSICRUCIAN DREAM
by Christopher McIntosh

1. Henry Adamson, *Muse's Threnodia,* quoted in Knoop, Jones and Hamer, *Early Masonic Pamphlets* (Manchester, 1945); p. 30; cited in Frances A. Yates, *The Rosicrucian Enlightenment* (Boulder, CO: Shambhala, 1978), p. 211.

2. J. J. Bode, *Starke Erweise* (Leipzig: Göschen, 1788) p. 25.

CHAPTER 14. MASONIC CIVILIZATION
by Richard Smoley

1. David Stevenson, *The Origins of Freemasonry* (Cambridge: Cambridge University Press, 1988), pp. 19–22.

2. John J. Robinson, *Born in Blood: The Lost Secrets of Freemasonry* (New York: M. Evans, 1989), pp. 164–6.

3. Ibid., pp. 152–5.

4. Michael Baigent and Richard Leigh, *The Temple and the Lodge* (London: Jonathan Cape, 1989), pp. 34–7.

5. Robinson, *Born in Blood,* pp. 17–36.

6. Ibid., p. 166. (Robinson may be in error about this phrase being in ritual.–Ed).

7. Ibid., p. 212.

8. Baigent and Leigh, *The Temple and the Lodge,* p. 120.

9. Christopher Knight and Robert Lomas, *The Hiram Key: Pharaohs, Freemasons, and the Lost Scrolls of Jesus* (Rockport, MA: Element, 1996), p. 313.

10. Baigent and Leigh, *The Temple and the Lodge,* p. 119. See also Frances A. Yates, *The Rosicrucian Enlightenment* (London: Ark, 1972), p. 211. Emphasis in the original.

11. Stevenson, *Origins of Freemasonry,* p. 102.

12. Yates, *Rosicrucian Enlightenment,* pp. 171–92, 210–1.

13. Thomas D. Worrel, "The Initiatic Symbolism of Freemasonry," *Gnosis* 44 (Summer 1997):18–23.

14. A worker named Hiram is mentioned in the biblical account of the Temple's construction; see 1 Kings 7:13–45. But he is a worker in brass, not an architect; there is also no reference to his murder.

15. Knight and Lomas, *The Hiram Key,* pp. 9–17. In some versions, the first two blows fall on Hiram's shoulder and the nape of his neck. See Edmond Gloton, *Instruction maçonnique aux Maîtres-Maçons* (Paris: V. Gloton, "5950"), pp. 56–7.

16. Harold W. Percival, *Thinking and Destiny* (Dallas, TX: Word Foundation, 1946), pp. 680–6. See also W. Kirk MacNulty, *Freemasonry: A Journey Through Ritual and Symbol* (London: Thames and Hudson, 1991), pp. 28–30.

CHAPTER 15. HEAVENS AND HELLS
by Gary Lachman

1. Aldous Huxley, *The Doors of Perception and Heaven and Hell* (New York: Harper and Row, 1990), p. 83.

2. George Trobridge, *Swedenborg: Life and Teaching* (New York: Swedenborg Foundation, 1992), pp. 114–5.

3. Wilson Van Dusen, *The Presence of Other Worlds* (London: Wildwood House, 1975).

4. Ralph Waldo Emerson, *Representative Men* (Boston: Houghton Mifflin, 1930), pp. 102–3.

5. Helen Keller, *My Religion* (Garden City, NY: Doubleday, Page, 1927), p. 207.

6. Van Dusen, *Other Worlds,* pp. 53–4.

7. Emanuel Swedenborg, *Journal of Dreams* (New York: Swedenborg Foundation, 1986).

8. Emanuel Swedenborg, *Heaven and Hell* (New York: Swedenborg Foundation, 1984), p. 43.

9. The literature on the hypnagogic state is extensive and comes from many fields. Of particular interest is P. D. Ouspensky's investigations in the chapter "On the Study of Dreams and on Hypnotism" in *A New Model of the Universe* (New York: Knopf, 1969). A relatively recent work, *Hypnagogia,* by Andreas Mavromatis (London: Routledge and Kegan Paul, 1987), relates hypnagogic phenomena to psychic abilities.

10. Emanuel Swedenborg, *The Universal Human and Soul-Body Interaction* (Ramsey, NJ: Paulist Press, 1984), p. 37.

11. Swedenborg, *Heaven and Hell,* p. 32.

12. In a work that antedates Jung's treatment of alchemy by several years, the psychologist Herbert Silberer describes the autosymbolic character of hypnagogia in detail. See *Hidden Symbolism of Alchemy and the Occult Arts* (New York: Dover, 1971), pp. 233–8.

13. Emanuel Swedenborg, *The Word Explained,* quoted in Van Dusen, *Other Worlds,* p. 28.

14. Emanuel Swedenborg, *Spiritual Diary* (London: Swedenborg Society, 1977), vol. 1, p. 29, and vol. 5, p. 158.

15. Swedenborg, *Heaven and Hell,* pp. 26–7.

16. William Blake, "Europe, a Prophecy," in *William Blake: The Complete Poems* (New York: Penguin Books, 1979), p. 229.

17. Van Dusen, *Other Worlds,* p. 117.

18. Swedenborg, *Heaven and Hell,* p. 330.

19. Ibid., p. 42.

20. Ibid., p. 355.

21. Ibid., pp. 489–90.

22. Ibid., p. 502.

23. Quoted in Wing-Tsit Chan, *A Source Book in Chinese Philosophy* (Princeton: Princeton University Press, 1973), p. 59.

24. Swedenborg, *Heaven and Hell,* pp. 312–3.

CHAPTER 16. BLAVATSKY AND HER MASTERS
by K. Paul Johnson

1. John King, the best known "guide" of early Spiritualism, was a "rough ex-pirate who loved recounting his adventures" and "appeared first in the early 1850s to a farmer-medium living in Ohio, and later would control the famous Italian

medium Eusapia Palladino." See Marion Meade, *Madame Blavatsky: The Woman Behind the Myth* (New York: Putnam, 1980), p. 136.

2. C. J. Jinarajadasa, ed., *Letters from the Masters of the Wisdom,* second series (Adyar, India: Theosophical Publishing House, 1973), pp. 80–1.

3. Ibid., p. 85.

4. Ibid., p. 86.

5. Aided by his wife Alma, an English medium, Theon disseminated his teachings in a journal entitled *La Revue Cosmique,* published in Paris. His most eminent convert was Mirra Alfassa Richard, who later became "the Mother," Sri Aurobindo's partner in his Pondicherry ashram. Richard incorporated Theon's teachings with those of Aurobindo. Theon spent the last forty years of his life in Algeria, where he died in 1927.

6. Sylvia Cranston, *HPB: The Extraordinary Life and Influence of Helena P. Blavatsky, Founder of the Modern Theosophical Movement* (New York: Putnam, 1993), p. 132.

7. Jinarajadasa, *Letters,* p. 108.

8. H. P. Blavatsky, *Letters of H. P. Blavatsky to A. P. Sinnett* (Pasadena, CA: Theosophical University Press, 1973), p. 171.

9. H. P. Blavatsky, "Letters of H.P.B. to Hartmann," *Path* (March 1896): 368–9.

10. Blavatsky, *Letters to Sinnett,* p. 111.

11. Ibid., p. 334.

12. Blavatsky, "Letters to Hartmann," pp. 369–70.

13. Ibid., p. 370.

14. Ibid., p. 371.

15. Ibid., p. 372.

16. Franz Hartmann, *The Talking Image of Urur* (New York: Lovell, 1890).

17. Ibid., p. 285.

18. Ibid., p. 287.

19. H. P. Blavatsky, "On Pseudo-Theosophy," in *Collected Writings,* vol. 11 (Wheaton, IL: Theosophical Publishing House, 1973), p. 46.

20. Ibid., p. 47.

21. Ibid., p. 49.

22. H. P. Blavatsky, "Why I Do Not Return to India," in *Collected Writings,* vol. 13, pp. 158–9.

23. H. P. Blavatsky, *The Key to Theosophy* (Los Angeles: Theosophy Company, 1973), p. 301.

CHAPTER 18. RENÉ SCHWALLER DE LUBICZ
by Gary Lachman

1. Christopher Bamford, introduction to R. A. Schwaller de Lubicz, *A Study of Numbers* (Rochester, VT: Inner Traditions, 1986).
2. R. A. Schwaller de Lubicz, *Nature Word* (West Stockbridge, MA: Lindisfarne Press, 1982), p. 129.
3. R. A. Schwaller de Lubicz, *Symbol and the Symbolic* (New York, NY: Inner Traditions, 1978), p. 40. A comparison with Whitehead's ideas on the two modes of perception, "presentational immediacy" and "causal efficacy," as well as his notion of "prehension," adds to our understanding of Schwaller's "symbolique."
4. *A Study of Numbers,* p. 27.
5. *Nature Word,* pp. 101–2.
6. Ibid., p. 51.
7. *Symbol and the Symbolic,* pp. 82–3.
8. Take a line A–C, and section it at point B so that A–C is longer than A–B in the same proportion as A–B is longer than B–C. That's phi, the "golden section." For its relation to "symmetry breaking," a central concern of current cosmology, see John Anthony West, *The Serpent in the Sky* (London: Wildwood House, 1979), p. 75.
9. *Symbol and the Symbolic,* p. 89.
10. *Nature Word,* p. 135.
11. Ibid., p. 102.

CHAPTER 19. G. I. GURDJIEFF
by Richard Smoley

1. James Webb, *The Harmonious Circle: The Lives and Work of G. I. Gurdjieff, P. D. Ouspensky, and Their Followers* (New York: Putnam, 1980), p. 13.
2. P. D. Ouspensky, *In Search of the Miraculous: Fragments of an Unknown Teaching* (New York: Harcourt Brace Jovanovich, 1949), p. 45.
3. Ibid., p. 50.
4. Webb, *Harmonious Circle,* pp. 25–6.
5. For the earliest reliable description of Gurdjieff, see "Glimpses of Truth," written by an anonymous student in 1914, reprinted in G. I. Gurdjieff, *Views of the Real World* (London: Arkana, 1984), pp. 3–37.

6. Ouspensky, *In Search of the Miraculous,* p. 7.

7. Thomas de Hartmann and Olga de Hartmann, *Our Life with Mr. Gurdjieff* (San Francisco: Harper and Row, 1983), p. 39.

8. Ibid., pp. 37–9.

9. Webb, *Harmonious Circle,* p. 196.

10. Ibid., pp. 236–7.

11. Ibid., pp. 280–2.

12. Boris Mouravieff, "Ouspensky, Gurdjieff, et les Fragments d'un Enseignement inconnu" (N.p.: Centre d'études chrétiennes ésoteriques, n.d.; reprinted from [Brussels] *Synthèses* 138 [November 1957]), p. 15. Emphasis Mouravieff's.

13. G. I. Gurdjieff, *Life Is Real Only Then, When "I Am"* (New York: Dutton, 1981), p. 94.

14. G. I. Gurdjieff, *Beelzebub's Tales to His Grandson* (New York: Dutton, 1973), p. i.

15. Gurdjieff, *Life Is Real,* p. 41.

16. Ibid., p. 5.

17. Ibid., p. 93. In fact Orage did have a romance with a woman named Jessie Dwight of the Sunwise Turn bookshop, and later married her.

18. For Olga de Hartmann's account of the rupture, see de Hartmann, *Our Life,* pp. 155–60.

19. Webb, *Harmonious Circle,* p. 473.

20. Ibid., p. 475.

21. Ibid., p. 449.

22. Ibid., p. 315.

23. Ouspensky, *In Search of the Miraculous,* p. 99.

24. Mouravieff, "Ouspensky," p. 18.

25. Ouspensky, *In Search of the Miraculous,* p. 102.

26. Robert Amadou, "Gurdjieff et le soufisme," in [Paris] *Question de* 50 (1989): 54.

27. Ibid., p. 55.

28. 2 Peter 3:10.

29. G. I. Gurdjieff, *Meetings with Remarkable Men* (New York: Dutton, 1969), p. 39.

RIGHTS AND PERMISSIONS

ABOUT THE EDITOR

JAY KINNEY is co-author, with Richard Smoley, of *Hidden Wisdom: A Guide to the Western Inner Traditions.* He was publisher and editor in chief of *Gnosis* magazine and has written and researched extensively on esoteric spiritual traditions for more than thirty years. He lives with his wife, Dixie, in San Francisco.

To read about *Gnosis,* visit www.Lumen.org.